Through a child's memories, Tina story which illuminates the indomitable courage of the human spirit in the face of numbing hardship and extreme poverty. This is a moving account of the fierce challenges, even humiliations, which faced many eastern European religious immigrants as they tried to carve out a new life in North America. Laced with humor and the author's marvelous recall of daily life, this is a book about faith and the virtues of hard work. It also reveals much about the formation of character in a young girl who, in spite of overwhelming odds, succeeds in achieving her dream of becoming a nurse. A wonderfully inspiring story.

-Lee Snyder, President Emeritus, Bluffton University and author, *At Powerline and Diamond Hill: Unexpected Intersections of Life and Work* (Cascadia)

Tina's book brings an amazing story to her readers; many will relate to and identify with some of her experiences. There is a larger history here about immigrants which is missing from standard history books. Her remarkable memory unearths both mundane and memorable events in the daily life of the family. Her style of writing emerges with powerful expression; so much is said in the wonderful short summary sentences at the end of paragraphs. Readers will be thrilled at Tina's rise from that "Monument to Poverty."

-Margaret Dutton, School Superintendent, Ret., long-time neighbor and friend

If you enjoy reading stories about the "old days" and pioneer times, and stories about how people in different countries and cultures live, then you should enjoy this story of Tina's life, growing up in a small community in Manitoba, one of the youngest daughters of a family who had left their native adopted country in the Ukraine to make a new life for themselves in a new country. It's the age-old story of God's people having no continuing city here on earth. When the freedom to worship God as they wished was in jeopardy, they decided to leave all they knew that was dear to them and make the journey across the Atlantic Ocean to a new land and a new life.

Each person's and each family's story is similar but distinctly different. And Tina's story is no exception. You will also be interested to learn what part a new camera plays in this story.

-Margaret Shetler, Archivist for PNMC and the Pacific Northwest Mennonite Historical Society

Frontispiece

"My name in the newspaper that day meant everything to me. At first sight, it meant I had passed the big Registered Nurses' State Board exams. But it meant so much more than that. It meant an end to personal poverty. Although I had no money in the bank or in my pocket, I would now be able to make my own way in the world. Those prospects would raise me above the poverty level of mere subsistence. The RN signature after my name gave me self esteem and assurance. I was no longer dependent on the mercy of others. I had not sought fame but value and self status in the world around me. I had learned a skill and was capable of serving humanity. I was no longer an immigrant child working in the fields or in rich people's homes. Canada had been very good to me and my immigrant family." (A quote from the book)

IMMIGRANT DAUGHTER

A monument to poverty

*Blaine
Enjoy
Tina Kauffman*

BY
TINA KLASSEN KAUFFMAN

authorHOUSE®

AuthorHouse™
1663 Liberty Drive
Bloomington, IN 47403
www.authorhouse.com
Phone: 1-800-839-8640

© *2012 by Tina Klassen Kauffman. All rights reserved.*

No part of this book may be reproduced, stored in a retrieval system, or transmitted by any means without the written permission of the author.

Published by AuthorHouse   04/12/2012

ISBN: 978-1-4685-5092-4 (sc)
ISBN: 978-1-4685-5091-7 (e)

Library of Congress Control Number: 2012902157

Any people depicted in stock imagery provided by Thinkstock are models, and such images are being used for illustrative purposes only.
Certain stock imagery © *Thinkstock.*

This book is printed on acid-free paper.

Because of the dynamic nature of the Internet, any web addresses or links contained in this book may have changed since publication and may no longer be valid. The views expressed in this work are solely those of the author and do not necessarily reflect the views of the publisher, and the publisher hereby disclaims any responsibility for them.

This Story

is dedicated to

daughters

Patricia Sue (Kauffman) Stutzman

and

Lynette Rene (Kauffman) Plank

and

our grandson Nathan Plank

who have been,

and still are,

the source of much joy.

CONTENTS

PREFACE.. ix

ACKNOWLEDGMENTS xi

FOREWORD... xiii

INTRODUCTION.. 1

PART I Russia to Saskatchewan 1885-1937 2

A Monument to Poverty 3

Introduction to Russia 8

Once upon a Time 9

Grigorjewka 13

War and Revolution 20

Health and Death in Russia 30

From Emigrants to Immigrants. 32

Trying to Make It.. 37

Financing a Farm 41

Born in Canada... 43

Child's Play 45

Paper Dolls 53

Our Parents' Two Worlds 56

Water 60

We Didn't Care 63

Saturday and Sunday... 65

Laundry Day.. 70

Important People in our Lives 74

Four Seasons 85

Dresses.. 92

Borsch, Verenichi (Vereniki) and Cheelchi 94

Medical Trivia 100

The Rush Lake School 104

Christmas 114

God and Church in an Unchurched Place.................. 119

Depression's Final Blow... 122

PART II Manitoba to British Columbia 1937-1948...... 125

A New Beginning.. 127

Nordheim 133

Oasis... 142

Pickles, Prips and Piety 147

Christmas Eve.. 150

The First Year.. 152

Bicton Heath 160

A School Enterprise 165

A Manitoba Blizzard 168

Fork River... 172

Fire and Ice 177

Adena 181

Aunt Tina Koop 183

The War.. 185

From the Sweat of the Brow.................................... 190

Leaving the Farm 197

PART III British Columbia to Jordan 1948-1959 201

British Columbia 203

The Mennonite Educational Institute 208

Becoming a Nurse... 213

Life After Graduation.. 224

Jordan 227

EPILOGUE PART I Reflections on my Parents............ 234

EPILOGUE PART II Ray and I and our Children.......... 245

APPENDIX I Names 246

APPENDIX II Letters 251

ABOUT THE AUTHOR.. 257

PREFACE

WHY DID I write this story? There are several reasons. Perhaps the primary reason is that I moved away from my family, church, country, ethnic family and all who share my history. Once I had left the warmth of the "womb" from which I came, I realized that the story of my people was unique. Many stories of immigrants were lost because no one recorded them. I wished my parents and grandparents had written their stories. I wanted to preserve what I remembered about our parents' stories as they told them to us, even though at the time I did not want to hear them.

Because our daughters grew up with my husband Ray's family, church, ethnicity and in his country, rather than mine, I wanted to record the other half of their heritage so it would not be lost. I included more than history. The story reflects the social, economic and religious climate of those days. These small or ordinary aspects of daily life also reflect the light and happy times of children at play. They reflect a child's acceptance of what is and not what should be. The way we lived was the norm for children who had not experienced anything different. What may have seemed trivial was what life was made of when there was nothing else to clutter our young minds.

Had it not been for the encouragement of my friend and coworker at Senior Services, Maureen Flynn, this story may never have been written. She had a great curiosity about these Mennonites who attempted to live out their faith. But she was also interested in their culture and history since the story was foreign to her.

Finally, I enjoy collecting and recording data. I recognize that some of the story is sad. War and Revolution play havoc in innocent people's lives. Poverty is cruel. But is there not some sadness in every person's life if he/she is honest enough to tell it? The joyful part of life is that God is the author of our lives. The faith of our fathers and mothers is also evident throughout the whole story. My story stands in a long tradition. I quote from Psalm 78, "I will utter things hidden from of old, things we have heard and known, things our fathers have told us. We will not hide them from their children. We will tell the next generation."

In 1997 I finished my amateur production and in 2010-2011, I revised the story for publication.

Tina Klassen Kauffman

ACKNOWLEDGMENTS

MY THANKS TO my sisters, Annie, Lena and Justine, and my brother Henry, for reading the original story, correcting and adding information that I did not have. Nettie, then in a nursing home, contributed before she was incapacitated. She has since died. Another brother, George, had he lived, would have been a valuable resource.

Our deceased parents deserve credit for telling us about life in Russia before the war, about World War I, and the negative changes that the Russian Revolution of 1917 and its aftermath wrought in the lives of Russian citizens. They spoke often about all the members of their own families. Without them I would have no story to tell. Information about Grigorjewka came from them and from a booklet called <u>Das Dorf Grigorjewka</u> (The Village of Grigorjewka), written by George (Gerhard) F. Loewen. In 1996 Lena, Henry, Justine, Ray (my husband) and I toured Ukraine and saw the village ourselves.

For the history of the Mennonites, Cornelius J. Dyck's book, <u>An Introduction to Mennonite History</u>, was a good source. Thanks to Grandpa Unger, Mother, Aunt Lizzie and cousin Peter Klassen for written family statistics.

Thank you to those who encouraged me to write and to buy a word processor, which I used in the early stages of the book (we have long since purchased a computer.) Thanks to my husband Ray for respecting the time and space I needed to produce this story. I acknowledge Jim Ellis who transferred my old manuscript from floppy discs to a computer disc. I thank my niece, Donna Bergey for compiling, formatting and typing. I am grateful to both Jim Ellis and Josh Henninger for valuable computer assistance. A heart-felt thank you to Lee Snyder for hours of editing and fine tuning. I am indebted to Melanie Springer Mock for publication counsel and encouragement.

Thank you to Margaret Dutton, my neighbor, and Margaret Shetler, my friend who encouraged me to publish the story, and most of all my husband, Ray, who wanted to see the story published from its conception.

FOREWORD

DURING THE DISCUSSIONS leading to the merger of two Mennonite
bodies, Mennonite Church (MC) and the General Conference Mennonite
Church (GC) in 2002, I was often asked what I thought of the idea,
typically from those who opposed it. One of my standard responses was
that yes, I was in favor of integration for a number of reasons. For once
we're getting together and not splitting, and secondly, the pool of stories
for each group will be enriched by those of the other. *Their* stories will
become *our* stories. Among the significant stories I had in mind were
those of extreme suffering of Mennonites in Russia during the anarchy
and chaos of the Bolshevik Revolution. Then came drought, famine,
disease, and finally, the devastating reordering of society under Lenin
and Stalin. Some 21,000 escaped the terror and migrated, primarily to
Canada. Their stories of fortitude, faith, and courage are instructive for
MCs, whose European experience and eighteenth-century migrations are
but distant memories.

Tina's story, *Immigrant Daughter*, is a story of suffering, poverty,
fortitude, and faith in Russia and in Canada.

From her parents' Ukrainian village of Grigorjewka comes a rare
story. When an occupying German officer tried to persuade Mennonites
to take up arms against their Russian neighbors, they refused. They were
unwilling to sacrifice nonviolence, a core component of their faith, even
in desperate times. As a result, the Russian peasants responded in kind and
refused to harm their Mennonite neighbors. Nevertheless, Tina's parents
with five children were among those who left the village and migrated
to Canada in 1925. Tina traces that journey, and describes the difficult

adjustment to all things new in southern Manitoba, and then in southern Saskatchewan.

Tina was born in a two-room shack in Blumenort, Saskatchewan. She writes graphically of their struggle to survive on the Canadian prairie. In their stark poverty, there was much her parents could not provide for their children, but they did give Tina something of great significance—her own story.

This is more than a plodding litany of events strung together to fill pages. In many places it reads like a novel. She writes of Dust-Bowl life on the prairie in poetic language that seems to form pictures on the page.

Take for instance such delightful coupling of words as the following: She writes of despair as "Hope dissipated just as the few drops of water evaporated." It was more than just a feeling; it was visible: "The despair written on Mother's face showed in the set of her muscles and the wrinkles of her skin." When insects invaded the prairie, she writes that "grasshoppers reigned without opposition. They jumped and danced before us when we walked across the dry ground. Could the plagues of Egypt have been any worse?" The years in Saskatchewan were not just hard, they were "bitter and poor." Though her father planted seeds and looked for a harvest, instead "We had harvested rocks, thistles, dust, grasshoppers and army worms." And water! Water was so scarce that it "has to be begged into existence."

With vivid word pictures, Tina describes daily life, her siblings, parents, neighbors, ministers, friends, and her school. Her frightening and stern teacher, Mr. Dyck, was "as unbending as a ruler," yet Tina endured and succeeded, eventually earning a Registered Nurses diploma in British Columbia.

When they finally escaped Saskatchewan, they left behind "Two black stacks of mown thistles . . . like two black tombstones to witness the end of farming in the dust bowl." In spite of the family's best efforts, "The army worms dealt the final blow. We had to leave. We had been defeated." And yet, all was not lost, because "in our hearts we carried hope. Farming could get only better."

Perhaps most remarkable of all, Tina expresses no bitterness, no lament, for the life not lived, for things not possessed. She is evenhanded and even-tempered in her telling. She credits her parents for passing on their faith. While it was understated, still they "had prepared us to recognize the oasis when we came to it. We drank deeply from its free-flowing waters."

And, it seems Tina has been drinking deeply ever since. In better times, Tina moved with her parents to the Fraser Valley of British Columbia. Then she struck out on her own to work in Vancouver and study in New Westminster, until she gained an "honorable profession" as a nurse. To enhance her faith she attended Canadian Mennonite Bible College in Winnipeg, and then to share her faith she volunteered to serve with MCC in Jordan. During orientation at Akron, Pa., she met Ray Kauffman. After two years of service—Tina in Jordan and Ray in Europe—they married in Germany and moved to Albany, Oregon, where they raised their daughters, and where they continue to live. And there she wrote this book, a gift to us all.

John E. Sharp, History Instructor, and author of *A School on the Prairie; A Centennial History of Hesston College, 1909-2009.* Hesston, KS

Introduction

For those readers who know the Russian (Dutch, German) Mennonite story, my attempt to explain the historical predicament in Russia will seem simplistic. I have no intention of rewriting the history which many historians have done more completely. For those to whom this history is foreign, you should know that it is intrinsic to the story of my people's dilemma.

To update the story I would like to add that the German Lutheran, Catholic and Mennonite colonists in Ukraine were growing in population and prosperity but remained German culturally.

They also loved Russia, their homeland.

Although in some respects privileged, these German colonists were always second class citizens. Lenin and Stalin eventually felt threatened by them, their own loyal citizens. Therefore these Germans living in Russia were discriminated against, and eventually treated ruthlessly by the Soviets. In fact, all Christians were persecuted by the atheistic Bolsheviks, though Christians were not the only persons who were tried, brutally tortured, imprisoned and sent to labor camps. Russian citizens and Polish prisoners, or anyone living in Russia, could become subjects of suspicion and experience the same terror. Knowing this history validates the desire of many Russian citizens to seek a new homeland.

There may well be inaccuracies in distance measurements, and oral interviews and their interpretations in my story. For these I apologize.

PART I

RUSSIA TO SASKATCHEWAN
1885-1937

A Monument to Poverty

The children wake up at the Montana/Saskatchewan border. Sleeping is their favorite pastime while we travel. We leave Havre and Malta, Montana, behind us and drive north watching for familiar signs. "Blumenhof" the big bold letters on the green sign say. This is where Dad registered my birth two years after my family came to Canada. We stop to take a picture of the sign, our daughters and me. No doubt the two room shack in nearby Blumenort, where I was born has been razed long ago. I would like to see the village but the dusty gravel road is as attractive to Ray as it would be to a Columbia River salmon. We do not leave the asphalt highway. So we pile back into the Pontiac and continue to drive north to Swift Current, about 100 miles from the U.S./Canadian border.

Road sign along Hwy. 4, Saskatchewan, 1969 Tina with Patty and Lynette.
Home again—my birthplace was near Blumenhof, Sask.

"Are we there yet?" Patty asks hopefully.

"No, but I see the big red barn," I point "That is where my Uncle Peter Unger lived. Oh, the big UNGER'S DAIRY sign that covered the whole barn roof is no longer there. No doubt someone reroofed the barn."

"How far till we get there?" Lynette wants to know.

"About 20 miles." Finally, "See, there is a sign. Rush Lake," it says, and the arrow points left to a little town a half-mile north of the highway. It nestles in a shallow valley created by the rolling hills around it. Later we'll explore the town but I'll save that for now. We drive two miles farther east on Highway #1 beyond the sign until we see a house to the right near the road. Ray makes a right turn down a short dirt lane at the edge of a farmer's field.

The weathered, gray, two-story house stands silhouetted against a clear blue sky in the summer of 1969. It stands like an orphan alone, surrounded by the green prairies of southern Saskatchewan. A modern irrigation system is obviously being used to produce such a scene of green grain. The Trans Canada highway creeps shamefully close to the once private farm yard. In the 1930s the road ran a respectable half-mile from the home place. But now the house stands in unpainted nakedness for every traveler to see. Its summer kitchen has been ripped away from its east end. There is no evidence of the unpainted barn and the equally unpainted granary that stood on the same yard years ago. But the house stands tall and erect, having yielded only the exterior paint to the sandblasting of the storms we knew too well.

Ray turns off the ignition. The girls, eight and six, tumble out of the car and dash toward the house where Mom had been a child. Ray and I follow and enter the east door where the added summer kitchen had been. Now, like then, the south door is boarded up. The girls explore the downstairs in two minutes. We stand in the living-kitchen-dining room. On Saturdays the room also served as a bath room.

To the left I can visualize the black wood stove. I can see Mother standing over the front burner trying to make waffles with a borrowed waffle iron. Her fuel was dry cow chips. They produced more smoke than flames. Desperately she says, "How can I cook without fuel?"

The table and bench had been placed along the south wall. The table was always covered with an oil cloth. My place at the table was in the middle of the bench between Henry and Lena. The rest of the family sat on wooden chairs around the table. Dad always sat at the head of the table with Mother on his left. Here we ate many Old Country foods like borsch, perischchi (perishki,) verenichi (or vereniki), plumi mous and cheelchi with fried onions. At other times we did not eat as well. A meal consisted of bread soaked in milk, or bread and coffee.

My eyes follow the walls around the room. The Singer sewing machine had been next to the door to the bedroom. On the floor I see the outline of the cellar door. It was through this cellar door and down the steps that Mother sent Henry to fetch a potato so she could prepare a poultice to cool a new burn on my left jaw. In the cellar she stored carrots, potatoes, onions and cabbage. In crocks she had pickled pig's feet, tongue, heart, zillchees (head cheese), dill pickles and sauerkraut.

The frame door to the pantry had held Dad's razor strap on a nail. We enter the narrow pantry under the stairway. The empty shelves were only a little less bare than they had been 35 years ago. Then we had a scanty supply of dishes. Today there is no coffee, sugar or lard, or even an empty Roger's Golden Syrup pail.

Back in the living room, old plaster has fallen from the slats on the wall and lies in pieces on the wooden floor. Cobwebs fill the corners where the walls meet the ceiling. The unpainted floor looks the same as it did then, including the cracks between the boards. Oh, this was a cold house! In winter it let the freezing cold in and in summer the hot dust blew freely through all its cracks and crevices.

The bedroom, now empty, had held two beds. Our parents occupied the full bed in the northwest corner. Justine and I slept in a small, homemade wooden bed with a straw mattress in the opposite corner.

The bedrooms upstairs await our visit. The girls are eager to climb the stairs but several steps are broken. Lynette, afraid she will fall through the holes, takes my hand. We all take long strides across the holes to the next step. These are the steps that I sprinkled with water and swept with a broom. I had seen Nettie do this before and when she saw me imitate her, she was angry because I messed up her steps. "I'm glad you're not my mother," I told her. "I'll feel sorry for your children."

When we approach the second floor we hear frantic fluttering of many wings. Alarmed, the pigeons take flight through the holes in the roof left by missing shingles. Bird droppings are everywhere. Here in the east room the older sisters had slept. George and Henry had shared the southwest room. We called the northwest room the "junk" room because it served as a catchall for the few things we stored there. Flour and sugar in 100 pound sacks had been carried up there by Dad. I was impressed with the way he hoisted the heavy sacks onto his back. His limp did not seem to impede him. In 1921, at the age of 36, a falling roof in Russia had struck him down and broke his hip. It was never set properly.

Memories fill my mind and I am a little girl again.

In this house I would remember not only where everyone sat at the table, or where everyone slept, but I would remember my first feelings of pleasure and pain. I would remember the events that created those feelings. I would remember not only the Old Country foods Mother made, but I would remember the new foods that my sisters tried to introduce to this immigrant family. I would experience the dreadful poverty in which we lived. But I would not remember what brought us to this house in 1929. I would learn these circumstances from my parents and older siblings.

Today, on this beautiful summer day in 1969, the tall gray house stands as a staunch reminder of one immigrant family's rendezvous with poverty. I will call it "A Monument to Poverty."

The Klassen house, Rush Lake, 1977

Introduction to Russia

Nineteen hundred and twenty-five was the year my parents, Gerhard Klassen and Anna (Unger) Klassen, with five children, Gerhard, Aganetha, Anna, Helena and Heinrich, set foot on Canadian ground. They knew not a word of English and knew nothing about their new homeland. Their name, Klassen, is Dutch, their language is German and their citizenship is Russian. Their faith is Mennonite. Let me give you a brief summary of how they changed from Dutch to German—not to Russian—no, they insisted they were German because they had retained their German tongue, culture and Dutch/German blood lines. They lived in German colonies in Russia and spoke German in school and church and business.

ONCE UPON A TIME

A VERY LONG time ago my ancestors lived in The Netherlands. Let me tell you why they left the land of dykes, windmills and tulips.

Once upon a time a man by the name of Menno Simons lived in Holland. In fact, he was born about the same time as Martin Luther. It was in the late fifteenth century. Both men were well educated and both became priests in the Roman Catholic Church. It was Luther who opened Pandora's Box when he posted his 95 Theses on the door of the castle/church in Wittenburg, Germany, in 1517. The Protestant Reformation was born.

Menno Simons remained in his secure priestly post long after Luther's name became well known in Europe. Menno Simons heard of the reforms and had his own doubts about the church. When his brother, who was an Anabaptist in West Friesland, in The Netherlands, was executed, Menno was shocked. He could not agree with the executioners. He became conscience stricken about his own comfortable life and he knew he had to leave the priesthood and the Catholic Church. He became an Anabaptist in 1536 and became a leader in the Anabaptist movement.

The Anabaptist movement, begun in Switzerland, in 1525 was not a clone of Luther's Reformation. The Anabaptists agreed with Luther's reforms but believed he did not go far enough. "Anabaptist" was a nickname which means to "baptize again." This group believed in a voluntary believer's baptism only. They re-baptized believers who had been baptized as infants. They believed in the separation of church and state and in nonviolence as a way of life. Although Catholics and Reformers both saw the Anabaptists as dangerous radicals, Anabaptism spread rapidly. Late in the 1520s and in the early 1530s hundreds of Anabaptists in Europe were martyred by drowning, beheading and burning.

Dirk Willems, for example, was an Anabaptist who escaped his pursuer, a sheriff, by fleeing across a frozen pond. His persecutor fell through the ice during the pursuit. Dirk heard him cry for help. He turned around and rescued his pursuer. The burgomaster on the other side of the river ordered the rescued sheriff to arrest Dirk. He was burned at the stake on May 16, 1569. In 2000, Ray and I with other tourists stood on the very spot in Asperen, The Netherlands, where it is thought the execution took place.

When Menno left the church in 1536 and was baptized, he expected to be persecuted. His expectations were fulfilled. As an Anabaptist pastor and leader in The Netherlands, Menno Simons traveled, preached and wrote about the Anabaptist faith and life, based on what the Bible taught. He married and had children.

When both Catholics and Reformers sought to take his life, Menno went into hiding. However, from his hiding place he dared to travel to Germany and Danzig and back to Holland to preach.

Menno Simon's followers became known as Mennonites. Persecution became so intense as to cause dispersion. Many of the Dutch Mennonites fled to Prussia. Mennonites from other parts of Europe fled also. Some came to North and South America. The last Dutch martyr died in 1574. In time, Mennonites grew to become one of the largest groups of Protestants in Holland and were prosperous. They flourished in commerce, the arts and professions. For this story, I will confine myself to my ancestry only.

History records that many of the Dutch Mennonites were artisans and merchants, using the northern Baltic Sea trade routes of their day. Due to persecution many Dutch Anabaptists emigrated from The Netherlands and settled in the Vistula delta of Prussia and in the city of Danzig. Today it is called Gdansk, Poland. Immigration began in the 1530s and continued for decades. Mennonites had a continuous existence in what is now Poland for over 400 years, until the end of

World War II. In 1945 they retreated with the German army as the Soviet army marched west.

The lowlands of the Baltic Sea coastal inland were swampy. The Dutch Mennonites knew how to drain the swamps and build productive farmland. They had reclaimed land from the sea and swamps in The Netherlands. The cost was high. Many became ill with swamp fever and died. Some Dutch families with surnames like Friesen, Klassen, Dyck and others survived. The survivors built a new life there. They kept the Dutch language for many years, but eventually they spoke German even in their churches.

When my mother wanted us to adhere to the German language in the 20th century, I reminded her that our Dutch ancestors had set a precedent—they changed from one language to another, and so would we.

Mennonites were tolerated in Prussia, but not fully accepted. Catherine the Great, a German princess, was born in Prussia. At the age of sixteen she married Peter the III of Russia. She succeeded him as ruler of Russia in 1762. The very next year she invited Germans to settle the lands vacated by the Turks in southern Russia. On October 19, 1786, two Prussian Mennonites, Jacob Hoepner and Johann Bartsch, were sent to Russia to see the land and to meet with Czarina Catherine. A year later they returned with favorable reports.

The first emigrants left Danzig on March 22, 1788, by wagon train. Their first destination was Riga, Latvia. After that their route went south along the Daugava River and the Dnieper River. They arrived in Ukraine a year after their departure from Danzig. This first group of immigrants settled west of the Dnieper River, on a tributary called Chortitza River. The new settlement was called either the Chortitza settlement, or the Old Colony, because it was the first Mennonite settlement in Ukraine which was under Russian rule.

By the year 1803, 400 more Mennonite families from Prussia were settled in fifteen villages and farmed 89,000 acres of land. This was the Molochna colony. By the end of the 18th century and early 19th century, about 10,000 Prussian Mennonites followed other German colonists and settled in the Ukraine.

Among the many privileges offered to new Mennonite immigrants were the promises of religious freedom and exemption from military service. Mennonites, in turn, were not to proselytize members from the Russian Orthodox Church. The privileges promised were not significantly different from the promises to other immigrants including Lutherans and Catholics. Russian colonial policy at that time wanted to keep foreigners separate from the native Russian population. This suited the Mennonites well. They wanted to control their own villages.

Prussian immigrants continued coming until 1859 and settled in three major areas. I will discuss only the Old Colony because this is where my family settled. These immigrants started their new lives in Ukraine with only the possessions in their wagons. They were poor. They experienced many hardships common to pioneers. But many prosperous years were sandwiched between their arrival in the Ukraine in 1789, and the major exoduses starting in 1874 and continuing in 1923. They had come with few possessions, and after World War I, the Revolution, and the famine they left with few possessions, just like Job.

GRIGORJEWKA

NINETY-SIX YEARS AFTER the first Prussian Mennonites arrived in the Ukraine, my dad, Gerhard Klassen, was born in Burwalde, a small German Mennonite village in the Chortiza colony. His birth date was April 7, 1885.

My mother, Anna (Unger) Klassen, was born on May 27, 1888, in Plujewka, another German Mennonite village in the Chortiza colony. A year later her parents, Peter and Helena (Nikkel) Unger, moved from Plujewka to Grigorjewka.

This village had been founded in 1888. Because of the population growth, land had become scarce in the Old Colony. The Mennonites bought new land in distant places to create daughter colonies. Grigorjewka was one of several villages in the Ignatiev colony, 250 kilometers east of Chortitza.

The Ungers arrived in Grigorjewka with six children. From oldest to youngest they were Jakob, Maria, Helena, Katharina, Peter and Anna, my mother. Four more daughters would be born in Grigorjewka: Aganetha, Justina, Margaretha and Elisabeth (Liese). Liese remembers her parents telling her that they had dug out a room-sized hole in the ground in which the family lived. The dwelling had one window.

Dad's family came to Grigorjewka later. The precise year is unknown but it was after his mother's marriage to her third husband, Isaak Schroeder, in October 10, 1895, and his death on August 21, 1907. My parents both spoke of this village with great affection. It was located between the 45th and 50th parallel. Kharkov was its nearest large city. Grigorjewka lay seven kilometers east of Gawrilowka and seven kilometers west of the Barwenkowo railway station. In 1996 the odometer of the Ukrainian van we rode in, clocked the distance from Zaporozhye, a city along the banks of the Dnieper River, as 253 kilometers northeast. Over a hundred years ago, without cars, this settlement was far removed from the Chortitza colony nucleus of Mennonites where their ancestors had arrived 100 years earlier.

When speaking about their home village of Grigorjewjka our parents described the village in glowing terms. It was a new village with one central street lined by white picket fences on each side of the street. Each farmer was allotted a farm yard on which to build his house with attached barn and plenty of land to plant fruit trees between the picket fence and the house. Houses were adequate for their large families. Rooms were identified as "the front room, the corner room, the big room, the bedrooms and the kitchen." The house contained a built-in stove/oven made of home-made brick. This could serve as a heater for the house or an oven to bake bread. A brick outdoor oven fueled with straw was used in summer. The smell of freshly baked bread wafted in the fresh air.

The vegetable garden was planted behind the house. The houses annexed the barns which made the access to the barn easy. The fruit trees bore pears, cherries, plums and apples. "If only you could have picked apples from a tree," Mother said, implying how unfortunate we were in Saskatchewan when we ate an occasional apple from a box of store-bought apples. These families dried enough fruit to last all winter. They had not yet learned to can fruit. Our parents spoke of Ukraine's mild climate where tomatoes ripened before frost turned them black. The taste of watermelons grown in Canada could not be compared to the sweet flavor of Ukraine's product. They also grew mulberry bushes whose leaves fed the silkworms, which in turn made threads of silk for them to use.

The arable fields were outside the village, producing wheat, oats, barley and rye. Possibly there were other crops also. At first only horses were used to work the fields. The early binders did not bind the sheaves. Instead, Mother remembers having to secure the sheaves with small bunches of grain stalks to serve as twine, which was hard work. The village mill ground their flour. It was no secret that plenteous white bread and plump wives indicated prosperity.

Field labor was done by the family and by the Ukrainian peasants living around them. My cousin, Jake Pauls, who lived with Grandma and Grandpa said that, "Grandpa never worked." However, no doubt he worked when he was younger. They were poor at first but he prospered. He wove basket trunk-like containers with lids and latches into which my parents packed their meager supplies to come to Canada much later.

On the farm our grandparents raised chickens, ducks, pigs and cattle. Butchering pigs late in fall was a festive occasion in which relatives and neighbors were invited to help with the meat processing. The custom, which I remember, was carried to Canada, and will be described later.

A Russian cow herder was hired by the village. Every morning he walked down the main street and gathered herds from each farmer's gate. He took them to the common village pasture to graze. In the evening he returned them to the village. Mother remarked how well the cows knew to which farmyard they belonged. They stopped at their gate and waited for the gate to open. Their owners unlatched the gate and let them in. The German Mennonites also hired Russians to work in the fields and in their homes.

Grandma Unger earned some spending money from selling butter and eggs. Her daughters thought she was becoming a bit stingy with her eggs and butter in the family's cooking. One day Grandpa overheard one of his daughters instruct her sister saying, "Always use more butter or eggs than Ma tells you to because she is trying to save the butter and eggs to sell so she has more money." With a chuckle he asked his wife, "Is that true?"

Living in a village with about forty other families provided many social occasions. Community and church life was important. My mother and her siblings attended elementary classes in the attractive brick school. Mother learned to write a beautiful Gothic script. German was the language of school and church. The school building also served as their church. Families visited each other on Sunday afternoons for a Faspa of coffee, zwieback and perhaps platz. Messages about a funeral or about a visiting speaker could easily be written on a note and passed from one house to another. The villagers also selected their own village mayor. Young people met to sing in the choir, and for social gatherings on Sunday evenings. They sang German folk songs and played circle games. Walking a girl home from these house parties could be the beginning of a serious relationship. From this setting many of the young people found their future spouses.

The colonists needed little from the big cities. The village met most of their needs. Life was good. They did not know yet that they needed electricity, indoor plumbing, telephones, or cars.

Although the Mennonites did not socialize with the Russian population, they were not immune to their way of life. Germans were impressed with the Russian greeting at Easter time. "Christ is Risen!" one would say. The response was "He is risen indeed!"

At Easter time both German colonists and Russians made Paschi. It is a sweet bread made of yeast and a bountiful supply of eggs, and baked in round coffee tins to make tall loaves. When the dome of the risen dough reached the top of the can it was ready to bake. The aroma of baking paschi even excelled the smell of bread baking. It tasted best when it came straight from the oven. After the loaves cooled, they were frosted with powdered sugar and cream icing. Colored sugar or tiny decorative candy was scattered over the icing. My sister, Justine, said it is sold in Regina stores today. Many Ukrainians came to Canada when our parents did and introduced their foods to Canada. I even saw Paschi in an Orthodox church on the Mount of Olives near Jerusalem.

Mother told of a young Russian suitor, accompanied by a matchmaker, coming to see the Russian maid employed by Grandma Klassen Friesen Schroeder. The matchmaker asked the suitor to walk across the room so the maid could see he was not crippled. Mother laughed at this primitive way of choosing a spouse.

Our parents thought the three-day Russian weddings were an oddity. But Mennonites celebrated three days of Christmas which they did not think was odd at all.

Like Catholics and Lutherans, Mennonites used a catechism to teach their faith to the youth. The catechism consisted of questions and answers about Mennonite doctrine. Every baptismal candidate who wanted to become a member of the church was expected to learn the answers to the catechism questions by memory. During the months prior to baptism, the sermons in the worship period were based on the teachings in the catechism. The minister asked the questions and the youth stood up and answered with memorized responses. The answers were based on Scripture. The Bible reference was given after each response. The catechism also became an annual review for those who were members of the church. This method of instruction continued in Canada through my teen years. Sometimes a candidate read the answers rather than giving the answer by memory. This was one of Dad's pet peeves. Everyone should memorize the material, he thought. Annie adds insight on Dad's sensitivity: "Dad's eyesight was too poor to read and learn catechism so he and a friend went to the garden where his friend helped him memorize. Learning to memorize via a helper had not come easy. Maybe that was why he was critical of those who didn't memorize."

In Grigorjewka baptism was a prerequisite to marriage. This muddied the waters of a believer's baptism. Kornelius Friesen, Dad's half brother, told of his experience. When youth reached their late teens they were expected to be baptized. When he was about to be baptized, a spokesman testified to the leadership about the youth's good character. But they did not ask him about a new birth, and young Kornelius knew he had no conversion experience to share. Uncle Kornelius became disillusioned with the Kirchliche church (later known in Canada as the General Conference Mennonite Church). He did not think the church was evangelical enough so he left and became a member of the Mennonite Brethren Church.

Grigorjewka's Mennonite life span was short. It existed only about 40 years. Our parents lived in the village from 1889 to 1925, in its best years, when they left for Canada.

In August, 1996, Lena, Henry, Justine, and Ray and I visited Grigorjewka. We had heard that the entire village had been destroyed by fire and by the German army retreating after the Soviets defeated them at the battle of Stalingrad in 1943. We were delighted to see that the village exists and thrives. A Ukrainian woman living there today acknowledged that Germans had lived in her house before she arrived in Grigorjewka in 1933. The architecture of most of the houses indicated that Mennonites had not built them as they lacked the distinct features of Mennonite buildings. One of those features included the rounded upper end of a window. Ukrainians built rectangular windows.

We roamed the vacant school yard in Grigorjewka and found brick rubble. We realized it was rubble from the school Mother had attended.

We visited the cemetery, but all German gravestones had been removed. One large concrete marker had been pulled over on its face. It may have been a memorial to the German soldiers who died in a train crash in about 1917 or 1918. The German Mennonites had been commanded by the German army to dig a mass grave and bury them.

Many of our family's relatives had been buried in this graveyard including my Klassen grandmother and my oldest siblings, Helena and Gerhard Klassen. There was no stone to mark their place.

Gerhard and Anna (Unger) Klassen, Grigorjewka,
Ekatrinoslov, Ukraine, January 25, 1911

Firstborn Helena, died at age 3, 1915

My parents and bro. Gerhard (George), 1916

War and Revolution

Three years before World War I began, my parents, Gerhard Klassen and Anna Unger, married in Grigorjewka, Gouvernement Charkov, in the Ukraine. He was 25 and she was 22. The year was 1911. They did not know that their quiet world would collapse before their yet unborn children were ten years old.

Many changes took place between the Mennonites' immigration in 1789 and World War I. The Mennonites had come during Catherine the Great's rule. They had lived under five succeeding rulers since then. In 1914 Czar Nicholas II ruled. Catherine's promises were no longer valid. One agreement had been freedom from military service; now men were drafted.

Some of this ethnic group felt threatened as early as the 1870s. The draft exemption status was at risk which led to 18,000 immigrating to North America beginning in 1874. Among these immigrants of the late 19th century were Grandma (Nikkel) Unger's two older brothers, Johann and Jacob Nikkel. They settled in Kansas. Immigrants in that area are credited with introducing Russian red hard wheat to the United States. Two of Grandma (Nikkel) Unger's siblings immigrated to Brazil.

Before World War I the Mennonites in Russia prospered. They were engaged in agriculture and manufactured farm implements. They also established various institutions. Among the institutions were Mutual Aid, a Home for the Aged, orphanages, hospitals, a mental hospital, a school for deaf mutes, a girls' school, and a school for young men. None of these can be credited to the villagers of Grigorjewka. The village was too new.

The Bolshevik Revolution took place in far off St. Petersburg in 1917. In 1918 Czar Nicholas was shot. Now the Mennonites took notice. Changes were in the air. Chaos was obvious. No one seemed to be in charge.

As Russia changed, the German Mennonites' independence from Russian society became threatened. Records and official correspondence had to be in Russian. They had to support Russian institutions as well as their own. Teaching Russian in school became mandatory. The Mennonites' military exemption remained threatened. The Russian peasants were restless and they were jealous of their more prosperous countrymen.

Some of the reforms were not enforced immediately. For example, the Gregorian calendar replaced the Julian calendar in 1918. Two of my sisters, born in 1919 and 1922 were given Julian calendar birthdays. Lena's birthday is January 21 by the Julian calendar but she was born in early January according to the Gregorian calendar. When she celebrates her birthday on January 21 now, she is already several weeks past her actual birth date. In1924, when my brother Henry was born, the Gregorian calendar determined his birth date.

Approximately 120,000 Mennonites were living in Russia after World War I. Many had died during the war. More died in the 1921-1923 famine. Typhus claimed others and Influenza killed yet more. Among the latter was my mother's sister, Helena (Unger) Pauls and her husband, Heinrich. She had tuberculosis but she died of the flu. Our own parents lost their first two children, ages three and one of, scarlet fever and measles three days apart.

During the war and revolution the villages were overrun with the White Army, the Red Army, the German Army, and various brutal bands of militia. There were Bolsheviks, Mensheviks, and the most brutal of all, the Machno terrorists. Nestor Machno proved to be the Mennonites' worst enemy. Machno had lived among Mennonites and had worked for them. He knew them well and even spoke the Low German dialect they spoke at home. In his opinion he had been underpaid and he came to seek revenge. The roving bands wanted roasted chicken today and eggs tomorrow. The villagers tried their best to hide their food so they would not starve.

The battle front between the Red Army and the White Army went back and forth through some areas up to 23 times (C. J. Dyck in An Introduction to Mennonite History). Grigorjewka was not as hard hit as some other villages. Sagradovka, where my brother-in-law, John Redekop, lived as a boy, suffered beyond reason. Two-hundred forty people were killed in the month of November, 1919. The villagers took up arms to defend themselves against those who came to destroy them. Tragically, self-defense led to their own destruction, rather than their salvation. Villagers were plundered, raped and slaughtered. Anarchy ruled.

As a child I saw in our family friends' home a snapshot of four men from the same family in coffins at the same time. Starvation killed others.

During the 1920s, American and Canadian Mennonites formed a relief agency called "The Mennonite Central Committee" (MCC) to help their brothers and sisters in Russia. John Peters, my brother-in-law, remembers as a boy receiving rice from MCC. Long after his 80th birthday he volunteered at the MCC thrift store in Clearbrook, BC, six days a week. Mother reported Russian beggars coming to the door. Grandma gave them each a bowl of dry beans. They were nutritious and went a long way.

She remembered the soldiers from Germany who were billeted in their homes. They felt a kinship with these young men. They shared a common language and heritage but they were now considered the enemy of their countrymen. They communicated in German. The German soldiers found a home away from home in so-called enemy territory.

An officer in this army called together a meeting of the villagers to try to persuade the people of Grigorjewka to take up arms to defend themselves against their Russians neighbors, if a future occasion called for it. They refused to do so. They were a nonviolent people by faith. Soon after this meeting with the German officer, the pastor of the Grigorjewka Mennonite church was on the road riding on his wagon when he caught up with a Russian pedestrian. He stopped his horses to give the man a ride. This man spoke freely to the pastor whom he recognized, saying he had been at the meeting himself and had heard the minister refuse to cooperate with the German officer by taking up arms against their neighbors. Mennonites had chosen not to shoot at them. He said, "We won't shoot at you either." And they didn't. The German officer admitted in the end that had they done so, they would have been defeated.

The Russian cauldron continued to boil. Native Russian and Mennonite farmers had to give up their horses to the bandits who requisitioned them, leaving insufficient horses to work the fields.

Five years after World War I ended, the Russian revolution was well on its way. Conditions were getting worse instead of better, so the Mennonites fled their beloved Ukrainian soil in search of peace, religious freedom, and a place to farm. From 1923 until 1930 a steady flow of emigrants left Russia.

Grandpa Unger's brother, Abram Unger, waited for the 12:00 noon train at the railroad in Barwenkowo, Ukraine, in July 1924. The train was late. In fact, the train was so late that Abram and his family, with many others, spent the night on the platform of the station. Many relatives had come to see them off. When the train had not arrived by the following morning, the Abram Unger family returned to their home in their village. Here his wife made cherry pancakes and Abram took some to the railway station for the travelers to eat. One-hundred seventy-five persons from Grigorjewka emigrated that summer, but Great Uncle Abram never left Russia. Did he not believe Russia was getting worse?

For a short period of time, early in the revolution, from 1921-1924, the desperate situation in Russia calmed down. The Communist government announced plans for their economic policies. The smaller factories were allowed some freedom to set their own quotas, and the small land owners could work their land as they wanted. They were obligated to deliver a quota of products to the government and were at liberty to sell the rest. However, the shortage of horses hindered them in the production of farm products.

Many Mennonites thought the tough times were over. But "the pause" proved to be only a calm before the storm. It may be that Uncle Abram was one of the people who thought the crisis was over when he decided to go back to his home in Grigorjewka in July, 1924.

Uncle Peter Harms, married to Mother's sister Justine, (see "Important People in our Lives" chapter) did not want to leave Russia. His village store was doing well. Things were becoming more stable; nonetheless, his wife had premonitions that something was about to happen. One night when coming home to Grigorjewka in a buggy with a load of goods and a Russian driver, robbers sprang out from the trees on both sides of the road. Peter shouted "GO!" and used his whip. The horses sprang forward and they escaped. Now he was ready to emigrate.

Aunt Justine said her husband had tried to rescue Margaret Pauls, (daughter of Helena Unger Pauls) one of the five orphans left when their parents died within days of each other. Margaret lived with her late father's sister, a single aunt. Peter went to Miss Pauls' house to offer assistance to emigrate but the elder Miss Pauls became irate and chased him from her yard. So Margaret remained in Russia when her three siblings came to Canada. In 1994 one of Margaret's granddaughters visited the rest of her family in Canada. She, her Russian husband, and her two little daughters attended a family reunion (which we also attended) in Winnipeg. They were new Christians. To help them in their ministry, they took home a guitar from Canada. We spoke to each other in Low German since she knew no English and I knew no Russian. Stories abounded.

Twenty-one thousand Mennonites immigrated to Canada in the 1920s. Among them were most of my parents' relatives. Some Mennonites remained in Russia, including Mother's brother Jacob and his family. Although Canada was the country of choice, 4,000 emigrants went to Paraguay, including Mother's sister, Tina, and her husband, Abram, who was Dad's brother, with their family. Reports from earlier immigrants to United States and Canada were favorable, but Paraguay was an unknown. Paraguay took people with health problems while Canada was more selective. And Grandma's two brothers had lived in the U.S. for many years.

While people were streaming out of Russia to avoid the evils of the revolution, the revolutionary turmoil continued. The various roving bands, or armies, arrested innocent people for suspected wrongs. The midnight knock became a reality for many families including Uncle Jacob. We have no details about the reasons and circumstances of his arrest. We know that the communists tried to eradicate ministers of the gospel, leaving the church without leadership. But Uncle Jacob was not a church leader. Censorship of mail out of Russia kept the victims' relatives ignorant of many of the hardships they suffered.

Some people told of miraculous escapes from would-be captors. Mother told of an anonymous man who was walking across a barnyard. He heard men approaching. He knew he would be in trouble if they saw him. Everyone was a potential captor. Where should he hide? There was no place he could duck into without being noticed. He pressed his body against the barn wall and prayed. The suspected enemies walked by but they were kept from seeing him. Was it divine intervention? Mother thought it was.

Another story was about a man trying to be invisible to the potential enemy. He too heard the approach of men in a farmyard. He dashed for a nearby straw stack and burrowed himself in the straw. The rustling straw was noisy and the two men walking through the yard heard it. "Listen!" one man said to the other. Just then some chickens ran about the barnyard rustling the straw on the ground. The second answered, "No, it was just the chickens." The man in the stack had been delivered from potential imprisonment.

Some stories were too terrible to bear. And we did not want to hear them.

My parents with five children left Barwenkovo, Russia, via train to go to Riga, Latvia, in the autumn of 1925. Getting a passport and a visa at this point had not been a problem. They had packed two hand woven reed basket trunks made by Grandpa Unger. They contained some clothes, bedding, a brass Russian hand basin and a baby fork for Heinrich (Henry), a year old. From Riga they sailed across the Baltic Sea to Southampton, England.

In Southampton British physicians screened the healthy emigrants from the unhealthy. Emigrants feared being separated from their family members. If emigrants did not meet British health standards, part of the family could be detained in England while the rest of the family sailed across the Atlantic to yet another foreign country. Not knowing the English language made this prospect a real threat to the family's unity. The ailing members were treated in England before joining their families in Canada. Thankfully, my family was healthy and passed inspection.

In 1930 the emigration ceased. Russia closed the doors of exit. My parents' families are examples of how many families were torn apart by various emigrations.

This is a summary of where my parents' siblings settled:

The UNGERS: (my mother's family)

Peter and Helena (Nikkel) Unger, Mother's parents, came to Canada and settled at Hasket, Manitoba.

Jakob Unger, their oldest remained in Russia. We know he had three children by his first wife, and one son named Berni by his second wife. We know he was imprisoned in Siberia and then released from prison in 1964 when Nikita Khrushchev was in power. We have his letter written in 1933.

Maria (Unger) Pauls and her husband, Jakob Pauls, with their family settled near Morden, Manitoba.

Helena (Unger) Pauls died in Russia in 1918 of influenza after childbirth. Their last baby died at birth. Helena's husband died of the flu about ten days later. Their oldest daughter, Helena, died of tuberculosis a year later. Another daughter, Margaret remained in Russia and married a Wiens. Their three remaining children came to Canada with Grandpa and Grandma at about the time our parents did. They were Maria, Heinrich and Jakob. These three visited their sister Margaret in Russia before she died. Her life had been very hard.

Katharina (Unger) Klassen and her husband, Abram Klassen (Dad's brother) and their children immigrated to Paraguay. They were Helena, Peter, Gerhard, and Abram. They adopted a daughter whose name was Margaret. This aunt's trachoma of the eyes kept her out of Canada. We called her Tante Tin. After her husband, Abram died she married Isaak Hildebrand in Paraguay. How well I remember the airmail letters from Paraguay with the return address and name of Isaak Hildebrand. Not knowing we could buy peanuts in Canada she sent us a small package of raw peanuts from Paraguay. I knew we had double cousins in Paraguay. One of those, Peter Klassen (Aunt Katharina and Uncle Abram's son) visited BC in 1980 or so, where we met him and his second wife, Margareta.

The youngest six children of the Peter Unger family and their spouses with children came to Canada:

Peter Unger and his wife, Katharina (Tina Unrau). Swift Current, Saskatchewan, and Abbotsford, BC.

Anna (Unger) Klassen, our mother, and our father, Gerhard Klassen. **Rush Lake, Saskatchewan, Fork River, Manitoba, and Abbotsford, BC.**

Aganetha (Unger) Harms and her husband, Peter Harms. Whitewater, Manitoba.

Justina (Unger) Harms with her husband Peter Harms, (no relative to Aganetha's husband). Rush Lake, Saskatchewan, and Chilliwack, BC.

Margaretha (Unger) Warkentin and her husband, Johann (Vahng from the Russian Ivan) Warkentin. Winnipegosis, Manitoba.

Elisabeth (Unger) Buhler, the youngest of the survivors, and her husband, Isaac Buhler, settled at Haskett, Manitoba, where her parents made their home. Tante Liese Buhler lived in Manitoba until her death in January, 2011, just days short of her 112th birthday. She was the oldest Canadian known at the time of her death.

The Unger siblings now lived on three different continents and some never saw each other again. Those in Canada saw each other, seldom at first and more often later as the financial conditions improved. My Unger grandparents could boast of over sixty grandchildren.

The KLASSENS: My paternal grandfather was Gerhard Klassen.

Grandma Helena (Loewen) Klassen Friesen Schroeder died in Russia in 1923 of a stroke. Her three husbands had preceded her. David Klassen, her oldest child, we think lived in Siberia. It is possible he went there because of the availability of land. All we know is that Uncle Abram Klassen had written to David's son in Siberia. His name is not known. This was information given to us by our double cousin, Peter Klassen, when he came from Paraguay to visit Canada in 1980. Do we have Klassen cousins in Siberia? Maybe.

Abram Klassen married to Mother's sister, Katharina Unger, went to Paraguay in 1930 and died a few months after immigration. He could not tolerate the heat and the food in Paraguay.

Gerhard Klassen, our father, married Anna Unger, our mother, and settled near Rush Lake, Saskatchewan in 1929, and at Fork River, Manitoba in 1937, and Abbotsford, BC in 1948.

Aganetha (Klassen) Peters and her husband, Kornelius Peters settled in Blumenort village, post office Blumenhof, Saskatchewan. Later they lived at Hanley, Saskatchewan.

Katharina Klassen was single and settled in Winnipeg, Manitoba, until she married Abram Koop, in 1930 or 1931. They lived near St. Anne until they moved to Fork River after we moved there in 1937. They lived only a half mile from our place. They adopted one son, Victor.

Kornelius Friesen, Dad's half brother, with his wife, Maria (Guenter), lived near Steinbach, Manitoba. They moved to B.C. later.

Julius Friesen, also Dad's half brother, and his wife, Helena (Unger), settled in Winnipeg, Manitoba.

Heinrich Schroeder, Dad's half brother died while serving in the Russian army in about 1921.

Franz (Frank) Schroeder, married twice. His second wife was Maria Klassen. They lived first in southern Manitoba, then at Winnipegosis, and finally they moved to B.C.

Their offspring, many of our cousins, became important to us while we were growing up. Some of them became our best friends and enriched our lives. I met all of those in Canada, but because of age differences I didn't learn to know all of them well. Distance also prohibited us from getting to know each other well. Of those in Russia and Paraguay, we met only Peter Klassen. At an Unger family reunion in 1994 we met a granddaughter of Margaret's from Ukraine.

All of the above mentioned Unger and Klassen siblings and their families had lived in the Ukrainian village of Grigorjewka at one time. It can be assumed they would have lived out their lives there, and perhaps in neighboring villages, in an ideal world, not shaped by the political and military upheavals of early 20th Century Russia.

Many of the former Grigorjewka residents came to Canada. Those who did not, moved to other German Mennonite villages in Russia. The whole village of Grigorjewka was sold to the Russians (Ukrainians).

Later a fire destroyed the buildings on six of the farm sites in the village. During the 1930s the fruit trees were not sprayed with Paris Green and they died of caterpillar infestation. The white picket fences, of which the landowners had been so proud, were burned as fuel. The last news of Grigorjewka was that the whole village was destroyed by the German army. But as noted earlier, it was rebuilt by Ukrainian Russians.

When our parents spoke of Grigorjewka they remembered a proud and beautiful Grigorjewka whose trees would always bloom and whose houses would never burn. They loved their village, their people, and the way of life experienced during Grigorjewka's golden years.

1925 emigration photo. Back: son Gerhard, father Gerhard, front: Anna, Helena, mother Anna holding Heinrich (Henry), front left missing Netha (Nettie) cut out later because she needed a picture of herself at school

HEALTH AND DEATH IN RUSSIA

MARRIAGES ENDED IN premature death, not in divorce. Babies died after birth, not by abortion. Remarriages were common. Children were raised by one biological parent and a stepparent. Children had step siblings and half siblings. Dad remarked that having step fathers was not a lot of fun.

Statistics kept by Grandpa Unger in Russia in 1894, by my mother in Canada, and by my cousin Peter Klassen, in Paraguay in 1980, came to life when I processed our common history. Information is incomplete but I have enough data to conclude that their health care was grossly inadequate.

My parents had no dental care.

They both needed glasses and neither had them.

Dad's broken hip in 1921 was never set properly.

These were not life threatening but they were handicaps.

Tuberculosis killed Dad's father, Gerhard Klassen, at age 32, in 1891. He left a young widow with five children. Three of their children had died only weeks after birth. Their deaths were undiagnosed. What killed the widow's second husband, Martin Friesen? What caused her third husband, Isaak Schroeder, to die before he was old and while he had young sons? Why had four of their babies died? Aunt Tina (Katharina Klassen) Koop, an older sister, told me they had all been beautiful, healthy babies at birth.

Grandma was only 47 when her third husband died. She considered marrying a fourth time but this time she consulted my dad. He advised her not to marry. Did Grandma's need to get married multiple times indicate her need for a husband to work her farm? Does Dad's advice indicate that he was now old enough to work the farm himself? He was 22 when stepfather Schroeder died in 1907.

We do know that Grandma Loewen Klassen Friesen Schroeder died of a stroke in 1923, as stated earlier. She had been very obese. What would her cholesterol count have been? Dad loved foods high in cholesterol and carbohydrates and never knew they caused his stroke.

We do not know the cause of David Klassen's death All we know is that he is not on the family picture taken in about 1911.

Other health issues included trachoma, a contagious disease of the eyes, which had no treatment at the time.

There is an account of a newborn baby in Mother's parental family who screamed for the entire two weeks of her life. Then she died. A little brother died at the age of nine months.

I have mentioned earlier Mother's sister Helena who died of influenza after childbirth, and of the deaths of her husband, their newborn and their fifteen year old.

Finally, my parent's first two children died within three days of each other in 1915. They had measles and scarlet fever at the same time. Mother was devastated. Her lap was empty until July of the same year when (Gerhard) George was born. Many years later, when we lived in the pit of poverty, she said she was glad now that the first two had died. They had been spared all the misery that the war, the revolution in Russia, and the drought in Saskatchewan had caused. But five of her Russian born children did survive those hurdles and seven of us lived through the depression in Canada.

From Emigrants to Immigrants.

Southampton in England would be remembered by eight-year-old Nettie for the peanuts she ate there for the first time. Lena, almost four, remembered a small doll Dad bought for her in England.

Dad's problem with the English language began in England. He remembered a conversation he was trying to have with an Englishman. I believe it involved money. The man was saying "eleven" to Dad. "Eleven" sounded a lot like "Loewen" to Dad, in German. His mother's name had been Loewen. He wondered what the Englishman wanted with that name.

After our family's visit to Southampton they set sail across the Atlantic Ocean on the S.S. Minnedosa. On the ship from Southampton to Canada, Dad inquired about the location of the dining room. The German word "Essen" means "to eat." Dad was guided to the rest room.

The autumn seas rocked the ship until the whole family, with the exception of one-year-old Henry, became very seasick. One of the family stories is that nothing deterred him from crawling through the mess on the floors.

The voyagers approached the Gulf of St. Lawrence and sailed through the Gulf until they reached Quebec City, Quebec. They disembarked on November 25, 1925, after a 19 day voyage. Mother reported that the city of Montreal looked black and dirty. From Quebec, the Canadian Pacific Railroad took them to Manitoba. Our parents never saw eastern Canada again. The Canadian Pacific Railroad company provided transportation for the Russian immigrants whether or not they had money for their fare. Our parents' destination was the little town of Kleefeld in southern Manitoba, where Dad's half brother, Kornelius Friesen lived. He and his young family were very recent immigrants themselves.

Physically the family was in Canada. But emotionally they were still in Russia where they had left friends and relatives behind. For those left behind, the sufferings of Stalin's purge had just begun. Through the years my parents learned about the terrible events of people being scattered over the globe, and the reality of the prisoners in Siberian Gulags—labor camps, forests and prisons. News actually came very slowly and rarely. (See Appendix II for a letter from Uncle Jakob. He dares not detail the events of his life.) Stories in books today tell of the persecution and torture of many, including Christians in the Gulags, and of deaths on the way to Siberia and in Siberia. Many refugees escaped Siberia and trekked to China, but we do not know how many died in the effort.

As the immigrants arrived in Canada, some like uncle Frank Shroeder did not have money for the family's train fare. He and others like him owed their fare for at least fifteen years after their arrival in Canada.

I remember that when I was a young teenager at Nordheim Mennonite Church at Winnipegosis in the 1940s, such debt became a church concern. Immigrants who had not paid their debt were urged to do so. Some families were unable to pay while others had no sense of obligation. The congregation was grateful to the Canadian railroad company and was embarrassed about the longstanding debt. The church collected money from the members and paid the debt for everyone in the Mennonite community, whether or not they were involved with the church.

After my family's arrival in southern Manitoba they went to live with a family by the name of Reimer. They were earlier Mennonite immigrants. We do not know how far from the Friesens and from Kleefeld they lived. Hundreds of Mennonites from Russia had arrived here during and after the 1874 immigration. Hundreds more like Uncle Kornelius' family, and ours, arrived in the 1920s. The area the Mennonites moved into was called the East Reserve.

Our parents did not know the Reimers. Whether the Reimer's motive in taking our parents and five children in, was compassion, we do not know. Mrs. Reimer gave birth to a new baby and wanted household help from Mother. Mother had a one-year-old herself and four children age ten and under. Mother had never worked for others.

One of Mother's responsibilities was washing the new baby's diapers. This was not a problem until she found the stack of diapers. Mrs. Reimer had stacked soiled diapers without rinsing them after diaper changes. Mother was indignant. Every woman ought to know that one rinses diapers after a baby soils them. For Mrs. Reimer to expect Mother to do what she herself found too dirty to do was too humiliating. She took the problem to Mr. Reimer. He understood. No doubt they had no flush toilets, but Mrs. Reimer rinsed soiled diapers after that.

Mother enjoyed telling us about the canned peach she and Dad ate in the basement of the Reimer home. They had not eaten peaches before and were not familiar with canning foods. The canned peaches on the shelves looked delicious. Since the Reimers provided them with food, they were not stealing if they tasted just one. They opened the sealed jar and took only one peach and closed the jar. It was certainly good to eat. Years later when she understood canning, she laughed as she thought about a whole jar going bad because they had wanted to taste one peach.

No one remembers how long they lived with the Reimers. Perhaps a year? Or was it just over the first winter? No one old enough to tell the story was more than six years old at the time.

Here in the East Reserve our parents saw the spectacular northern lights for the first time. They had never heard of these dancing lights in the northern sky. They were terrified! We children grew up knowing about them and accepting them as a delightful break from the monotony of the clear, cold and starry skies in the winters of Manitoba. Like an unfocused beam of light from a giant flashlight, the lights bounced and spread over the entire northern dome. Under the flashing sky we walked over a crisp, white world, crushing the snow beneath our feet until it squeaked on the frozen soil.

Pristine winter nights were at their best under a big white moon illuminating the barren landscape for miles around. In Manitoba, the howl of coyotes pierced the cold air. It was a world of clean air and cold beauty, but harsh to our touch.

The first years in Canada proved to be like the winter nights, cold and harsh, but not nearly as beautiful.

Canada

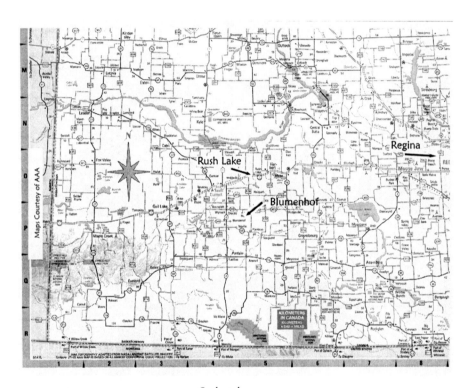

Saskatchewan

Trying to Make It

How DOES AN immigrant family find its place in a new world? Our parents, like others, had left the warmth and security of the German Mennonite village life. They had received help from the Reimers but they understood from the outset that this was a temporary living situation. Neither did they want to be dependent on others. There was no Mennonite village as they had known it in Russia where they could put down their roots. In Canada farmers lived on farms miles away from each other. They could not understand the language of their host country. Neither did they know the culture, politics, economy, or the resources that might be available to them. They were without a voice and without power. Added to these difficulties were Dad's extremely poor vision, poor reading skills and his heavy limp—although the latter was the least of his problems.

Dad had always been a farmer. It was the only way of life he knew. It was the only skill he had. But he had no farm, no implements and no horses to work for him. He had no money to purchase what he needed. When his sister Aganetha's (Nettie) husband, Kornelius Peters, invited him to come to live near them at Blumenort, Saskatchewan, our parents decided to take their family there. This location is just north of the Montana border. It was about 300-400 miles west of the Reimers and the Friesens. It would be good to live close to his sister, whom we called Tante Neta Peters. Mother's brother Peter Unger would also be within a day's drive with horses.

Blumenhof would be their post office but they would live in the little Mennonite village of Blumenort nearby. It was not anything like the village they had left in Russia. Here, each man was on his own, which meant no close community life even though they would be living near Mennonites.

They moved into a two room shack in Blumenort, which means a "place of flowers." The shack was grossly inadequate for a family of seven. Mother, Dad and Henry slept in the only bedroom. George, Nettie, Annie and Lena slept on the floor of the other room which served multiple purposes. Every night Mother spread the children's bedding on the floor and every morning she picked it up and stacked it in the bedroom. They needed the floor space during the day.

Dad worked for farmers to earn money to feed his family and to buy a farm. While working for an English speaking farmer he was told to catch a certain horse in the pasture. Dad and the farmer chased the horse while the farmer repeatedly said, "Catch him!" Dad thought he understood. At last Dad caught the horse. But the farmer still said "Catch him!" Dad thought he must have misunderstood. He let the horse go! Now the farmer was irate. He let Dad know in any language that to "catch" means to apprehend and not release him.

The English lessons were hard.

Dad was working away from home when a hailstorm hit Blumenort. Mother was home with her brood of children. Lena recalls how Mother stood at the window waiting and watching for Dad to come home to safety. She anxiously watched the hail smash into her little shack; and, near tears, she fretted and prayed. Can you imagine her fears about being left alone with her children in a foreign country, without money and without a language, fearing her husband had been killed in the storm?

When the storm was over Dad came home unharmed. He had found a straw stack and burrowed in the straw until it was safe to walk home.

George and Nettie had attended the village German school in Russia. Now at school in Canada, all my siblings names were translated into English. Gerhard was changed to George; Neta became Nettie; Anna was now Annie; Helena was abbreviated to Lena and Heinrich became Henry. In Blumenort they attended school but they had a problem. They had to learn English. George was ten when they came to Canada. He was never able to catch up to the grade of his peers. He learned to speak English well but it was too late to help him in the lower grades. Then he had to drop out of school early to help Dad with finances. He was not ashamed to tell the world he had the equivalent of a fifth grade education.

During World War II he joined the navy. He was aware that the navy required a tenth grade education so he told them he qualified. He was afraid he would be drafted into the army and he did not want to serve in the army. Nettie was eight when they arrived in Canada so she had an advantage over George. She became a very good student.

For a short time our family lived at Pamburn, not far from Blumenort. Annie remembers someone taking the children to church in a canvas covered car.

It was at Blumenort, in the two-room shack, that the four oldest children were awakened one November night and taken to the neighbors. Lena remembers Dad carrying her, not quite six years old. At the neighbor's house they slept on the floor, next to a wood heater, which was very hot! No one wanted to sleep near it so they took turns sleeping in the hot spot. Outside a blizzard raged.

In our parent's shack, while Henry slept, Mother waited for Dad to return with a self proclaimed midwife. Early on a Sunday morning, November 6, 1927, Mother gave birth to their fourth living daughter. They named me Tina. Dad registered the birth in Blumenhof, the town. Dad was 42½, Mother 39½, George 12, Nettie 10, Annie 8, Lena not quite 6 and Henry had just turned 3. King George V reigned in the British Empire. McKenzie King was the Prime Minister of Canada.

My family was still making adjustments necessary to live in this foreign land. They accepted land measurements in acres instead of Desjatins. Miles replaced Wersts. Instead of Rubles they thought dollars. A Russian "Poot" did not have a comparable weight in Canada. But forty pounds made a poot. They had thought kilograms in Russia rather than pounds and meters instead of yards. And what was a foot or an inch? And temperatures in Fahrenheit meant absolutely nothing. How can 32 degrees be freezing when everyone knows freezing starts at 0 degrees? As long as I lived at home we had the Reaumur thermometer. And when I think about temperatures as they were in the prairie provinces in winter,

I think Centigrade. These measurement adjustments were only a small segment of our lives.

Becoming Canadian in culture, language, etiquette, dress, education and just "knowing the ropes" in our new world was a challenge that we hoped was not too obvious to those around us.

Financing a Farm

Two years before I was born, my parents and older siblings emigrated from the Ukraine to Canada in the autumn of 1925. In Russia Dad had worked his thrice widowed mother's farm. Before they left Russia they had been impoverished by the events of World War I and the Russian Revolution. There was no money for fare to Canada. Grandpa Unger, Mother's father, paid for the fare. Neither did my parents have money to buy a farm in their new country.

For four years Dad had worked for other farmers but he knew he needed his own farm. He also needed livestock and farm implements. In 1929 he and Mother bought a 160 acre farm near Rush Lake, Saskatchewan. They needed $600 to buy this farm in their new country. They knew nothing about Canadian banks or farm loans but they knew their relatives.

A niece, Mary Pauls, had been orphaned in Russia, at the age of 13. For three years she had made her home with our family. Now she was married to a well-to-do farmer by the name of Driedger. My parents wanted to borrow money from him. When asked, he consented. Dad would repay him with profits from his new farm. I will call this phase Plan A.

Plan B: Peter Unger, Mother's brother, operated a dairy farm near Swift Current, Saskatchewan, and might need a farm hand. His own children were attending school. George, the oldest in our family, would become this farm hand.

Uncle Peter Unger agreed to pay George a salary, but Uncle Peter would withhold a portion of the salary (we think half the salary) and would send it directly to Mr. Driedger in Osler, Saskatchewan, to pay Dad's debt.

Because of the 20 miles between the Unger's at Swift Current and our home at Rush Lake, George would make his home with the Ungers for the several years it would take until the debt was paid.

Was plan A simply to borrow money from Mr. Driedger with the intent to pay him from future farm profits, or did Plan A include Uncle Peter and George from the outset? We think Dad planned to pay Mr. Driedger with farm profits. We believe Plan B evolved after the first or second crop failure. Because all the players in this financial game are deceased, I cannot be sure how the plan was conceived.

Our parents did not know the geology or history of the Palliser Triangle in which Rush Lake was located. (Information about area found in The Rural Municipality of Excelsior, No. 166). It had a long history of drought and crop failures, and the land was covered with rocks thought to be left in the debris of a melting glacier eons past. They did not know either that the Friesens, who owned the land before us, had left this land because of the frequent droughts.

George was 14 when we moved to Rush Lake in 1929. He attended Rush Lake School with Nettie, Annie and Lena, a beginner. Nettie remembers walking in his wake because his body sheltered her from Saskatchewan's cold winds. Although no one knows exactly how old George was when he dropped out of school, he was probably between 14 and 16. He was a teenager in a foreign country and left his family home to live with the Ungers 20 miles from home. We had no phone and he had no transportation. He worked to pay off a debt he had not incurred.

What no one knew in the summer of 1929 when Dad bought the farm was that the stock market would crash in the fall of the same year. Neither did anyone foresee the long drought of the 1930s. My family had just bought a farm and moved into the heart of the depression's dust bowl. They were doomed to failure but they were unaware of this. The rainfall in 1929 had been 144.5 mm, a little less than six inches.

What the family was aware of was my birth two years earlier. What my parents knew by the time they bought the farm was that in the spring of 1930 they would have another child. Justine became the ninth member of this family.

BORN IN CANADA

JUSTINE'S BIRTH IN the old gray house two miles southeast of Rush Lake was attended by Mother's sister, Justine (Unger) Harms, who lived in Rush Lake. Consequently she was named after this aunt. Our mother's grandmother's name had been Justina Driediger Nikkel.

Complications arose and Dr. Leach, the only physician in town, was summoned. Those family members who were old enough to remember are not sure what the problem was but Annie thinks the baby's color was not good. Whatever it was, Dr. Leach resolved the problem and left mother and child in good condition. He was hired by the municipality at a salary of $4,000 a year. He was allowed to charge $3 for a house call but for this call he charged nothing. (Information from The Rural Municipality of Excelsior, No. 166)

One of the most oft told stories about Justine's birth was that Annie cried. Annie says she cried because she knew we did not have enough forks, knives and spoons to feed another child. Annie was ten years old. Justine thinks Annie cried because she didn't want HER! Justine never went hungry for lack of a spoon.

When Justine was old enough to understand that she had not moved into the old gray house with the rest of the family, she asked where she had been. With a twinkle in her eye Mother told her she had been waiting for us under the cellar steps. That was the end of our sex education. There was no pregnancy, stork, hospital or cabbage leaf.

Justine was the last of nine live births. It was difficult for Mother to remember a particular incident in each child's life, so she generalized by saying, "One of you did this or that." As an adult I realized our parents certainly did not need more children in their lives than the ones they had brought from Russia. Justine and I were superfluous. But I remember Mother saying, "Parents are not allotted a limited measure of love to be divided between all the children. Each child brings its own love with it."

Mother also said we had all weighed about ten pounds at birth. How did she know when in Canada we had no scales? Did they weigh home-delivered babies in Russia? She kept no records of our childhood. Nor do we have baby pictures. However, in her memory there were no two children as precious to her as the first two born and buried in Russia.

Although Justine and I were born in Canada and our births were recorded in the Vital Statistics Department of Regina, Saskatchewan, we were born into an immigrant family. We experienced many of the same challenges that immigrants experience when trying to adjust to a foreign country. But Justine and I never had to learn the English language in school like some of our older siblings did. They brought the English language home to us. Our parents spoke Low German to us, a language that was spoken in Russia by German Mennonites, and was retained after immigration to either Canada or Paraguay. The origin of this quaint language was probably from the dialect of German spoken in the Vistula Delta (now part of Poland) at the time. It is neither real Dutch nor German. It is also related to English. It was spoken by Mennonite people who came from Holland to Prussia and then to Russia. Our nearest neighbor, Mr. Beisel, visited us frequently. From him we learned conversational High German. We were never aware of lessons in linguistics. We were multilingual without trying. But most of all we were Canadians! Mother proudly called us her "two Canadians."

CHILD'S PLAY

IN THE WINTER of 1930-1931 Justine was not yet a year old. Mother was 42. Justine was able to sit by herself but was too young to walk. The old frame house was very cold. Fuel was scarce. I remember that Mother used straw to fuel the stove since we did not have a tree on our farm to chop down for wood. Mother placed Justine on the floor in front of the black cook stove and told me to play with her to keep her happy. I liked my little sister and was happy to play with her. I was three.

Our play ended abruptly when I felt a searing burn on my left jaw. Mother had dropped the hot metal stove lid lifter. Instinctively I flexed my neck to the left and clenched the metal. Mother quickly removed it. She commanded Henry to go down to the cellar to get a raw potato which she grated and wrapped the gratings in a cloth to make a poultice. She put it on my jaw to relieve the pain of the burn, but the scar remains to this day.

Until Justine was old enough to play with dolls, Henry and I played together. We never played with dolls. He was interested in playing outside when the weather allowed. The farm provided entertainment for us two pre-school children. It also provided information about reproduction.

On the way to the barn Henry told me that eggs were laid by hens. Incredible! He invited me to crawl into a corner of a stall to watch a hen lay her egg. We crouched down to become as invisible to the hen as possible. He told me to be very still. We saw her in her nest. We waited. With a little effort on the part of the hen, the egg was laid just as he had said. I was impressed with his wisdom and with the birth of an egg.

His next lesson was about pigs. He told me that pigs come out of their mother's bodies just like the egg had come from the hen. He was unable to prove this to me at that moment because none of the pigs were in the process of giving birth. After seeing the miracle of an egg being laid, I believed him. His word was reliable. But he neglected to tell me that pigs do not lay eggs. For many years I visualized pigs laying piggy-sized eggs that hatched into piglets just as I knew hen's eggs hatched into chicks. When at last I saw the birth of pigs, the myth was dispelled.

Henry and I played in the grain bins of the granary on the hill. Dad did not want us in those grain bins even though it was so much fun to bury ourselves in the wheat. He seemed not to be concerned about us suffocating in the wheat as much as he was about us damaging the bins and spilling the precious kernels. In winter Dad buried smoked ham and sausage in the wheat bins to preserve them until spring. The cold winters provided a natural deep freeze. In warmer weather the meat was safe from field mice and flies.

If we weren't allowed to play in the granary, we climbed to the sloping roof of the granary with our hands full of rocks. Once on top we practiced our throwing arms by pitching the rocks as far as we could. One of the rocks flew no further than Henry's head! Ouch! He held his hand to his head over his temple where the rock had struck him. I was terrified! What if he were permanently injured, or what if he died? What if he told Mother? He recovered and did not tell Mother. I was spared a scolding.

Henry and I played on the binder while it stood idly on the yard between harvests. The binder served as monkey bars, although we had never heard of monkey bars. The binder provided many different bars and angles on which we could sit, climb or hang. The primary purpose of the binder was to cut grain and to bind it into sheaves with binder twine. The sheaves dropped behind the binder to be set up in stooks (Canadian, or shocks in the USA). Binders were drawn by four horses. Every farmer needed a minimum of four horses to pull farm implements.

The tongue of the farm box wagon also had a dual purpose for us. Normally it was used to haul water from Belter's well, or to haul grain, but we found that the tongue could be used on which to place a plank to create a teeter totter. It was from this improvised teeter totter that I fell and dislocated my right elbow when I was six. My parents drove ten miles to an uneducated chiropractor. He told me to straighten my arm and the joint snapped into place. He had learned that procedure somewhere.

The old tires left by the former owners of the farm became toys. Our farmyard was located in the flat bottom of sloping hills. Henry and I each rolled a tire to the top of the west hill with considerable effort. Once on top, with sticks in our hands, we guided the tires to roll down the hill. I could not run fast enough to keep up with my rolling tire. It was out of control. I ran to follow.

New ducklings waddled with their mother on the same hill. My tire rolled directly over one unfortunate yellow duckling. When I caught up with the tire I saw the duckling lying crushed to the ground. I was horrified! What pain I had caused an innocent duckling. I knew the duckling would die under the warm summer sun and that any loss was a big loss. Mother would scold me. I chose not to tell her and to live with my guilt rather than to tell her and get a scolding.

Guilt found me again when I sat on the kitchen window sill. "Get off the window sill before you break the pane," my parents warned me. I did break it—right in front of everyone. This time it was not boarded up like some of the others before had been. There was little money but somehow the broken glass was replaced with a new pane in the window frame.

Henry read the first English children's story to me in the upstairs of our house. What power he had in being able to read the whole story of the "Wizard of Oz." Of the book Lena says, "The school had the book. I was reading it when I was about 12. I had convulsions one night and Mother thought I was dying. She thought I shouldn't be reading a book such as 'The Wizard of Oz.' I dared not finish it. After the convulsions I had to eat brain from a pig to cure me. It helped," she says in jest, "I never had convulsions again." The cause of a single convulsion is not known. Mother was unable to censor books for her children because she did not read English. She was just making sure Lena was not reading bad books. She knew a remedy for convulsions.

My family: standing: Henry, Nettie, George, Annie, Lena, Sitting: father
Gerhard, Tina, Justine, mother Anna, 1931

Back: Lena, Annie, Nettie, front: Tina, Justine, Henry, 1931

Books. Other than the German Bible and the German picture Bible book in black and white we did not have another book in the house. Mother borrowed the thick classic Martyrs' Mirror from a friend at one time but that was not at all attractive to me.

Henry was the only one in the family to own a pair of skates, a puck and a hockey stick. He played hockey with the town's boys on the Rush Lake ice rink. He says:

> *They were used skates and in terrible shape. I think I had them for only one winter in Saskatchewan. I think we paid a dollar but I don't know if they were bought with our parents' money or with my gopher trapping money. Or maybe they were a Christmas gift from our parents.*

From Henry: *One of my earliest memories I have of childhood is standing on the bench behind the table and against the wall in the Rush Lake house and crying because I didn't want to go to school. That was in August, 1931. My crying didn't help. To school I went. However, butchering pig day could not be missed by a young boy. A blizzard could keep us from going. 'Helping Dad' qualified in our parents' view.*

> *Dad was very near sighted which created many problems. One was that he could not see the tracks the drill made in spring while seeding. In order not to sow double, or to leave unseeded strips, one must see the tracks. So I stayed home to walk in the drill tracks in front of the horses. In that way Dad could follow me and see where he had last gone.*

> *The fields he seeded ran east and west and were not quite a mile long. I think it was going against the sun that he could not see. So in the morning I walked east to the end of the field. Then I could ride back west, and repeat the same over and over. In the afternoon the directions were reversed.*

> *The drill is a machine with discs that cut into the ground. A box, the width of the machine was mounted on the top, into which*

the seed was placed. Small rotating gears in the box forced out an even amount of seeds into the spouts and placed the seed in the soil behind the discs. Dad's drill was only eight feet wide with disc spacings of six inches.

That drill went along to Fork River in 1937 where the wooden wheels were replaced with steel wheels. I bought it at the farm auction in 1948 for $45, I think, and used it for a few years. Dad had already taken off the wooden tongue and replaced it with a tractor hitch.

Lena says my staying home from school caused the teachers to wonder why I stayed home and apparently our parents were admonished. I did not remember that part.

George had the dubious honor of being the oldest of seven living children. Mother was pregnant with him when the oldest two died in Russia. He was a welcomed child. The nine years difference between the two boys was not conducive to bonding. Consequently Henry tried to play with Lena who was almost three years older than he, or with me, three years younger. Years later he complained that when he tried to play with Lena, Annie would steal her away and when he played with me, Justine stole me away, leaving him alone.

Because I was younger I do not remember George, Nettie and Annie playing. I barely remember George living at home. Lena says she and Annie played with paper dolls cut out from the Eaton's catalogue. It was probably from them that Justine and I learned to play with paper dolls. They were free.

Lena and Henry played farming. Outdoors they built their farms next to the south side of the house. Little twigs found in the yard became miniature fence posts. They pushed them into the dirt just like Dad pounded his posts into dirt. String unraveled from flour or sugar sacks substituted for barbed wire. Much as Cinderella's pumpkin became a chariot, a breast bone from a chicken we had eaten was transformed into a horse.

Lena's play became art. She learned to live within the boundaries that poverty provided. I heard our parents call her "the golden one" because she was good natured and demanded little. At Christmas time when the children at school exchanged names to buy 25¢ gifts for each other, she withdrew because she knew there were no 25¢. She never told our parents about the exchange.

Lena took me to the edge of the slough (dugout) while it still held water from the winter snow. At the edge of the pond where the mud was just the right consistency, she scooped mud into her hand while I watched her make a well-shaped cup and saucer. She could not leave it unadorned. She created a little mud flower and stuck it to the cup's outer side. Later in life she used her skills in making flower arrangements in the MCC store in Clearbrook, B.C. She also dabbled in painting.

At school we celebrated Valentine's Day by giving Valentines to our friends. Days before the 14th of February the teacher set up a box with a slot in it. This was the Valentine mail box. We dropped our cards into the slot. Our Valentines were distributed on Valentine's Day. Lena made her own cards. With simple water paints and a brush she created the best copies of store bought Valentines imaginable. She allowed one coat to dry before applying a second coat. When the colors were bright and shiny the cards were complete.

Lena wanted to sew doll clothes from left over dress scraps but Mother would not allow her to use the thread she had bought with precious pennies. Lena improvised by pulling fibers from the woven fabric. The fibers were not as strong as thread, but her talent needed an outlet. For my seventh birthday she presented me with a little doll dress she had sewn by hand. She was almost thirteen. It is the only birthday gift I remember given at home, to me or to anyone else.

Birthday gifts were not given. Was it because it was not part of the German Mennonite culture or was it because poverty prohibited it? The only recognition given us on our birthdays was the comfort of sitting on a pillow at meal time. Celebrations of a small kind can be done without money. A doll's dress and a seat on a pillow were special. Adult birthdays were sometimes honored by receiving guests.

Justine and I spent many happy hours playing with our dolls. Justine owned a little tin stove on which we pretended to cook. Our favorite food items were raisins, sugar and cocoa. In our toy dishes we mixed sugar, cocoa and water. We almost had chocolate. I liked it then already.

Mother got tired of my frequent requests for these goodies. She told me to quit asking. But how could we play house without them? I sent Justine to ask Mother for food. Mother quickly called to me, "Don't send Justine either!" Poverty caused Mother to be irritable.

Two of the most coveted toys in my young life were, first, a table and chair set to play house, and second to own a doll with hair and with eyes that opened and closed. We learned to do without. When I had daughters of my own I provided them with these things. The table and chair set had not been one of their dreams and was not used as I had imagined. I was merely fulfilling my dreams. We were given used dolls at the school Christmas concert but they did not have hair or eyelids with lashes. Henry was luckier at the concert. He received a sand powered windmill. Instead of wind propelling the blades, the sand we poured into the center top of the mill created pressure to turn the blades. His unique gift was much more interesting than ours.

We did not know yet that one brand new doll was to be ours in the future.

PAPER DOLLS

DAD HAULED WATER summer and winter on our farm. At the same time, George lived with the Ungers in Swift Current while he worked on Unger's dairy farm. Henry and the three older girls were in the Rush Lake school. Justine and I were preschoolers at home with Mother. We played with paper dolls cut out of the Eaton's catalogue.

The Eaton's catalogue was free. It was shipped to us from Winnipeg. When it arrived in the mail, Justine and I quickly leafed through its pages to claim all the prettiest models in the prettiest clothes as our own. But it was only after six months, when the catalogue was replaced with a new one, that we had permission to cut the figures out with Mother's sewing scissors. We were careful to cut on the lines of the dolls so that every figure was perfect. Justine and I cut out entire families of dolls—mothers, fathers, and large families. For six months our paper families ate, slept, worked and went to school. Eventually the oldest children married and had families. Life became too complicated. It was time for a new catalogue. We were assured of a new catalogue every six months only if Mother had ordered from Eaton's during that time. Because she did not read English, the older girls helped her order the few yards of fabric she could afford to keep us clothed. Next season we went through the process of choosing new dolls for new families. We never tired of this simple play because it reflected the only life we knew.

Wallpaper samples from the catalogue were free even though we never ordered paper as long as we lived in Saskatchewan. Our paper dolls needed houses. Wallpaper pasted to old notebook covers made attractive floors and inch high walls. A water and flour paste worked well. Our houses had only one level, probably because we did not know how to build steps and a second floor. In our make-believe world we made all the rooms that any doll family could desire. While Mother baked bread and Dad farmed we played with paper dolls.

Bread baking on a warm day created warm memories and other problems. Before the advent of quick starting yeast, Mother used yeast cakes. She thought yeast cakes were very modern compared to the starter dough they had used in Russia. Her mother had taught her to save some dough from week to week, and had added ingredients to that small leaven to make more. But modern yeast cakes were soaked in water the night before baking bread. In the morning she mixed scalded milk, salt and lard. After this was cooled she added the flour and yeast.

Mother made big batches of dough so the baked bread would last at least three or four days. She used a big mixing bowl in which she kneaded the dough until the yeast produced air bubbles. These popped while she was kneading. When the dough was smooth and elastic, she covered the dough with a clean flour-sack dish towel and put the dough in a warm place to rise. This was on the shelf of the cook stove. When the dough had risen, she kneaded it down to let it rise a second time. She emptied the bowl on the flour sprinkled oilcloth on the table and shaped the dough into three or more loaves. Dad had made some bread pans to hold three loaves. They were made of strong metal. Mother never washed these pans but at every baking she coated them with a little butter or lard. They were black with baked-on oils for as long as I remember. She placed three loaves side by side in the pans to let the dough rise again. When risen well above the top of the pans, the loaves were then put in the oven to bake. One hour later she pulled out the loaves from the oven, filling the air with the aroma of freshly baked bread. Real butter on this bread with a glass of cold milk was the best thing this side of heaven.

The problem with baking bread was that the house became hot. We had no screens on our windows. It became essential to ventilate the house. Outside in the barnyard, flies had multiplied even faster than our paper dolls had indoors. With our windows open the flies found a warm welcome to swarm over uncovered and unrefrigerated food. They lit on bread and on smoked ham. They liked to lay their eggs wherever they desired. The flies tickled our faces, arms and legs. They were uncontrollable pests. We had no refrigeration and no plastic bags.

Swarms of flies occupied the kitchen during the summer. Mother, Nettie, Annie, Lena and Henry did what they could to get rid of them. There were three major methods of trying to empty the house of flies. The number one choice was to catch flies with fly catchers hung from the ceiling. They were the long yellow, sticky paper things we bought in little canisters. We pulled the tab and the strip came out in a coil. Although very effective, we could not always afford the luxury that these little devices provided.

In the absence of a modern fly catcher we resorted to the number two choice of ridding ourselves of flies. Justine and I watched as the older members of the family armed themselves with flour-sack dish towels, aprons, or whatever was on hand. First they closed all the windows. Then they lined up in a row at the west side of the kitchen, and together they fluttered their towels above their heads in pursuit of fleeing flies. They moved their battle line forward slowly toward the open door. Recognizing the absurdity of the situation, they broke out into a roar of laughter while they approached the door. Of course, it was impossible to drive out all the flies in one attack so they initiated a second attack from the original defense line at the west wall. After this was completed the door was closed. The screen door kept the flies out.

The third method of killing flies was the lethal fly swatter.

When the action was over Justine and I returned to our dolls. They were easier to control than the flies. Unwittingly our family had entertained us with an activity more exciting than paper dolls.

Our Parents' Two Worlds

Our parents missed the village life they experienced in Ukraine. They missed community life, their extended families, their common language and their small world where they were at home and felt secure.

In Canada, by contrast, Mother and Dad lived in isolation. They lived alone on a farm two miles from town. The nearest neighbor was one quarter mile away, over the hill. Although Mr. Beisel spoke High German, and they communicated, he did not share their history. He visited often and relieved the monotony but he could not replace a village. Aunt Justine lived in town.

At Rush Lake, there was no German Mennonite church they could attend. They missed the spiritual nurture that they had left in Russia. The United Church of Canada did not appeal to them because they could not understand English. The nearest German church was ten miles away and too far to go with horses.

The Rush Lake school was taught in English. School attendance was mandatory, fortunately. Our family had to speak English. Our parents spoke little English and could not monitor what their children were learning. They had no control. There was no German Mennonite mayor to whom they could go. They had to trust a foreign culture to influence their children. They were limited to signing our report cards and coming to concerts in which we participated. In the meantime, we were learning English fairy tales and nursery rhymes which were foreign to our parents. We enjoyed school and learned to sing "God Save the King" and "Oh, Canada" just as enthusiastically as the children from English speaking homes. But our parents had no voice.

At home our parents forbade us to speak English. Of course, they could not stop us. Our English vocabulary was soon better than our German one. We always spoke Low German to our parents. In Russia our parents had understood the language spoken in their own home. In Canada, our parents depended on their children to translate the English world to them.

Our aunt and uncle, Peter and Justine Harms, owned one of the two general stores in Rush Lake. Our parents were able to communicate with them in German. The Harms were exposed to English in the store. They asked customers to point to items on the shelves and to name them in English and thus they learned English.

Shopping had been different in Russia. It had been acceptable to bargain for the price of an item. In Canada that was taboo. I was embarrassed when Mother and I were in a store and Mother asked, "How much?" when she could see the marked price. The clerk read the price to her in English and Mother answered, "Too much." The clerk did not offer another price and we did not buy the item.

We all laughed when Mother reported seeing a topless young Canadian man on their way home from town. To be seen without a shirt was indecent by Old Country standards. Mother wanted to tell the man she could give him fabric for a shirt. When asked how she would have said it in English, she said, "Come to me. I give you to shirt." The sentence structure was correct in German. But we all laughed at her attempt.

Our parents talked fondly of the many evenings they had spent playing the table game of "Mensch Aerger Dich Nicht," with Mother's sister Margaret (Unger) Warkentin and her husband Vahng (John). It was similar to Parcheesi but the game consisted of two round tracks. The outside track was the size of a large pizza drawn on cardboard. The inner track was the size of a dinner plate. Buttons served as men and home-carved dice were free. The name of the game meant "Man, Don't Get Angry." Although our parents taught us to play the game they did not play it with us. We were unable to play it with the fervor with which they had played it in entirely different circumstances, when they had been happy in Ukraine.

Rush Lake, Saskatchewan, made little news and when it did, it was of little concern to our parents because they did not know most of the people in town or in the country. They hungered for news of their old friends and their relatives. There was no telephone, radio or television. The post office was two miles away. This is where we received the German "Rundschau" and the English "Free Press." When she got the "Rundschau," Mother searched for news about people she had known in Ukraine.

Our parents could not censor the Winnipeg Free Press but the subscription was allowed. The older girls read the "What Should I Do's," a Dear Abby-like column. When I could read I began with the funnies. In retrospect I am surprised that we always subscribed to the newspaper because we did not have money for nonessentials. We were being integrated into Canadian culture.

Mother's brother, Peter and his family from Swift Current, visited sometimes. He was the first person to inform us of his radio. Wide eyed we listened to his description of this new invention. He said the voice from the radio was almost indistinguishable from that of a voice spoken in the room. That was news. It was a battery operated radio since there was no electricity.

Shortly after this news flash, our parents heard about a German religious program to be aired on the radio. Since we had no radio, they decided to take the box wagon and all their children to the Unger twin bachelors who had one. Without a telephone they were unable to notify them we were coming. So without an invitation we arrived at their place several miles away one winter evening. They graciously allowed us to listen to the 15-minute, static-plagued broadcast. Mother, not understanding how radio programs were funded, wondered aloud why this message on this wondrous apparatus was a mere fifteen minutes long. What a hunger our parents had to hear the word of God in their own language. After the broadcast we literally bounced home in the springless wagon over frozen ground.

The letters to or from relatives always began with "Liebes Geschwister," (Dear Siblings). Usually the first line read, "We are all well, thank God." At that time I thought it was the only way to begin a letter. Now I realize they were truly grateful to have healthy families. They had no money for medical expenses.

Grandma and Grandpa Unger were concerned about all their children. They had paid the fare for some of their children to Canada, but they could not provide them all with farms. They were mostly poor. Our grandparents' primary concern was for their son in Russia and their daughter in Paraguay. They urged the children in Canada to send ten dollars each to Tante Tin in Paraguay. I recall our parents debating this issue. They simply could not send money. They had none themselves.

When Tante Tin's son, Peter Klassen, visited British Columbia in 1980, I met him there. He was impressed with the wealth of his cousins. No one is poor any more. After he and his wife returned to Paraguay she wrote that he lay on the couch feeling depressed.

In the 1930s, hearing about family members who were less fortunate than we made our parents grateful to be able to live in Canada. Even though we were poor we never feared the midnight knock on the door like Uncle Jacob did. Our only enemy was poverty. We listened to Mother reading the German letters and we would remember what we heard.

Our parents had experienced the bad times in Ukraine but liked to dwell on the good times before the war and the revolution. Like the Israelites they remembered the "flesh pots" in Russia. They remembered the prewar years when they had fruit, gardens, green fields and fat animals.

We did not know what we were missing. Rush Lake was the only place we knew and whatever we experienced here was the norm. Our world was very different from the world in which our parents had grown up. They needed us to build the bridge between their Old Country and our new one.

WATER

In our parents' new world the warm west wind blew across the thirsty brown prairie. Dry, powdery dust welcomed the chance to fly with the wind. The air was thick with soil from Mr. Beisel's farm not far to our west. The soil from our farm flew just as gleefully over fences and barns to plague the Pedes, our neighbors to the east. Dry Russian thistles (tumble weed in the US) rolled across the open fields and piled up against barb wire fences. Dust flew into every crack and crevice in the house. Window sills became laden with a layer of dust. Year after dusty year came and went without relief.

Mother and Dad struggled daily with the poverty inflicted upon them from the drought in Saskatchewan and by the impoverishing consequences of the war and the revolution in Russia. How could they feed us and how could they clothe us? Without rain the new farm could not produce enough grain and fodder to make a profit. Instead of rain from the sky, we had wind, dust and grasshoppers.

This new farm had no well. Dad tried to dig a well without success. Henry thinks he dug fifty feet deep. He says,

> *It was dug by hand, one man with a spade in the well, and one man with a bucket and rope pulling up the dirt with a winch. He emptied the bucket and let it down for more. There was no cribbing while digging—terribly dangerous for such a deep well. If there had been water, cribbing would have been a must.*

Discouraged, Dad stopped digging. He was destined to continue hauling water. Later the gaping hole, half filled with debris, reminded him of his great attempt and of his failure to succeed. Unfortunately he had no money to pay a well driller.

The dugout south of the house created by an earlier owner, collected water during the spring thaw. The animals drank the water as long as it lasted, but during a drought it did not last through the summer.

Wooden barrels sat under the eaves of the house, waiting for rain, but they were empty. Mother liked rain water especially to wash clothes. In winter she could help provide water when there was snow. But not in summer!

The Belter's well failed at least one summer. For us, without a well, Dad had to haul water from the creek west of Rush Lake. Henry thinks it was at least five miles from our farm on the west side of town. He loaded the wagon with five barrels and he had to haul water every other day.

Every cow, horse, pig, chicken and duck depended on the water Dad hauled home in barrels. He filled those barrels with a bucket full at a time.

In the house we depended on the water from barrels for cooking three meals a day, drinking, bathing once a week, washing clothes every other week and cleaning the house every week.

When Dad arrived at home with the barrels on the wagon we saw wooden lids floating on the water. The purpose of the wooden lids was to prevent spillage, but we saw that the water had sloshed over the tops and ran down the sides of the barrels and froze.

Annie says, "The sun dried out the barrels when they weren't full and would become very leaky or runny. Dad tried to seal the cracks by filling them with rags and the use of a knife." The consequence of this was that Dad nicked his left forefinger with the knife. It became infected and sore. A little piece of rust had entered the wound. The result of that was amputation of the finger up to the second distal joint. He went to town to see the doctor and he came home minus one finger. The phantom finger was always the coldest in severely cold weather.

In winter time the freezing temperatures and water hauling created a dramatic scene. Of course, Dad used a sleigh instead of a wagon. But he got so cold while filling the water barrels with a bucket, one at a time. The cold miles going home added to his misery. Upon his arrival at home we heard the sleigh's runners squeak as they were drawn across the powdery snow. The ground under the snow was frozen solid. Next we saw the billowing clouds of warm breath from his own nose and mouth and that of the horses. Icicles hung several inches from the horses' chins. White hoar frost covered the woolen scarf wound around Dad's head and the furry flaps of his cap.

Dad was extremely sensitive to the cold; so in this unbearable frigid climate, he despaired. He remembered the mild winters in Ukraine. They had snow and frost but it was tolerable. He remembered the abundant water that the village wells in Grigorjewka provided. There had been enough for men and beasts. He remembered one drought in the history of Ukraine. It was 1921 and all of Russia had a famine. But Grigorjewka had not suffered like many villages had. They had not been hungry. But in this new country, Dad counted crop failure after crop failure.

About Saskatchewan, Henry says, "One summer, I think in July, we had what our parents called a 'cloud burst' which overflowed the dugout." That was an exception. The living conditions were so dire that even a 'cloud burst' was memorable.

We Didn't Care

Gerhard and Anna (Unger) Klassen, our parents, had been in Canada only two years before I was born. Our parents wanted to talk about their lives in Russia and about families and friends they had loved. We did not want to hear about Russia or about the people we had never seen. It was acceptable to hear about Uncle Jakob left in Russia, or about Tante Tin in Paraguay, but please don't make us listen to a lot of people's sufferings. Our older siblings had been ages one to ten when they left Russia and, except for George and Nettie, they did not remember very much. To us younger children, the War and the Revolution had happened "Once upon a time." We did not understand why they happened or how our parents had been affected within the last decade. Yet they needed to talk about their experience.

Some stories were too terrible for us to hear. Lena recalls, "These were often bedtime stories—no wonder I had terrible nightmares. It seemed to me that the worst stories were told when they had company who shared their history."

Mother enjoyed telling us that Grandma's sixteen children, plus the children born to Martin Friesen and Wilhelm Schroeder in prior marriages, totaled thirty-one. They never lived under the same roof. Grandma Klassen Friesen Schroeder's obesity became a point of interest when Mother said she needed two chairs to sit on. On the family picture she uses only one chair.

Mother and Dad had lived with Grandma Klassen Friesen Schroeder in Ukraine. Mother said Grandma spoiled Frank, her youngest. Mother thought seven-year-old Frank was old enough to wash his own feet in a basin sitting on the floor. Instead, obese as she was, Grandma stooped over to reach those feet on the floor, and hinted broadly that Mother should be doing this instead of Grandma. Mother played too dumb to catch on.

Grandma died of a stroke in 1923 at the age of sixty-four, and two years before our parents emigrated. She died four years before my birth but it seemed like ancient history to me. We had not known her and we did not care about the people our parents had known in Russia. We children cared only about the people we knew in Canada.

Saturday and Sunday

"WEEKEND"—WHAT DID THAT mean to our family in the 1930s? This word we know so well in today's society was unheard of in our 1930s immigrant family. We saw Saturday as a day of preparation for Sunday. From our parents we knew Sunday was special. They remembered the congregation in Grigorjewka. But in Canada we had no church. Our parents taught us a routine that they had followed in Russia. Whether we had a church or not in Canada, we followed the routine practices they had established in Russia.

Cleaning was an item that was high on the list of things to do. We had only one room other than the bedrooms. That one room served multiple purposes. It was our kitchen. But we had no cupboards to wipe and no counters to clean. There was no electric stove where food boiled over to run into the burner wells. The nonexistent refrigerator did not take any time to clean. We had no microwave either. What did we have in our kitchen? We had a black cook stove that did not show dirt. It did have some black baked-on grease. The attached black cabinet above the stove may have had soot on the shelf from the pot or pan that had sat directly over the open flame. Mother emptied the ash compartment with a long-handled scraper by scraping the contents towards the door of the chamber and emptying the ashes into a bucket. The painted chairs in the kitchen were wiped every Saturday in preparation for Sunday. The oilcloth covering the table was wiped after every meal, but the girls examined the draping-down parts with special care on Saturday. We might have dropped some food from our spoons on its way from the table to our lips. Last of all the girls got down on their hands and knees to wash the unpainted wooden boards of the floor. The kitchen was clean.

The kitchen was also our dining room and our living room. The painted chairs were already clean after wiping them with a wet cloth. There was no china in a cabinet, no sofa, no upholstered chairs, no dusty television, radio or piano.

In each of the bedrooms we had at least one bed. They didn't need cleaning. Laundry day took care of the sheets only occasionally. Washing conditions were too difficult to provide clean sheets very often. We children never felt deprived of clean sheets because we did not know any better. No doubt, Mother grieved over the loss of the standards she had known in Russia. However, verbally she clung to a standard: "It is no shame to be poor but it is a shame to be dirty or lazy." To be patched was no shame either, but an open hole was. Mother would have delighted in patching all the holes in Levi jeans which we see today.

The bathroom. At the base of the stairs stood a Russian wash basin of brass on a crude wash stand. Every Saturday we polished the basin with the ashes Mother pulled from the stove's ash chamber. We rubbed the basin with a wet rag until it shone like new. While we were using ashes anyway, we got the cutlery out and polished the cheap flatware. Above the wash stand hung a towel. We all used it. A mirror hung at an appropriate level for adults to see themselves.

The black soot from under the stove lids became shoe polish. We all had one pair of shoes. We wore them hard all week when we couldn't walk barefoot. They were gray with wear. We inverted the stove lid and poured a little milk into the black soot. With a brush or a rag, we tried to mix the milk into the dry soot. Next we applied it to every shoe in the house. When the shoes were dry they were brushed until they shone.

The Singer sewing machine's black metal stand with its many curlicues was slowly dusted by little fingers with a little cloth. At the age on nine it became my first household responsibility. The older girls had other chores to do.

The only windows in the kitchen sparkled after a cleansing with wet Bon Ami from a bar. In summer the pesky flies left specks all over them. In winter a layer of ice covered them. With our warm little thumbs pressed against the ice, we thawed out a little hole to see through to the frozen outside. In winter the lamp chimney got smoky from much use. It too was cleaned on Saturday.

Dad shaved on Saturdays. All week he let his whiskers grow but on Saturday he took his straight razor and sharpened it on the razor strap hanging on the frame of the doorway to the pantry. He took down the mirror from the wall above the brass basin and a bar of soap from the stand. Now he propped the mirror on the kitchen table. He needed only a cup full of hot water before the shaving process could begin. With a shaving brush in his hand he sat down on a kitchen chair at the table for the weekly ritual. He dipped his brush into the hot water and worked it over the bar of soap until it made lather. He brushed the lather all over his jaws, but not over his mustache. A transformation began as he shaved the bewhiskered face, stroke by stroke, showing his smooth white skin. He was blessed with super white skin which he hated because a brown face was evidence of having worked like a man in the sun. His forehead was always white because he wore a wide brimmed hat in summer and a fur cap over his forehead in winter. Stroke by stroke as he shaved, he changed more and more into a civilized looking man. He always left his mustache which was very Russian. His Dutch ancestry showed not only in his skin but in his blue-gray eyes which were ultra-sensitive to the bright sun on the snow. He always squinted in the sun, as do some of his children.

We belonged to the generation where Saturday was bath day. In lieu of a bathtub, Mother brought in the galvanized wash tub. This was the same tub in which she had washed the farm laundry. It was also the tub in which last fall's sausage had been mixed with salt and pepper, before it was stuffed and smoked. Of course, it had been cleaned before and after mixing the sausage. Mother set the tub on two kitchen chairs facing each other. As soon as the bathing process began, one of our older siblings shouted, "After the kids to bathe!" Justine and I were "the kids," and because we were youngest we always bathed first—together. She and I were the only ones to start out with fresh water from the stove's reservoir. Hot water was added from time to time for the rest of the family. Mother washed our hair for us and liked the tub at chair level to save her back from stooping. We used bar soap. After we were finished, the tub was set on the floor with a blanket draped over the backs of chairs to provide a bit of privacy. Henry says, "Being the only boy among five girls, bathing was not my favorite thing." Towels? I think we had only two small towels so we all had to use them. Wash cloths were an unknown to us. We knew nothing about matching towels sets in the bathroom. Neither did we have cosmetics or hair blowers.

Bathing on Saturdays only was so common that when we came home from school Wednesday and told Mother that one of the Hammet girls had missed school because she had burned herself in the bathing process the evening before, Mother asked, "Why did she bathe on a Tuesday?" It was Nettie, I think, who brought home a curling iron. It had wooden handles with a rod and a sheathe at the other end. After heating the rod and sheathe over a hot lamp chimney a tuft of hair was caught between the rod and sheathe and rolled into a curl. No one had a permanent curl. However, I was one of many grandchildren to have inherited naturally curly hair from Grandpa Unger.

When possible, Mother baked on Saturday. She liked to have food on hand in case someone dropped in to see us on Sunday.

Sundays were special. No one worked. We stayed home most Sundays because we had no local church to go to. Mother sometimes took out the German black and white picture Bible story book to either read to us or to tell us a Bible story. Sometimes a Mennonite family came to see us with their buggy or sleigh. Sometimes we visited them. There were the Klippensteins, Andres, Enns, Harms, Dycks, and Krahns. The latter three had little girls to play with but only Mary Harms knew how to play with paper dolls like we did. The Krahns were said to be even poorer than we were. Was it possible? Mrs. Dyck liked to dress her family in very bright colors. Mother said she had been born into a Russian family and Russians liked bright colors. She was raised by Mennonites.

Very occasionally a traveling Mennonite minister came to visit the scattered Mennonites around Rush Lake. I remember using the United Church building for a Mennonite meeting more clearly than I can remember the meetings at Unger's vacant farm house. Here we sang:

He hears what I say
And He sees what I do.
My dear God writes
Everything down.

In German the lines rhymed but I did not like the song because it made me feel that God was trying to catch us doing something He might not approve of. Was God really like that?

Mr. Klippenstein taught the Sunday School lesson about Joseph and his brothers. My older sisters remember the Unger house meetings better than I do and have a picture of the young girls at a Sunday School picnic. Not having had a church in our lives, we younger ones did not know what we were missing. The older children knew that our Sundays needed a church and people in them. The time would come when their desires would be fulfilled. They needed only to wait.

LAUNDRY DAY

IMAGINE YOURSELF IN our kitchen with unpainted wooden floors, with only a wood stove to aid you in the task of washing the family's laundry. There is no other power, no machine and only a limited amount of water in the stove's reservoir. Water has to be begged into existence. As seen earlier, it rarely rains. This was long before running water and electricity became part of our lives. It was long before we had washers and dryers.

Now imagine collecting the laundry. What kind of laundry did we have to wash? There are seven children but no one has more than one or two dresses in her entire wardrobe. If there is only one dress per child, how can you wash it when it is cold and she has nothing to change into? Underclothes are made of white flour sacks. Bloomers, undershirts and slips. Sheets are also made of white flour sacks. But there is only one sheet per bed to cover up the straw mattress. The woolen comforter is encased in a print covering and is seldom washed. These bedding items must be dry by nightfall. Without a dryer, and in freezing cold weather, this is completely impractical. How do you solve all these laundry day problems?

Mother did it this way. She had to plan her day around water and fuel. She could wish neither into existence so she learned to do with little of either. In winter time she brought in tubs and boilers full of snow and thawed it in the boiler on the stove. In summer she used water Dad had hauled in wooden barrels from miles away. Because it was so hard to obtain, she used it to the maximum, as we shall see later.

Fuel was as scarce as water. Instead of hauling it in barrels, the family picked up dried cow chips. When we did not have enough from our own small herd, we asked the Robertsons for the privilege of picking up chips from their pasture to haul to our home. Cow chips make pathetic fuel. They provided much smoke and little heat. Mother used straw too, when it was available. At last, when we were destitute, we had coal. It was not our own. Government "relief" (welfare) provided us with coal. Mother stretched it as far as she could. Wood was not available. We had no trees, and to buy wood was not possible because we had no money. Besides, southern Saskatchewan was nearly bare of trees.

Relief also provided us with some store bought long johns and navy blue, fleece lined bloomers. Justine and I did not suffer from the lack of these like our older sisters had. Lena remembers the cold, bare ring around her thighs on the way to school where the too-short woolen stockings did not meet the flour sack bloomers.

Before Mother could make a sheet out of four one-hundred pound flour sacks, she baked dozens of loaves of bread until the sacks were empty. She unraveled the string that held the bag together and wound it into a ball to be used in many ways. It was free. To remove the large blue and red brand name from the side of the sack became a challenge. It had to be scrubbed and bleached over and over before the colors faded into oblivion. Mother had made large quantities of soap before wash day. She made the soap from lye and used animal fats. Detergent was not yet in our vocabulary.

Mother gathered up the scant clothing, sheets and towels and sorted them according to color; whites, colored and dark. She assembled her washing equipment from the adjoining lean-to. All she needed was a tub and a wash board. She set the tub on a kitchen chair. Then she poured water from either the boiler or the reservoir into the tub. She gathered up the white clothes to soak them in the water. Next she took the wash board and placed its bottom over the laundry while the top rested on the side of the tub. She took a chunk of homemade soap and put it on its ledge. One by one she lifted a piece of clothing out of the water and onto the washboard, rubbed soap all over it and started to scrub it up and down over the wash board. She wrung it out by hand and placed it on the table. When every white piece had undergone this process, she began to wash the colored clothes, and finally the dark clothes. No, I did not forget to mention any change of water between loads. Water was too scarce. But after the used water had served its purpose, Mother poured it out and put clean water into the tub. The scrubbing process began for a second time. Everything was scrubbed twice.

Henry reminds me that laundry water was used to wash the floor. And finally, he says, "After I had skates I tried to make a small skating rink with the dirty floor and wash water."

The laundry was not as sparkling white as ours is today when it comes out of our dryers. But Mother did her best. She sometimes shredded homemade laundry soap and added it to water in the boiler before she tried to bleach white clothes whiter. She started with cool water and clothes, then heated it till just below the boiling point for best results. She had no other bleach.

A third time she wrung the clothes out before she plunged them into a tub of rinse water with bluing in it. And lastly, she starched many of the whites and prints. There was no "easy care" or "wash and wear" fabric in those days. There was no polyester or nylon and there were few knits in our household. Most clothes were made of woven cotton which required ironing. Starch was meant to retard the soiling process as well as to give clothes a fresh appearance after ironing. Starch was simply a mixture of water and flour, boiled, and diluted to the right consistency.

Mother liked to hang clean laundry on the line to dry. In summer the dry warm wind blew and dried the clothes in a short time. In winter the laundry froze stiff as a board. Mother said the freezing process whitened the laundry. She knew it freeze-dried if she left it out long enough. But she could not risk leaving the laundry outside over night because a rising wind at night would break the clothes, leaving them looking like they had been cut with scissors.

Each frozen piece was taken from the line while fingers got colder and colder. The clothes froze to each other, the wash line and the clothes pins. Laundry was handled as gently as possible in an attempt to bring it into the house intact. It rested on the kitchen table until the stiffness was thawed out of it. After it was no longer in danger of breaking, it was hung up on lines in the kitchen. The fresh clean smell of outdoors filled the room. Hopefully everything would be dry in the morning.

When the clothes were dry the girls sprinkled them with water and rolled them up snugly. They were allowed to rest until the moisture was distributed evenly. The moisture made the ironing process easier and the clothes looked more finished. We had no plastics in which to put dampened clothes, but time took care of the moisture distribution. Before the ironing process began Mother had to be sure the stove could be heated to a temperature hot enough to heat the irons. Once the irons were hot, a blanket spread on the kitchen table served as an ironing board. Three irons were used alternately. The same iron holder fit all three irons. Ironing may have been tedious but it was a clean job. Neither did ironing redden or blister the hands like scrubbing could. Ironing was compatible with bread baking. We needed a hot stove for both functions. The fuel did double duty. Ironing and baking ensured a warmer house in winter and a hot house in summer.

Tina, Justine, cousins Frieda, Art, Mary, at the Harms, 1932

Important People in our Lives

I. THE HARMS

Mary Harms, with her dark, shiny, straight hair, shone like a diamond in my childhood sky. She was my cousin and next to Justine, the dearest playmate a little girl could have. Mary was over a year younger than I and a year older than Justine. Both of our families lost two children in Russia.

Mary, blest with a sweet and gentle personality, knew how to play with dolls like Justine and I did. She blended, conformed and never disagreed with us. She didn't care that our dolls didn't have real hair, or eyes that closed. She seemed not to notice that we did not have the material things their family took for granted. She improvised like we did when we had no chairs and table with which to play house. Long before we went to school we were playmates in our homes. At school Mary remained our best friend.

Mary's hair was as dark as ours was blonde. Hers was straight and stiff which ours was not. Mary's hair was cut in bangs across her forehead and straight across the back from ear to ear. Justine and I had haircuts identical to hers but Justine's thin, wispy hair and my curly hair made ours stick out all over while hers was flat, smooth and glossy.

Frieda, Mary's little sister, was too small to play with us. She messed up our orderly play the one time she tried. Even when she was older she was never one of us. Patsy Campbell in Rush Lake became her best friend.

Art, another memorable person, was my age and we were in the same grade in school. In third grade he became a threat to me when his grades were slightly higher than mine. Until then I enjoyed ranking first in class without trying. But he overtook me. He also taught me to cross my eyes.

Then there was Lena Harms. She was two years older than I and stayed overnight at our place at least once. Pete, Justine, and John Harms were the ages of our older siblings. Pete was George's best friend. Much later in life Pete had a lumber yard in Chilliwack, B.C. He was the wealthy one with the swimming pool. My brother George owned and operated the Sunrise Bakery in Cranbrook, B.C. Both died prematurely: George died of cancer at fifty-two, and Pete at sixty—of a heart attack, I think. The Harms had peanuts and candy kisses even when it wasn't Christmas. It was at their place that I first saw shimmering, molded red jello. They must be really rich I thought. They even had a car. It was what our parents called a "glass car" because it had glass windows and a solid body, instead of canvas parts. I remember that we sat in it once. What would it have been like to ride in it?

Justine and Lena Harms graduated from high school and became teachers. John became a dentist while in the army during World War II. No one in our family finished high school. Our oldest ones had to drop out of school to work and support the family.

Peter Harms, whom we called "Mr. Harms," was called just "Harms" by his wife, Aunt Justine. He had stiff black hair that was always cut in a brush cut, long before it was in style. I suspect it would have stood straight up if he had tried to comb it back or to one side. He owned and operated the General Store on Main Street in Rush Lake. We bought our few staples there instead of at his competitor's, Mr. Danzer, because Mr. Harms was related to us. He was married to Mother's sister, Justine (Unger). When we children had a penny or an egg to spend, we would have preferred to get candy at Mr. Danzer's store since he was more generous.

Aunt Justine was four years younger than Mother. She was about five feet, two inches, just like Mother. Our sisters were annoyed when Aunt Justine asked to see their underwear. Would she tell her next guest about the flour sack slips and bloomers they wore?

Aunt Justine, like most of the Unger clan, had droopy eyelids that gave the appearance of eyes that slanted down on the outsides. Under Aunt Justine's droopy eyelids, her eyes sparkled. They sparkled most when she was about to tell a real life story. I say "real life" because her stories were about real people, often about people we knew.

Aunt Justine loved comedy; comedy about human behavior at the expense of people. Just as a cartoonist exaggerates his character's most prominent features, she drew characters with words. To enhance the effect of her words, she changed the inflection of her voice. She embellished stories with amusing details, making the object of her story the brunt of belly-deep laughter. But as cousin Lena (Unger) Gemberling once said, "One can't leave the room if one doesn't want to be the object of her next story." Aunt Justine was a Mennonite Phyllis Diller.

But at least once she became the object of comedy in our home when she described how she attempted to stay cool on hot summer days. She told us she stretched out on her back on the linoleum of their living room floor and extended her arms and legs away from her body. What fun it was to visualize her fat body lying there with her arms and legs extending in four directions! She would have laughed with us. We liked Aunt Justine. She was fat and jolly. She was Mother's sister. She was Mary's mother.

II. THE BEISELS—OUR NEIGHBORS.

"Beisel is coming," was a frequent announcement made by anyone looking out of the west window of the old gray house. It was a frequent but welcome statement. The old man came down the eastern slope of the hill separating our two farmyards a quarter mile apart. He and his wife were our only close neighbors. He followed the wagon tracks, bare of vegetation. The packed soil was dry and cracked in drought-stricken Saskatchewan.

Mr. Beisel's visits interrupted the monotony of our simple lives for as long as I remember. His peculiar High German accent was different from ours. Our parents called him a "Kolonist." Just what that meant I do not know except that everyone with an accent other than ours seemed to fit that label. They were able to read the same language but his sounded different. At home we spoke Low German as has been stated before. Mr. Beisel understood every word, just as we understood him.

I became aware that he spoke High German rather than Low German when he spoke to me, and unthinkingly I answered him in High German. I remember it only because of his remark to my parents, "See, I talked Low German to her and she answered in High German."

He predicted that I would become a good dancer. Did he not know we did not dance?

Mr. Beisel spoke to our parents about many things. He liked to talk about religion. He had no church and was exploring the teachings of the Jehovah Witnesses. Our parents found little common ground with him. But they remained friends.

Why Mr. Beisel became more interested in Nettie's health than in anyone else's, he did not say. He told Nettie to walk from school to Harms' store every day at noon to eat an apple. He would pay for a bushel-box of apples. Nettie did so and none of us knew until Annie walked to the store and saw Nettie eating an apple. Having an apple to eat demanded an explanation, and Annie got it. It is doubtful that Mr. Harms was ever paid for those apples.

Mrs. Beisel shared the old farm house with her husband. Her background was different from his. She spoke the same Low German as we did. She came from the United States and brought jars of fruit with her. How long ago had it been canned? How long had she lived in Saskatchewan? She saved the fruit. Could it be that she did not want to share the fruit with her husband? They did not get along with each other, that much we knew.

Mrs. Beisel complained about the towels that her husband wore out too soon because he dried between his fingers too thoroughly. The unnecessary friction did it. I could not fathom this lack of generosity.

I do not trust my memory well enough to say she wore a black dress, a black shawl, black coat, and black shoes and stockings. But she left with me the impression of a woman looking like the wicked witch in Dorothy's Land of Oz.

Together the Beisels left us something we were not able to get rid of. Bedbugs. When they visited, their wraps were laid on our parents' bed. From there they spread to every bed in the house. For the next ten years Annie fought the bedbug population. She had no chemicals to fight them but she examined the joints of the beds where the foot of the bed connected to the side rails of our iron beds. Once Henry and I saw some loose paint on the old plaster wall upstairs and he told me there would be either flies or spiders under there. But when he removed the loose paint we saw bedbugs in hiding. They emitted a foul odor when crushed. Why was it Annie's responsibility? She took it upon herself. She probably could not adjust to sharing the house with bedbugs. She remained a meticulous housekeeper until her death in 2010.

Mrs. Beisel had money she did not share with "Aundres," as she called him. During the depression of the 1930s she lent $600 (amount not certain) to Mr. Harms, the store owner. She did not tell Aundres. Then on a very cold winter day she died suddenly, cause unknown. Mr. Beisel came over the hill to see us and exclaimed, "She didn't say a word about the money!" Our parents knew about the money but had promised secrecy. Whether the debt was ever paid, or whether he even discovered where it was, I do not know. If not, Mr. Harms was paid for more than the box of apples Beisel owed him. Mrs. Beisel would rather lose the money than let Aundres have it.

The death of Mrs. Beisel created a terror among the children in our home and in the home of the Harms. She was a woman who had not endeared herself to those who knew her. In death we thought of her more like a witch's ghost than an angel. This was the first death among my acquaintances. Justine and I felt safe in our parents' bedroom but the older kids were afraid to sleep upstairs. They were allowed to bring their blankets and pillows downstairs to sleep on the kitchen floor. Justine and I joined them just for fun. But when one of the Harms' children either imagined, or dreamed, seeing Mrs. Beisel's legs still walking without the rest of her body, it was scary. As time went by the kids moved back upstairs.

What we learned from Mr. Beisel was a language. From Mrs. Beisel we learned how not to live. After Mrs. Beisel's death the widower employed a young housekeeper. She was a new person to know and expanded our world. She associated with my sisters, but once I was allowed to go along to see her. She let us taste a sour cream prune pie. I had never tasted anything so delicious. I wanted my sisters to make it at home but we had no recipe. Years later I searched for a recipe and never did find one. She probably substituted prunes for raisins.

She introduced us to the guitar and to cowboy songs. She sang and played one or both of the following:

"I once was an old cowpuncher, though here I'm dressed in rags.
I used to be a tough one, boys, and go on great big jags.
Before I left my home, boys, my mother for me cried.
She begged me not to go, boys, for me she would have died.
My mother's heart was broken, was broken for its all,
And I'll not see my mother till the work's all done next fall."

In an environment that offered little to think about, anything new became indelibly impressed on our open young minds. *"I'll not see my mother,"* seemed sad to me. "Beat the drums slowly" is another song I remember:

"Beat the drums slowly and play the fife lowly,
And play the dead march as they carry me on.
Take me to the prairie and throw the sod o'er me,
For I'm a young cowboy and I know I've done wrong.
. . . There is another who's dearer than Mother
who'd weep if she knew I was dying alone."

This latter sentiment I could not understand but my sisters did. They told me it was the cowboy's sweetheart. I could not understand how anyone could be dearer than Mother and someone outside the family at that.

The young housekeeper did not stay long but she influenced us in small ways. Mr. Beisel was left alone and we moved away.

III. THE PETER UNGERS

Peter was Mother's brother two years older than she, and Grandpa Unger's namesake. Peter and his wife Katherina (Unrau), whom we called Tante Tin (and was our third aunt by that name) and family, lived at Swift Current on a dairy farm. The Ungers became important to us when George lived with them and worked for them.

Many years later Mary Driedger questioned that our debt had been completely paid by Peter Unger. After her husband died she found the bill of debt but she had no record of payment. After Dad died in 1960, Mary heard Mother say, "I am so glad I no longer have any debt." Mary replied, "What? No debt? You still owe me money for the farm."

When George heard about that he told Mother he had worked to pay the debt in its entirety. "Don't pay again," was his counsel. Virginia Unger said she worked to pay for part of the debt. Was Uncle Peter unable to send the money to Mr. Driedger? Was that why Virginia had to work for Driedgers? Dad died in 1960 and George in 1968 so this conversation occurred sometime between 1960 and 1968.

Uncle Peter was an educated man. He was the fifth child and the second son in his parental home. He alone obtained a higher education.

When he was young he aspired to become a missionary to China. The local village of Grigorjewka provided funds for him to attend a school in Switzerland. He received his education but he never went to China. The reason is not clear but it appears he was influenced by modernistic theology. The church was disappointed.

Instead of going to China, Peter married a student nurse from a Crimean hospital. Her name was Katherina Unrau. The High German spoken in her parental home suggested a more sophisticated family than Peter's, where Low German was spoken. He liked that. She did not graduate.

Together the young couple left Russia to go to the United States in about 1914. Peter's two uncles, Jacob and Johann Nikkel, had preceded him by three to four decades and settled in Kansas. Peter forgot to take their addresses with him so he and Tin had nowhere to go. They did not know the English language. They spread the map of the United States on a table and dropped a bean on it. They had decided to go to the State on which the bean would land. It dropped on Ohio, so Ohio was their destination.

They did not settle in Ohio for very long. They moved around to several states, including Kansas, Louisiana, and in Canada to the province of Saskatchewan. With Peter's limited English it was hard to make a living. But even when he prospered temporarily he could find no permanent place to satisfy him. He wandered on to the next place.

Peter's children, Otto and Virginia, were both born in the U.S. While Peter's family was on the west side of the Atlantic Ocean, Russia was at war. In 1921 the young Peter Unger family left North America to return home to Russia. They were detained in Germany where Willie was born. A letter from Peter's mother written to him in Germany tells of desperate conditions in 1921. The drought in 1921 was followed by famine. In spite of this, Peter and Tin returned to Russia where Lena was born in 1925.

When Peter's parents and sisters emigrated in the mid 1920s, he and his family left too. This time they settled in Saskatchewan. They bought a General Store in Rush Lake but sold it to the Harms before moving to Swift Current where they built a dairy. Their last child, George, was born in Saskatchewan.

When I learned to know this family early in life, Uncle Peter had a truck. He needed it to deliver milk in Swift Current. Once I was permitted to ride in the back of the truck. Uncle Peter had been to Rush Lake to see our parents. His wife, Tante Tin, gave Lena and me each a new tam. What a treasure. One was pink and the other was blue. Lena, Henry and I were privileged to go back to Swift Current with Uncle Peter to stay overnight.

On the way there the wind whizzed past our ears and blew off my new tam and deposited it in the ditch. A tam was a big loss but we dared not ask Uncle Peter to stop and pick it up. We could not impose. We were already indebted to him for taking us to his place.

While at the Ungers, Tante Tin wanted me to sleep in a bed in the house. This would separate me from my siblings who would be sleeping in the hay loft of the barn. Furthermore, the loft was a novelty. I asked Tante Tin to let me go with them. Of course, she did.

During the day I followed Willie and Henry to the railroad tracks that ran by their house. Willie actually had a penny to WASTE! He placed it on the rail. Then we stepped back and waited for the train. The train came as scheduled and we watched it roll past us. We looked for the penny. It was as flat as a knife blade but much wider across the center. The world was full of surprises.

Henry adds,

> I was able to go to Ungers for a week or two in summer holidays. A few times I went along with Uncle Peter to deliver milk in Swift Current. He would buy a candy bar or ice cream. Afternoons, Willie, George and I went swimming in the creek about a half mile west of their place. Willie could swim and dive and scared me half to death by staying under water so long. I was sure he had drowned.

Henry recalls a number of incidents from those holidays with the Ungers:

> They (the Unger boys) could earn 5¢ for each gopher they caught but they did not have the need for money so caught very few. At home I got 1/2¢ per gopher. I was making too much and the money was reduced to 1/4¢.
>
> There, our brother George also let me drive the truck on the field as they gathered sheaves to feed cattle.

One day we boys pumped a lot of water from the well to make mud pies, etc. When the cows came to drink there was not enough water in the well to satisfy their thirst. That is the only time I remember Uncle Peter really scolding us.

I went home by bus at least once. I had 25¢ for fare but the bus driver didn't take it. He gave me a free ride.

All the Ungers completed high school and most of them graduated from Bethel College in North Newton, Kansas.

One winter Uncle Peter even provided funds for Annie to attend the five-month Bible School in Swift Current.

In 1937 our cousin Virginia was one of two summer Bible School teachers who taught us in the vacant farm house where we sometimes met for church. Lena, Henry, Justine and I attended.

Several times Uncle Peter took our parents in his truck to see relatives—to Manitoba to see their parents and siblings, and to Osler, Sask., to see their niece Mary (Pauls) Driedger. Otherwise, my parents would never have gone further than their horses could take them.

We left the Unger family behind when in 1937 we moved from Rush Lake, Saskatchewan, to Fork River, Manitoba. But in 1948, Dad, Mother and I moved to Abbotsford, B.C. We purchased two acres of land located only a half mile from the Ungers. We picked strawberries in Uncle Peter's field and enjoyed him being our row boss. We lived on Townline Road and they lived on the intersecting Peardonville Road.

All of their children were either married or in school, but Virginia and her husband came from Saskatchewan to spend the winter of 1948-49 in B.C. Now we became adult friends. I looked to her for my Christian model.

I was twenty years old that fall when I started ninth grade at the Mennonite Educational Institute. One day I came home from school to find Uncle Peter visiting in our home. I was discouraged with school because the fourteen and fifteen year old students in my grade were immature and wanted to waste their time playing outside, rather than taking advantage of the wonderful opportunity to receive an education.

I considered going to Vancouver to work, although I did not relish the thought of doing housework for others for the rest of my life.

Uncle Peter listened. He valued education. In response, his words were something like, "Sure, the kids may be immature, and it causes you problems. But you can endure the annoyance for a short time in order to get an education. It's the only way to rise beyond what you have today." I finished school. He stood at the fork of my road and pointed the direction I needed to go. This family proved helpful to our needy family.

On December 23 of the same year, Otto and Henry Reimer (Virginia's husband), rode the four miles to Abbotsford with Uncle Peter in his truck. They crashed on the icy road. Uncle Peter died instantly. Henry died ten days later and Otto survived.

Years and distance separated us, but on July 10, 1993, the fiftieth anniversary of Otto and his wife Lena's wedding, we were delighted to meet all the Unger children again in the West Abbotsford Mennonite Church for their celebration.

I am getting ahead of my story and will return to Saskatchewan the way it was in the 1930s.

Four Seasons

Growing up, Justine and I were usually protected from severe cold in the winters. Yet I am sure the temperatures would have been the same as they are currently. Justine writes of a minus 32 degrees Celsius temperature in Regina in the winter of 1996. Henry writes that Manitoba has 40 degrees below zero. Justine and I were kept in the house. We seldom went anywhere, and when we did, we were well protected with warm blankets in the sleigh. I also remember how happy I was when George gave us muffs to keep our hands warm on the way to school.

The older siblings and our parents were not as well protected. They were old enough to remember how cold the house was. They remember their cold feet with chilblains, evidence of chronic cold. Henry's chilblains developed into open sores on his heels. In less severe situations feet were itchy and could be swollen. Hot foot baths in the wash basin relieved the itching and it probably assisted in the healing process. Warm weather was the best cure.

Dad particularly suffered and complained about the bitter cold. He had to brave the weather to take care of the animals in the barn which had to be fed morning and evening. He also had to clean the barn. His worst winter job was hauling water as described earlier. Usually a horse drawn sleigh took the kids to school. Here a barn housed the horse from 9:00 A.M. until four, when school was out. Henry was only twelve when he was in charge of unhitching the horse from the sleigh in the morning, and later in the day, hitching up to go home. This was a cold task for a boy his age.

When I was in third grade the big kids in school built a snow/ice slide on which to slide down on a toboggan. With a spade the kids cut blocks of driven snow on the school yard. Then they hauled them to the location where the slide was to be built. They piled the blocks on top of each other, staggering them. On one end were steps and on the other they formed a slope. When the slide reached the desired height they poured cold water from buckets on the slide to make it smooth and slippery. Jack Frost helped the process. Now the fun began. They climbed the steps and slid down the other side. The momentum carried them far beyond the base of the slide and down the natural incline of the rolling hill on which it was built. Once or twice they allowed the little kids to slide down even though we had not helped build the slide. What pure delight!

From Henry,

> *That slide brings back a painful experience or memory. Dad made a sleigh for us kids. It was made of crude angle iron runners and pieces of wood on top. He cut 'V's out of the angle iron to bend it in the front. With an iron brace and rivets it was the strongest built sleigh of all those brought to school. It was great to haul large blocks of snow to the slide. I was the hero to have such a sturdy sleigh.*
>
> *It was, however, not the best for sliding down the slide. On one such ride down, my close friend, William Wallace, reached out his hand—I don't know why—and a sharp corner, or a rivet, cut his hand quite badly. I got the blame and from hero was demoted to bad guy.*

At home we spent the long winter evenings at the kitchen table. It was the only place which was lit up by our one kerosene lamp. We could color with crayons, cut out dolls from the catalogue, or play table games like Mensch Aerger Dich Nicht or Chinese checkers on a piece of cardboard that had been converted into a game board. Our parents tended to guard the use of lamps. Dad had to use a kerosene lantern to feed the animals in the barn but in the house the lamp was not lit until well after dusk. It took money to burn kerosene. Mother could knit in the dusk but what could we do? Lena remembers the impatience she felt while we waited in the dark when it was necessary for Mother to take the lamp to another room for a few minutes.

In Saskatchewan, Easter came long before our white and brown world turned green again. In preparation for Easter, Mother brought a cake pan full of soil into the house and planted oats in it. She watered it regularly. We watched the green shoots come through the earth and we watched it grow into a spot of luscious green. This was a Russian Mennonite version of an Easter basket. Just before Easter we put boiled eggs into the green grass with a promise of new life to come. We never had commercial egg coloring. We tried pickled beet juice or onion peel.

I do not remember having any other Easter goodies with the exception of 1937 when George came home in his pickup truck. He brought us some. We played in the pickup bed while I held a chocolate covered marshmallow cookie in my hand. George had finished paying Dad's debt, and he no longer lived with the Ungers. He now lived in Regina with Mother's cousin, Mary Klassen, and with Mother's Aunt Margaret whom we called Gretchimum. George endeared himself to these ladies just as he had endeared himself to the Ungers.

Each spring held a new hope for rain, a crop and a garden. Dad worked the fields with a horse drawn plow and disc before he seeded grain with his drill. Year after year followed without adequate rainfall. Year after year hope died when the winds swept the prairie and carried the soil away. Russian thistles rolled across the fields dropping slivers in our yard to be picked up later by the soles of our bare feet. The despair our parents felt was transferred to us children but we never doubted that they would take care of us. "Children's questions sprinkled with sugar," Dad answered us when we asked childish questions. It meant the question was not worth answering. The answer pricked more subtly than the obvious Russian thistles in our bare feet.

Dad worked up the garden patch on the east slope of the rolling hill to the southwest of our house. Mother planted radishes, onions, beets, cabbage, potatoes, lettuce, carrots, parsley, dill, summer savory, sorrel and tomatoes. She needed the herbs to make the soups she had learned to make in Russia, and which we enjoyed eating. Annie adds,

*Also cucumbers. We had a barrel on a shaft between two wheels
and a large tongue attached. One of us would hold the tongue and
another help push it out to our dugout. We'd fill the barrel with
many pails of water, then push it to our cucumbers and water
every plant.*

The end of June marked the end of the school year. Summer holidays
were spent exploring the small world around us. Horses did not take
us far. We delighted in the growth of what we called "road roses." They
grew between the wagon tracks. They were hardy little flowers and did
well in an arid climate. Wild pink roses grew in the ditches beside roads.
Grasshoppers danced at our feet, while our parents hated the little beasts
that devoured our meager crops. Gophers enjoyed summers too and
multiplied underground. The mounds of dirt beside their gopher holes
showed us where their homes lay buried.

When Mary Harms visited I recruited her help in closing up the holes
with the gophers' dirt mounds. We shoved soil down the holes thinking
they would remain imprisoned. But the next morning we found the
mounds beside the holes just as they had been before we disturbed them.
They were free to eat Dad's crops again. Annie's and Lena's summers were
not as carefree as mine. They herded the cows in the fields to prevent them
from trespassing on fields that were not theirs to graze on. They had no
books or radio to break the monotony of their days. Boring!

Summers in Saskatchewan were brief. The slough was dry before
summer was over. And Dad hauled water for yet another year. The
dark clouds on the western horizon billowed and threatened to rain.
Occasionally a few big drops splattered into the dust. But there was not
enough moisture to relieve the drought. Although we had confidence in
the ability of our parents to feed and clothe us, they had good reason to
know they could not. At some time during the drought they applied for
"relief." We were given a small amount of money to survive. Dad hated to
receive help. The country had taken us in and had provided a safe haven
for his family. Now he became even more indebted to the government and

promised himself he would repay when he was able. The "relief" coal was used in winter to keep the fire from going out over night.

We are not sure how much our family was given each month. Henry suggests,

> *Apparently application was made according to need. But our parents were told that any money taken would have to be repaid. Therefore they took just enough to survive. One Mennonite family at Swift Current is said to have actually paid some back, before all was canceled. I don't know what we got in the beginning but I thought it was $25 per month the last year.*

Yet, I think each person in the family was allotted so much. Nettie said at one time that by working for a wage as a maid, she made $2 more per month than if she had received relief. I thought she mentioned $12 a month if she worked versus $10 if she stayed home.

Henry adds,

> *There was some other help at times. I think it was the Red Cross that sent blankets distributed by the municipality. Seed grain was received in spring, I think government sponsored. Ontario sent trainloads of vegetables and apples to the prairies. Also a very large apple was thrown to us from a passing truck when we walked home from school one day.*

It was perhaps the last summer we lived at Rush Lake when one of our old horses knew it was his last day to live. He came to the porch of the house and stood there patiently waiting to get some attention. The horse had never stood there like this before. Each of us in turn went out to pat or stroke its old hide. When it had received its due respect it walked away and died.

August and September yielded some vegetables from the much deserved garden. It was time for harvest but again and again there was little to harvest. After Labor Day we returned to school. We enjoyed school, but

I did not like to get ready for school because it involved having my frizzy hair combed. We had no brush which would have eliminated the pain of a comb pulling through my hair. Nettie enjoyed creating order out of my hair while I stood very impatiently. Mother had little sympathy, saying, "The crows will build a nest in your hair," as she smiled.

Henry had another problem. He did not like to have his ears washed. Mother told him she would plant potatoes in his ears if he didn't let her wash them. He asked innocently, "Why not corn instead?" I was learning to recognize sarcasm. In September we started counting the days until Christmas with great anticipation.

When the autumn frost had come to stay, our parents butchered one or two pigs. A sense of festivity accompanied this event, a tradition imported from Russia. In Russia the villagers invited friends and relatives to come early in the morning. They ate breakfast and lunch together and sent spare ribs home for the helpers to eat for supper. Some of these customs continued in Canada.

Mother started her day with boiling water on the kitchen stove. Sometimes she borrowed a large metal cauldron. And later, we owned our own cauldron in which to boil water and to render lard. The men carried the scalding water outside where they poured it over the slaughtered pig in a trough. Then they shaved off the bristles. Outside they hung it, dressed it and cut it up.

Sometimes our parents let us stay home from school to watch these exciting activities. One of my favorite procedures was the preparation of intestines to make casings for smoked sausages. To clean the intestines they had to be turned in-side-out. One person held the end of an intestine, carefully telescoping it while the second person trickled water from a teapot spout down the inverted casing.

Once the intestine was completely inverted, it was held against a solid piece of wood or a cutting board while the right hand of the cleaner used the dull edge of a knife to scrape the mucus from the casing. It became partially transparent. Next they rinsed the casing and soaked it in salt water. The meat to fill the casings had been ground by a hand operated chopper. In the clean galvanized tub they mixed it with salt and pepper and nothing else. Here the adults tasted the raw meat for saltiness. They worked the meat until it was just right. But what did this mean? Some suggested throwing a handful of the ground meat to the ceiling. If it stuck to the ceiling it was ready to stuff. I never witnessed this test of readiness. The blades of the meat chopper were replaced by a spout. Now one adult turned the handle to propel the meat through the chopper while a second adult slipped the casing over the spout and regulated the amount of meat filling the casing. One long sausage after another came into being. The end of each casing was twisted with fingers to close it off. Now the yard-long sausages were ready to smoke.

This pork was the primary source of meat for the family for a year, although during the next summer chickens supplemented the pork. Therefore it became necessary to prepare many meals without meat.

Because of the meat preservation difficulties without refrigeration, it was important to eat the meat in the correct sequence. Liverwurst and ribs were eaten first. Then we ate pickled head cheese (zill chees), tongue, heart and feet. After that we ate smoked sausage and lastly, ham. The latter two meats were smoked and then stored in the grain bins where they naturally froze in the frigid weather. Cracklings were covered with lard in crock pots in the cellar. They lasted for months. Mother served fried potatoes with cracklings, or they were fried for breakfast and eaten with brown bread. They were made of the meat that Americans use to make bacon. Russian Mennonites made no bacon, but their cracklings were delicious. We used lard for all frying and most breads.

After the fall butchering, the next major event would be Christmas.

DRESSES

ALTHOUGH I HAVE only three or four pictures of Justine and me as little children, we are wearing the same dresses on three of them. The pictures were clearly taken on three different occasions, and in different seasons. One picture shows snow on the ground. Dad's brother-in-law, Abram Koop took that picture when he and Aunt Tina (Dad's sister) were on their honeymoon in the late autumn of 1931. On another picture our older sisters are wearing summer dresses. On the third are the Harms children, who wear long sleeves but there is no snow. I suspect Justine and I had only one dress each. I think I remember that particular dress I wore. In our community, no females wore pants.

When I was little I suddenly became aware that the right sleeve of my dress, between my wrist and my elbow, was very shiny. In the absence of Kleenex my sleeve had brushed under my nose countless times. Was the dress ever washed in winter? Or in summer? What did I change into? Annie recalls,

> At one time I had only one winter dress with a white collar and cuffs. On Saturday I took off the collar and cuffs and washed them. Then I sewed them back on and I was ready for Sunday and another week of school. I don't know what I wore during the process.
>
> At school we had to change clothes for Christmas practice. I remember I had a bright yellow 'vanich' to keep me warm and how embarrassed I was.

92

A vanich is a sleeveless undershirt, or vest, with full wide shoulders. It was homemade.

Justine had a white dress at one time. She was standing on the porch of our summer kitchen on a Sunday morning, ready to go to house church. She demanded my instant attention when she commanded, "Tina, look what I can do!" She promptly jumped off the side of the porch and into the mud below. Dish water was dumped there on a daily basis. The ground was not frozen. She was a muddy mess in her white dress. Mother soon appeared and was obviously not pleased. "Now what will she wear? I have a notion to leave you both at home!" I was frightened. We were too little to stay home by ourselves. I thought she was grossly unjust. I had not jumped into the mud nor had I done anything to make Justine jump. What she changed into I don't know, but we were not left home alone.

The older the children in the family were, the more they were aware of the poverty. There was an advantage in being second youngest. I never knew I did not have enough dresses.

Borsch, Verenichi (Vereniki) and Cheelchi

Let us pretend briefly, that Mother had all the ingredients she needed to make Russian Mennonite meals. In reality, she was often short of vegetables in winter. In mid winter the eggs she had saved in the cellar were not necessarily good any more. She was always mindful of the meat shortage.

In summer she delighted to say "Go get me a handful of parsley from the garden." How much is a handful? Does it mean your hand full or mine? Does it extend beyond the grasp of a hand or is it entirely contained in a hand? I wanted to know how many stems were a handful. Mother did not measure any of the ingredients she put into soup or a dough.

Borsch required dill and parsley. Mother used old hens to make borsch although she preferred beef. She grew potatoes, onions, cabbage and tomatoes. She stored the first three items in the cellar. She did not yet know how to can tomatoes. She dried dill and the roots of parsley.

Sorrel, dill and onions made a tasty green borsch, or "summer borsch." She needed ham, buttermilk, and potatoes for this soup. "It is the onion, and not the dill that gives borsch its good flavor," she said.

Green bean soup required summer savory, ham, potatoes, onions, and of course, green beans. We grew all the ingredients for these soups on the farm if we had enough water to keep them growing. Any of these soups was an entire meal. We did not use crackers. But we ate bread with the soups. Mother never heard of sage, rosemary, marjoram, basil or oregano. Neither would she have known how to use them.

When Mother wanted to make red borsch or chicken noodle soup, she started by catching a chicken in the yard. She liked the old hens best because they provided more flavor. She needed one of us to hold the hen's head over the chopping block while she held the body in her left hand and an axe in her right. I could not watch the axe fall. I turned my head away. She scalded the dead hen in a bucket, pouring boiling water over the entire body. The feathers were easy to pull out after scalding. Next she lit a match to some crumpled up newspaper and held the hen over the fire to singe off all the hairs. Now it was ready to wash and cut up. She saved all the giblets which Dad enjoyed, and we did too. While the chicken was boiling Mother added the vegetables, or made the noodles—if it was to be noodle soup. She rolled the dough as thinly as she could. If there was enough time she allowed the sheets of dough to dry in the room. This made it easier to cut the noodles very fine. To make fine noodles was an art. She cut the sheets of dough into one and a half to two inch strips, piled them up and started the slicing process. Dinner was almost ready.

I almost lost my left forefinger at duck killing, Henry says. This time it was I who held the head of the duck over the block of wood with my left hand and the axe in my right. I chopped once but the head was not completely detached. I struck for a second chop but Mother pulled on the duck to tear the remaining skin and with her pulling, my hand went on to the block and the axe came down on my two fingers. I was twelve years of age. My tendon was cut so I could not straighten my forefinger. I went to the doctor all by myself. He put iodine on it and bandaged it. No stitches. The tendon healed on its own. The scars remain.

He also writes,

Mother plucked ducks alive. Feathers made warm quilts. With every pull of the feathers the duck quacked. I felt sorry for the ducks. 'It doesn't hurt me at all,' she said.

I remember her doing this and I pled for compassion for the ducks, but she argued that the ducks were molting anyway and their feathers scattered all over the yard. Why not get them before they fell? She plucked only on their breasts where fine feathers and down are found.

Henry remembers,

> *Even the chicken's head was cleaned and cooked. That was Dad's favorite. After eating all the skin off the head he split the head in half and sucked out the brain with one big 'Whoosh.'*

Mother needed a sharp knife in the kitchen. Dad used a whetstone wheel to sharpen knives. The whetstone was set up in a frame with foot pedals. The peddle rotation made the whetstone go round and round through a trough of water made with a piece of rubber tire. Then he applied the knife to the whetstone. Later, in Manitoba, I stood aghast watching him sharpen our stainless steel plated table knives. He did not care that they were never made to be sharpened. "The purpose of a knife is to cut," he said. The knives rusted without their stainless steel plating.

The seasons of the year dictated Mother's menus. She could dry dill, parsley roots and summer savory. She could not dry sorrel leaves, green beans or tomatoes. So she cooked bean soup in winter. Served with brown homemade bread it was very nutritious. But many of the meals Mother made were starchy and fatty.

For example, Rollkuchen (Krullers) were very starchy and fatty. She served these alone, or with borsch when times were good. Verenichi (vereniki) were cheese pockets, or cottage cheese ravioli. At that time we had never heard of ravioli and thought verenichi was a Russian specialty. Mother made a noodle dough but rolled it out and cut it into rectangles of about five by six inches. Into these rectangles she dropped a mixture of dry cottage cheese mixed with egg yokes, salt and pepper. Now she brought up the sides of the rectangle and pinched the tops together. Then she pinched the ends together. For the first meal these were dropped into a pot of boiling water and cooked a few minutes. She scooped them out and served them in a bowl. She fried ham or sausage if she had some. If she did not, we simply ate them with cream gravy. The leftovers served fried the next day were delicious. A variation was to fill the dough rectangle with fruit, but in Saskatchewan that was only a dream most of the time.

Cheelchi were coarse noodles. They too were served with ham or sausage if we had them. Sautéed onions and vinegar topped the noodles. We never had ketchup, and I still prefer vinegar to ketchup.

Large flat pancakes without baking powder (now known as crepes) comprised a whole meal. I think of crepes as gourmet, perhaps with more eggs than Mother's pancakes. She served hers with sugar or Roger's Golden Syrup. We wrapped the pancakes around our forks to make a roll. We dipped the end of the roll into a bit of sugar on our plates and popped a bite into our mouths. We didn't know what a balanced meal was so all this tasted very good, and still does today.

Mother made a meatless soup of noodles and potatoes. She used the same herbs and spices as she did for noodle soup. I thought it was best with a tablespoon of vinegar in a soup bowl. She called it Butter Soup because she added melted butter when it was ready to serve. We used vinegar over cooked beans and over pickled pork from the cellar. Vinegar made cold foods like pig's feet, heart, and head cheese go down a little better.

Before Mother had jars and before she knew how to can, she tried to preserve gooseberries in pop bottles that the kids picked up beside the road and brought home. To clean them she put gravel and water into them and shook them well. The gravel scoured them clean. We filled the bottles with gooseberries slowly through their narrow necks. She used corks to close them. Of course, the corks blew off in the cooking process but she put them back on. When they were cooled she dipped them into paraffin and hoped the berries would keep. In winter time she coaxed these berries out with a knitting needle and made mous.

Mous was not "mouse" or "mousse". German mous was a sweetened fruit soup made of milk or water and thickened with a little flour or cornstarch. Almost any fruit can be used to make mous. Plume Mous was the queen of mous. It had dried prunes and raisins, plus any other dried fruit one might have on hand. Dried fruit was very much a part of the Russian Mennonite culture and cuisine.

With mous Mother often served French toast, or Rea Rei—a German kind of scrambled egg. Sometimes she served fried potatoes with it. But with Plumi mous she preferred ham.

The Ukraine had provided our parents with plenty of fruit. They dried fruit to preserve it. In Canada they had to buy dried fruit in the store but it was considered a necessity.

Perischchi were fruit pockets made with pastry dough and filled with fresh fruit. They were made much like verenichi (vereniki). The difference was in the kind of dough, which was closer to pie dough, and in the difference in the cooking method. We added sugar and flour to the fruit in the perischchi and baked them in the oven. What scrumptious individual pies they were! This was not dessert, this was dinner.

To make noodles, verenichi, cheelchi or rollkuchen, Mother needed eggs. Chickens do not lay eggs in winter when it is very cold, so Mother saved autumn eggs and stored them in the cellar. How long do eggs keep? She could never guarantee the condition of an egg in winter unless she broke it into a cup. If the yolk had begun to invade the white of an egg, she discarded the egg. Then she could not make dough that required eggs.

We did not eat chicken in winter. We needed the hens to lay in the spring. We also needed them to become clucks which had patience to sit on a nest of eggs for three weeks. Tiny yellow chicks pecked their way out of a shell after three weeks and the life cycle began again.

Like the chickens, the cows sometimes went dry in winter prior to calving. For short periods we went without butter. We substituted brown lard. Brown lard was not quite pure enough to be lard, but the brown specks in it were not big enough to be cracklings. We never liked brown lard but with enough salt it was edible.

Everything Mother fried was fried in hot lard. Dad liked potatoes fried in enough lard so he "could lift them out of the fat." We children preferred our potatoes with as little fat as possible but we ate what Mother served. Cholesterol was not yet a household word.

In the absence of supermarkets and money, the produce in the garden was important. In summer we ate leaf lettuce mixed with cream, sugar and vinegar dressing. Cucumbers were good with salt or in whipped clabbered thick milk. Beaten clabbered milk became a cold soup when either cooked beans, sliced cucumbers or cheelchi were added. We ate fresh radishes and green onion tops. We ate green beans in soup but never as a vegetable by themselves. Fresh tomatoes were good either with salt, pepper, onions and vinegar, or with sugar. Vegetables helped Mother greatly in feeding the family. Although we knew nothing about vitamins, we ingested more of them in summer. There were no fresh vegetables in winter, so wilted potatoes and carrots from the cellar had to suffice.

Food changes were made very slowly. Dad was not fond of potatoes, and he said corn was cattle fodder. He preferred the pastas Mother made. A meat, potato, vegetable, salad and dessert meal was foreign to us. But we did enjoy peanut butter and Roger's Golden Syrup made in B.C., both Canadian foods introduced to our family before I can remember.

The older girls came home from school with new ideas about food. For the first time we had jello. What do we do with it? It sounded like jelly but we could not spread it on bread. It was dessert.

Another recipe the girls brought home required hard boiled eggs, lettuce and radishes in a cream dressing. What is it? We tried it in sandwiches and it was very tasty. Or was it a salad? And what is a salad?

Where did the foods Mother made originate? Some foods like borsch are clearly Russian. In 1996 we were served perischchi and verenichi when on tour in Russia. The pancakes Mother made were more like Swedish pancakes than American. Could they have originated in Holland? How much Dutch and German cuisine did our people retain? And where did fruit soups come from? My Jewish friend whose people came from Russia knew about fruit soups, such as Plumi mous, which was eaten cold.

In Saskatchewan where gardens were too dry to produce well, and where money was almost nonexistent, Mother had a hard time cooking like she had cooked in Russia. Years later when we lived in Manitoba and food was abundant, Mother remarked, "But we were never hungry." She was grateful.

MEDICAL TRIVIA

A GRATED POTATO wrapped in a handkerchief took the heat out of the burn on my jaw. To cure a headache Mother soaked a handkerchief in water and wrung it out. She poured a tablespoon of vinegar on the handkerchief and put it on our forehead. The smell of vinegar convinced us of its healing power. We had not heard about aspirin yet. Iodine was the only medication we had on hand, although I seem to remember having some ointment at some time. Dad's left forefinger needed more than aspirin or vinegar. It had to be amputated. Before the days of antibiotics or sulfa, amputation was the only cure for an infected finger.

Dr. Leach came to our house when Justine was born. Almost four years later she and I had the measles. While I was covered with a red rash, I was not sick. But Justine lay in bed, and we thought she was dying. Perhaps it was then that we became aware of Dr. Leach's red liquid medicine, which apparently worked because Justine recovered. Dr. Leach used the red liquid medicine for various disorders. It was bottled in a large glass container the size of today's ketchup bottles. The red color looked like the juice of canned plums. It had the consistency and flavor of canned plum juice. Did Justine recover because of the red medicine? What was in that red solution? Was it perhaps aspirin in the juice that took her fever away?

It was while I had the measles that I embroidered the little flour sack dish towel with the pink pitcher on it. It survived all the moves I made and I still have it. I was six. I needed medical help only once while we lived in the old gray house and that was when I dislocated my elbow.

Mother was the only family member to be hospitalized. She had a bladder problem. She and Dad dreaded hospitals more than any of their children because they felt powerless without knowing the English language. They could not communicate their needs to the hospital staff. The doctor ordered a no-salt diet but Mother did not understand the need to abstain from salt. In fact, she craved a dill pickle. When a young family friend came to see Mother, she persuaded her friend into going out and coming back with a dill pickle. The doctor and the nurses never knew, and she recovered in spite of the salty pickle. Mother laughed when she told us about it. She thought she outsmarted the doctor. The problem never recurred. Was it really a kidney problem as the doctor seemed to think, or was it merely a bladder infection? And what did they do for bladder infections before the advent of antibiotics and sulfas, besides pushing fluids?

The Beisel's little granddaughter experienced a ruptured appendix and had surgery. This was serious without antibiotics. Her grandmother's report about the girl's thirst triggered my deepest sympathy. She was not allowed to drink. Did they not have intravenous fluids in the 1930s? The child recovered and lived to show us her scar in the lower right part of her abdomen.

Sore throats were cured with hot milk and sugar. The remedy really called for honey but since we had none, sugar stirred into milk was fine. It certainly soothed the throat. Mother recommended wearing a warm scarf wound around the neck.

We were immunized in Rush Lake. I do not know who sponsored the immunizations. A nurse came to school and gave the injections. "Inoculation" was a big word for the process of scratching our skin on the upper left arm. We developed a scab and when it came off it left a scar. The older children had been immunized in Russia.

Nettie inherited Mother's farsightedness. "I needed glasses desperately," she said later. She lived in with farmers where she did housework for the farm wife and earned money for glasses. Mother was not fitted for glasses until she went with me to an ophthalmologist in New Westminster in 1954. The same doctor told me my eyeballs were shaped just like Mother's. I too am very farsighted.

Dental care was almost unknown to us. A dentist came to school when I was seven. My secondary teeth were replacing my primary teeth but they were coming in crooked. The dentist said the problem would correct itself by the time I was eleven. He recommended no treatment. They remained crooked because I did not have enough room in my jaws.

Henry says,

> *I must have been in grade three or four when a dental nurse came to school and examined everyone's teeth. I had eight teeth that needed pulling—four on each side. With permission from parents we who needed dental work were to go to a dentist in Herbert. I think two or three carloads full had to go from our school. Probably volunteers with cars took us. The dentist pulled four on one side and said that was all he could do at one time."*
>
> Henry remembers, *"I was to come back later for the other four. I had enough of dentists, and also shyness, to report to the teacher, and never told our parents or siblings that I needed to go back. I said only that he had pulled four. Surely it must also have been on the dental record but no one ever mentioned it again. Of course, I suffered with many toothaches after that.*

Henry also recalls that for toothaches

> *One remedy was a drop of red medicine on the gums. That burned so bad that you couldn't feel the tooth ache. Another was to take a few puffs of smoke from Dad's self-rolled cigarettes and hold the smoke in the mouth but not inhale. I can't really report any relief from the latter.*

The school supported good health habits by doing health checks every day. The teacher asked for a show of hands of those who brushed their teeth that morning. She walked along every row of desks to see everyone's fingernails while we spread our hands on the desktops. She noted whether our hair was combed. She asked us to raise a clean handkerchief above our heads. Confidently I pulled my one clean handkerchief from the bottom of my desk and held it up for her to see. If we had a perfect record she rewarded us with a small picture sticker at the end of the month.

Nutrition was poor and Mother lost all of her teeth. She remained toothless. I cannot remember her with her natural teeth. Her mouth was hollow long before she was fifty years old. She did not complain about this personal loss. We liked her toothless face. Many years later when we lived in Manitoba, she went to Winnipeg to buy dentures for $25. She came home with a mouth that looked far too full. We begged her to take her dentures out because she looked ugly with teeth. She listened to us and laughed till her round belly shook.

Dad suffered most from medical neglect. He failed to be fitted for glasses. He had tried non-prescription glasses, but they were of little use, so he gave up on glasses. I know we were poor and he could not pay a doctor, nor could he pay for glasses; but without knowing the English language, I doubt that all the resources had been explored. Dad's vision was a serious handicap until he died.

Our parents were grateful for the good health we enjoyed. No one had a major illness or accident while we were poor. Mother prided herself in not believing in all the home remedies in which some people indulged. Thank God, we did not need them.

THE RUSH LAKE SCHOOL

THE TWO-ROOM SCHOOL house was built on the rolling hill southeast of town. We walked north down a cinder sidewalk to get to downtown Rush Lake.

The town's most prominent structures were the five elevators on the north edge of town. The tall elevators had witnessed many prosperous years when business bustled in this farmers' nucleus. In the 1930s they waited quietly to hear the clatter of horses' hoofs and rattling wagons loaded with grain. The Canadian Pacific Railroad ran east and west past the elevators and paralleled Canada's number One highway one half mile south of town.

Most businesses were built along Main Street, which ran east and west, and along the road from the highway into town. That road and Main Street formed an L. The town boasted two General Stores, a town hall, a United Church of Canada building, a small hotel, a post office and a physician's office. Residential houses dotted the rest of town. Aunt Justine and Mr. Harms lived in a white frame house one block south of their store on Main Street.

The Harms' children climbed the gentle slope to school for ten months a year. We Klassen children came to school in a buggy or a sleigh, or we walked from our house two miles southeast of Rush Lake. A barn sheltered our horse while we went to class from 9:00 A.M. until 4:00 P.M. At first, Annie was in charge of the horse's unhitching and hitching and placement in the barn. Then Henry fell heir to this job when Annie dropped out of school.

The entrance to the school faced west. Broad stairs inside the building took us to the cloakroom directly in front of us. Here we shed our coats, scarves, mittens, helmets that covered our ears, and the above-the-ankle buckled overshoes. From the cloakroom the high school students went to their classroom to the north and the grade school students went to their classroom to the south.

Rush Lake School in 1977

The school was not large. I would guess there were about thirty to forty children in grades one to eight, but there were not nearly that many in high school.

I started school in September, 1934, when I was six. Annie was the only one in our family to go to high school that year. Nettie had dropped out of school a year earlier. Mr. Butterworth, the principal and high school teacher, had tried to keep her in school by offering her the use of his books. But our parents wanted to go to Manitoba to visit my grandparents. They had a rare opportunity to ride with Uncle Peter in his truck to see them. They wanted Nettie to help with the younger children at home. They also wanted her to work for wages. All her life Nettie regretted our parents' decision for her. School was something she excelled in, and she saw it as the only opportunity for her to "make good." The opportunity was taken out of her hands. George was working at Ungers' dairy at this time.

Lena entered sixth grade in 1934. Our parents had kept her out of school until she was seven, and would be eight in January. She also regretted that they had made that choice for her. Henry was in fourth grade. Lena and Henry anticipated meeting a new teacher that year. Until then Miss Peden taught the lower grades. Miss Daisy Jean Erskine took her place in front of the class that September morning, prepared to fulfill her role as a teacher in her eight-grade classroom. She was probably in her late twenties.

That morning and every morning after that, Miss Erskine took her place in front of the classroom and led us in The Lord's Prayer. She bowed her head and put her fingertips on the desk before her. She used "trespasses" and "trespass" instead of "debts" and "debtors." This was probably the first time I heard the prayer in English. What Miss Erskine said was engraved in my mind. Therefore, if she said "trespasses" and "trespass", then it was the right way to say it and anything else was wrong.

Every morning she led us in our national anthem:

O Canada, our home and native land,
True patriot love in all thy sons command.
With glowing hearts we see thee rise,
The true north, strong and free.
We stand on guard, O Canada,
We stand on guard for thee.

The Union Jack flew proudly on the flagpole. The maple leaf flag was not yet in existence.

Next Miss Erskine did the daily health check as described earlier. We used salt and the same toothbrush for years. No wonder that in Summer Bible School I was awarded a tooth brush for either learning Scripture verses or for attendance. I remember my disappointment. I wanted something frivolous instead of a tooth brush. But the teachers probably knew I needed a new brush.

About brushing teeth, Henry remembers,

Miss Erskine telling us we could use our finger came in handy at times. Forgetting to brush at home, a few pokes in my mouth with my finger and I could raise my hand, 'I brushed my teeth.'

One day at noon upon opening my lunch pail, my half apple was gone. Apples were a special treat, one that we had only occasionally. Now mine was stolen. I cried, and I don't remember, did I, or my sister tell the teacher? She went to the principal. Mr. Butterworth called me to follow him. I didn't know what was happening now. He took me to his home and let me choose between a peach, and I think the other was a pear or maybe an orange. I chose the peach. It was delicious, the first peach in my life.

Henry continues,

In 1936-37 I was sitting next to the windows in grade six. Arithmetic was after the first recess until 12 noon. I often sat daydreaming as I looked out the window till the daily 11:30 passenger train went roaring west. Then I had to hurry and get my work done.

In grade one in 1934 were five boys and two girls. Margaret Unger moved away and I was the only girl left. Grade one pupils sat facing Miss Erskine to her left near the east wall. Grade eight students sat next to the windows on the opposite wall. All the grades sat in sequence from left to right. Miss Erskine taught us phonics. If we knew the letters of the alphabet we could sound out most words. The first word we learned was CAT. When we mastered that word, it was easy to learn to read MAT, BAT, SAT AND RAT. Reading and writing required simple common sense.

Miss Erskine used flash cards with simple words or simple arithmetic to reinforce what she had taught. We enjoyed standing in front of the classroom while she flashed one card after the other to us. We stood with one foot in front of the other, and competitively barked out one word after the other. We shouted the words as fast and as loudly as we could. We all wanted to be first to answer.

In third grade, Miss Erskine gave us letters on wooden tiles similar to today's Scrabble tiles. She assigned words to each of us and we were to make a sentence out of tiles using the assigned word. Words and sentences came easily to me. I made the shortest sentence possible, which meant I expended little energy. Miss Erskine probably knew it. Then she gave me the word "if." I sat thinking about making a short sentence but the shortest sentence I could think of was, "If a dog bit me it would hurt." I was a bit perturbed that I couldn't think of a shorter one. I formed my sentence with my tiles on my desk. Miss Erskine walked the aisles and looked at the sentence. She commended me for my effort. It is the only sentence I remember.

Miss Erskine provided a solid foundation in reading, writing and arithmetic. Once when she looked at my handwriting she said, "You will certainly have to improve your writing if you want to write as well as your sister Lena." I was not offended, nor was I challenged. In my own mind I knew Lena was her own person and I was mine. This is how it is and that is how it will be.

Miss Erskine was not as adept at throwing balls as she was at teaching the three Rs. While watching her pupils play at recess a stray ball landed next to her. When she tried to throw it back, it went straight up into the air. She too was not perfect in all things. This thought comforted me when I became aware of how inept I was in sports.

Another area of my ineptness appeared when she tried to teach the older classes music without any instrument. She taught the scale, bass clef, treble clef and the notes: every-good-boy-deserves-favor for the lines and f-a-c-e for the spaces. I could memorize that but I could not understand how those things translated into singing notes. For the first time in school she taught something I could not comprehend. And I still can't. Sharps and flats were incomprehensible too.

Henry reports about music,

The music I know is thanks to a thorough teacher and Freddie Belter. Freddie was a bit slow in learning. He was in a lower grade but with one teacher and six grades (I think eight—author), grades were lumped together. Example: grades four to six took the same history. Music was divided into one to three and four to six, I think.

Freddie was very dense in music, but the teacher taught so the dumbest could catch on. I can still hear her almost screaming, 'The right hand sharp is always 'ti,' count down or up to 'do'. That stuck. It may have been Miss Peden as I can't really recall Miss Erskine ever yelling.

Construction paper and plasticine (play dough) were teaching tools too.

At school we were almost always able to forget the poverty at home. We had 5¢ Scribblers (note books), pencils, erasers and crayons just like the other children. At home Dad complained about the Scribblers needing replacement when they were full of our printing and arithmetic. He suggested we erase the penciled work from the pages so we could use them again. Perhaps he was the original recycler. That was too much! I could not bear to think of writing new work on pages smeared with erased pencil marks. I thought of the dog-eared corners of my Scribbler. I would not enjoy writing or arithmetic any more. I argued that the cost of the erasers would equal the cost of new Scribblers. In any case, we never had to use old Scribblers.

Once I had chewing gum. After chewing the flavor out of it I wondered if it would stick to the paper on a page of my Reader. I put it over a word. But when I tried to remove it, it took the print with it. It was the school's book. That error caused me many guilt-stricken moments. How could one explain damage with chewing gum? What would happen if someone found out I did the damage?

In our Reader the two children pictured were Jerry and Jane. The script said, "Jerry can catch a ball." "Jane can run." Any Reader that did not feature Jerry and Jane seemed like second class material.

Most of the time I ranked first in class and took it for granted that I was. In third grade, my cousin Art Harms was a close second. I did not feel threatened until my parents promised me a dime if I were first in class again. That was big money! They pressured me into telling Miss Erskine about the dime. I didn't want to, but for a dime it was worth doing something I did not want to do. Very timidly, I told her. I liked her very much but I was uncomfortable talking to her about this.

When the report cards were issued at the end of the month, my rank was first. When I checked with Art, he too, was first, but his grades were slightly higher than mine. I was not proud to be first when I knew Art was, but I got the bittersweet dime. I do not know why my parents coerced me into telling the teacher about the reward that I did not deserve.

Art's sister, Mary, my best friend, sat across the aisle from me in third grade. We were whispering across the aisle until I saw Miss Erskine stare at me. I quit talking. Mary's head was turned away from the teacher and could not see her stare. She wouldn't quit talking and I listened to her. Then Miss Erskine told ME to stand in the corner! Two of my favorite people got me into trouble.

In third grade our class gained one pupil. Freddie Belter had failed to pass third grade and had to repeat it. There was something different about Freddie. He was obviously obese but there was something else about Freddie. Every child in my grade was Caucasian, but Freddie looked Asian. His brother Lawrence, also in my grade, looked as Caucasian as the rest of us. I knew the little hotel was managed by a Chinese man. Then I overheard an adult conversation I could not understand. It was about Mr. Belter taking money for his wife's services. How did that explain Freddie? The Belters couldn't be very bad if they shared their well water with us.

The Hammett children brought milk from their farm to sell in town. During the day they kept the bottled milk in the school basement to keep it cool. One day a rumor circulated about Hammett's milk bottles being broken. That was all I knew. The same day, in the classroom, Miss Erskine asked, "Who knows anything about the milk bottles?" My arm shot up and when she called on me I said, "They are broken." That wasn't the answer she wanted. She already knew that. She wanted new information and I had none to give her. She dismissed me as the innocent that I was. I wondered why no one raised their hands. Obviously someone knew about it or it would not have happened. I had not heard of vandalism yet. I could not imagine anyone breaking milk bottles deliberately.

The school had a full basement. A wall separated the boys' play area from the girls.' Both boys and girls had separate toilets in their end of the basement. This was before we had plumbing or electricity. Lena says,

The toilets had holding tanks and in summer the contents were pumped out and taken to the fields west of Rush Lake. The doors had a rope attached to a pail. The pail hung down in the toilet. The weight of the filled pail pulled the door and closed it. Sometimes the stench was bad. Sometimes it wasn't.

We played in the basement when the weather was unsuitable for us to play outside where we had swings and a teeter totter. We also skipped with a jump rope, and played hop scotch.

Once day Miss Erskine called me in from recess. I was the only third grade girl and was playing with first and second graders. Justine was in first grade and Mary Harms in second. Miss Erskine asked me why I wouldn't let Annie Krahn play with us. Annie had tattled. True, Annie had not been playing with us but I certainly didn't know why. Miss Erskine excused me when she saw the story was totally new to me.

On one occasion Miss Erskine asked me to show her my overshoes. Most of us wore rubber soled and lined overshoes when it was wet or cold. The ankle-high overshoes kept the snow out and the warmth in. The problem was that Jerry Jenkins couldn't find his overshoes. Miss Erskine came to the cloakroom to help him search. My initials were printed in ink in the inside at the very top in the back. They were easy to see. When Miss Erskine asked about my overshoes I found only one of mine. To lose an overshoe would be a disaster. Thinking that perhaps only one of mine was initialed, (although I was pretty sure both of them were), I quickly found another overshoe in my size and put TK in it, complicating the search for

Jerry's overshoes. Poor Jerry could find only one overshoe. Miss Erskine was left to untangle the jumble, and at the end of the day we all wore our own pair of overshoes home. But there were three initialed TK.

Before we went home at four o'clock we sang the British anthem:

God save our gracious king.
Long live our noble king.
God save the King.
Send him victorious,
Happy and glorious,
Long to reign over us,
God save the king.

King George the V reigned in 1934. In 1936 he was dead and Edward VIII was heir to the British throne. However, he was never crowned. Even in our little town we heard of his scandalous affair with a foreigner and a divorcee. Edward abdicated the throne for Wallis Simpson, an American.

Lena adds, "That was at Christmas, and 'Hark the Herald Angels Sing' became:

Hark the herald angels sing.
Mrs. Simpson stole our king.
She had two men before and now
She's looking for some more."

George VI was crowned king of the British Empire. The coronation provided the school with an opportunity to celebrate. We left school for this rare event and walked to the town hall. We probably had a program to present to our audience. Miss Erskine took this opportunity to teach us about British Royalty, the throne and our history. Each child received a metal medallion as a memento of this occasion. My medallion is in my dresser drawer, but the accompanying taffy was eaten promptly.

After singing "God Save the King" at the end of each day, Miss Erskine followed us to the cloak room to help us get dressed for our cold trip home. She bound the long, hand-knit scarf around my head until only the eyes were exposed to the cold.

One summer day, on our way home in the buggy, Henry, Lena and I saw rocks piled up against the end of a culvert. The culvert lay under the dirt road onto which we would turn when we left the gravel highway a half mile from home. We traveled the same route every day and knew the rocks had been placed there this day. Curious, Henry stopped the horse to climb down to investigate. Henry and Lena removed the rocks. They peeked into the dark tunnel and saw a skunk. We were terrified. We had heard that the only way to rid oneself of the smell of a skunk was to be buried up to our necks in the ground. I'm not sure Lena and Henry believed this but I certainly did. They did not take time to block the culvert but instead jumped back on the buggy as fast as possible. We made the poor horse run up hill to get away as fast as we could. A half mile later we were safe at home.

On our way home from school in the 1930s we frequently saw men riding on the roofs of the train cars. We called them "bums."

At the end of June the school's closing was celebrated with a "Sports Day." We left the school grounds and played in a field west of town. I cannot remember it being a park. Various races such as the three-legged race and the sack race were fun to compete in. The bigger kids played softball. But the highlight of the day was to eat the annual ice cream cone sold by the Chinese man at the hotel. The price was 5¢.

CHRISTMAS

On Christmas Eve in 1935 the gray house was dark except for the dim light from the kerosene lamp on the kitchen table. The scanty curtains pulled across the top corners of the windows did not keep the light from filtering through the windows onto the snow outside. The light from the window reflected a poor immigrant family who was home for Christmas.

Even our handsome big brother, George, came home for Christmas. George was twenty and seemed so grown up. He had been a welcome child, born only three months after the first two children died in 1915. George smiled a lot. He was clearly glad to be home.

The house looked exactly like it did the other 364 days of the year. The stove, the table and sewing machine were in their usual places. They had not been moved to accommodate a Christmas tree. There was no baby Jesus, Mary, Joseph or stable. Nor was there an eastern star or an angel at the top of a tree. There was not one item of Christmas decoration to be seen. But we had snow. And we were happy. A spirit of excitement and anticipation pervaded the room. Joy sprang from our young hearts and shining eyes. We had counted the days until Christmas since September. Now it was almost here.

We knew Christmas meant celebrating Christ's birth, but we also expected something tangible; something different from any other day of the year. We did not know what we were missing by not having a church, and consequently no Christmas program in a church. We had a school and the school provided a Christmas concert, which was always the last Friday before Christmas.

We were often part of the Christmas concert held at the town hall. I was one of several dolls that walked and moved in jerky motions, like a mechanical doll was expected to move. We witnessed "The Star of the East" shining from a corner of the stage near the ceiling. Miss Erskine had cut out the shape of a star from a box and covered it with cellophane. Then she put a flashlight into the box. She really was a creative marvel! At the concert three wise men walked across the stage while the rest of the students sang "Star of the East." We even sang "Home on the Range" at one concert.

After our performance, Santa Claus made his appearance and gave us each a bag of Christmas goodies. The bag held peanuts and candy, but the best thing was the annual orange and an apple. One year Santa gave us secondhand dolls. They did not have hair and their eyes did not close. We were grateful for whatever we received. We had no idea who had collected used toys to give to poor children. Henry's sand mill was much more interesting. It could turn its blades around if we poured sand into the top.

Our parents attended the school's English program. I remember going home afterward in the family sleigh. We sat on the edge of a comforter that went down to the floor, under our feet, and up over our legs and into our laps. I looked up and saw the clear, starry sky overhead. No tall buildings obscured the view, and no electric light paled the starlight above.

Christmas at home seemed even more special than the school concert. Now we had only to wait until morning to see what we would get for Christmas. In 1935 Mother sensed my eager anticipation. She took me aside and became very serious. She said, "All gifts are merely tokens of the real gift at Christmas. God gave us His very best gift of all when He sent Jesus at Christmas. He is the reason for our joy, and not the material things we give." Quietly I absorbed this and was prepared to be disappointed this Christmas.

I was eight years old and just a little suspicious about Santa. Why did our store-owning cousins in town get so much more than we did? Santa did not favor children, at least not if they had been equally good. We knew the song about Santa coming to town to check on how naughty or nice we had been. This night I would know for sure.

Mother sent Justine and me to bed. I resolved to find out the truth, but I did not tell Justine about my suspicion and she was soon asleep. When all the children, except George, had gone to bed upstairs, Mother poked her head into the bedroom door and asked, "Children are you asleep?" I did not answer.

I listened. When I could no longer hear the sounds from the big kids, I heard the sounds of Christmas. Paper bags rustled. Peanuts and candy dropped into our enamel plates we had set on the table. I heard soft speech. I heard George laugh heartily. Above these lesser noises, I heard what sounded like a wind-up toy running across the bare wooden kitchen floor. Then I heard Mother reprimanding in a pleading voice, "George, don't play with them now, because if you break them they will have nothing in the morning." Now I knew I would be disappointed. I was too old for a wind-up toy. But for now, I knew the truth about Santa Claus, and that was satisfying.

On Christmas morning we got up early and rushed to the table. Beside the enamel plates holding the peanuts and candy, Justine and I saw an unwrapped wind-up car/motorcycle/policeman, all molded out of one piece of tin and painted in bright reds and blues. I was disappointed.

Dad had driven to Swift Current, twenty miles away, with horses and had chosen these toys. He was out of touch with his youngest daughters. We could understand spending only 15¢ for a gift, but we would have preferred 15¢ dolls to these little machines. That was the only gift given to us at home that Christmas. Now I knew why Mother's voice had been so plaintive the night before.

Annie adds,

> *You were lucky. When I was six years old, I got a pair of stockings. I kept asking Mother what I was getting for Christmas and she said 'schulchi.' So when Corny Peters came over, I asked him what schulchi meant in Russian and he said stockings, so I knew what my gift would be that Christmas. It must have been terrible for our parents.*

Lena says,

We'd be counting days till Christmas, starting in September. It was the one day in the year we got something—little as it was, but how we looked forward to the small gift and to the plate full of candy and peanuts and one apple. I remember saving my apple upstairs and it froze on me. The gifts were only pennies worth but our parents didn't have any money.

One year there were a few yards of cotton print on the table and that was to be dresses for Nettie, Annie and me. In spring Mother sewed the dresses and there was only enough for Nettie and Annie. Of course Mother knew when she bought it that it would be only for Nettie and Annie. Then in spring she bought another piece for me.

Poverty struck in every season and at every angle, it seems.

Next year we would celebrate!

On Christmas morning in 1936, we were truly surprised. A miniature chest of drawers awaited Justine and me. It was made from apple boxes and was stained brown. The drawer pulls were empty red wooden thread spools cut in half.

A big doll awaited us. She did not have hair or eyes that closed but she was new! Before long we knew she cost 89¢ in the Eaton's catalogue.

We also knew Dad had spent many hours in the hayloft of our barn, making the crude chest out of apple boxes. It would store our clothes and toys. The doll and the chest were both jointly owned by Justine and me.

Not only did our parents surprise us with their generous gifts, but George and Nettie had bought gifts. Both spent of their meager earnings. Nettie was only eighteen and worked as a house maid. From Nettie we received store bought paper dolls. They were of light weight cardboard and bigger than those we had cut out of the catalog. They came with clothes for every social occasion. We enjoyed dressing and undressing the dolls but had no understanding for the need of different clothing for different occasions. Their names were Peggy, Polly, Patty and Pinky.

George gave us muffs to keep our hands warm. Aunt Justine had made them for him. The outer shell was brown fur. Stuffing between the fur and the lining insulated the muffs. At each end of the cylinder was an elasticized opening into which we stuffed our hands. The side of the muff had a pocket with a zipper.

This was a Christmas to remember. Just wait until we tell our store-owning cousins in town!

God and Church in an
Unchurched Place

RUSH LAKE HAD only one small church, the United Church of Canada, whose white frame building stood near the town hall. We were familiar with the town hall where our school concerts were held. We had celebrated King George the VI's coronation there. But who used the church? We lived near Rush Lake from 1929 until 1937, but we were unaware of what took place at church on Sunday mornings. Our family never went to town on Sunday mornings so we may have missed the action. If there were services they would have been in English and our parents would not have been interested.

Our parents had attended church in Russia where the village church services were all in German. In Canada our parents did not associate with anyone who spoke only English.

During the eight years we lived at Rush Lake, the German families had no home church. The seven or eight families knew each other, and they shared a common language, faith and culture. They enjoyed visiting each other on some Sunday afternoons but no leader stepped forth to initiate structured meetings. There were many Mennonite families in the Herbert and Main Center areas and they had Mennonite churches. But without a car it was too far to go to church ten or more miles away. I have already mentioned the occasional services in either Unger's vacant farmhouse or the United Church building.

I remember that when Mother told the story of Jesus' crucifixion, I cried. He suffered so. I asked Mother whether God, who is almighty, could not have found another way to redeem mankind. She said, "No, it is the only way of redemption."

When Dad saw mysterious lights on the road, (See Epilogue: "Dad") Mother and Dad wondered what God was trying to tell them. They taught us to pray, and they read the Bible. They depended on God for their sustenance. God protected, provided, guided and gave meaning to their lives. I recall that my parents took us to the Unger bachelor twins' house to hear a fifteen minute German Mennonite radio sermon one winter.

In school Miss Erskine prayed the Lord's prayer and we sang "God save the King." In every letter our parents wrote or received it said, "We are in good health, Thank God." God's existence was not questioned by anyone we knew.

The summer of 1937 brought a two week summer Bible School to us. Virginia Unger, our cousin, was one of two young women who made arrangements to teach Bible School in Unger's empty farm house. They divided the group into two classes.

The lesson that impressed me most was an object lesson about nails and pins. The teacher poured out a container of these little nails and pins on the table. She told us they represented the people on earth. She held a magnet in her hand. The magnet represented Christ. She lowered the magnet until it was close enough to the nails and pins to be drawn to the magnet. She told us Christ was coming again to pick up those people whose sins were forgiven. The pins left on the table were like the people who would be left after Christ's coming because they had not asked God for the forgiveness of their sin. They would go to hell. Christ would take his own to heaven.

This illustration scared me, not for myself, but for those who would be left behind. I suggested to the teacher that the solution to the problem was very simple. We would ask God to forgive them. I was disappointed when she said it didn't work that way. Each person was responsible to ask God for themselves.

The theme song we sang every day was:
"My Jesus I love Thee. I know Thou art mine.
For Thee all the follies of sin I resign."

The words were engraved upon my memory.

It was at the end of this Bible School that I was given a toothbrush instead of a frivolous toy.

In September of that same year we moved from Rush Lake to Winnipegosis, Manitoba. Here we would find a thriving young church involving about forty families. We welcomed the opportunity to drink deeply from this spiritual oasis. If our parents had not modeled and taught us as they did, would we have been as eager to drink from the fountain of life? Our parents, too, survived the drought and drank the living waters.

Our Klassen family at Rush Lake just before moving to Manitoba in 1937.
Back row: Lena, Annie, George, Nettie, Henry, front: Tina, Dad, Mother and Justine

DEPRESSION'S FINAL BLOW

In the spring of 1937 Mother planted her garden on the eastern slope of the hill southwest of our house, just as she had done for seven years. For seven years we had lived in Saskatchewan's dust bowl. Dad worked the fields and seeded the grain as he had done every year since 1930, after buying the land in 1929. Perhaps this year we would have rain. Each year the dry west winds blew the dust from one farm to another. Dad continued to haul water.

The water level at the Belter's well, two miles away, had dropped and Mr. Belter told Dad he could no longer haul water from his well. The Hammetts lived further away and so did the Rhodes, but Dad was permitted to get water from their wells, as well as from the creek five miles west of our place. With a horse drawn wagon, this was time consuming.

The landscape remained dry and bare. In summer the Russian thistles grew and matured in these desert-like conditions. When the wind blew, the fully grown and dried stems broke above the arid soil to roll across the brown fields. One thistle raced after the other to reach its destination first. Blowing dust and thistles heaped up high at the barb wire fences, changing the landscape.

One summer day Mother saw a dark cloud above the western horizon. The increasing wind blew it high into the sky above us. The wind blew across our yard and into our faces. It blew through our hair. Mother called us to help her gather the clucks and their new chicks, and to take them to shelter. Before they were safe the threatening cloud released a few big drops of water. The drops splattered in the dust and the cloud was gone. Hope dissipated just as the few drops of water evaporated. The despair written on Mother's face showed in the set of her muscles and the wrinkles of her skin. Her eyelids drooped. "Dear God, why couldn't it have been a drenching rain?" Our lives depended on it. She and the older children continued to dip water from our dug-out with buckets to pour into a wooden barrel to water vegetables.

In these drought conditions, grasshoppers reigned without opposition. They jumped and danced before us when we walked across the dry ground. We were accustomed to grasshoppers because they came every year. But in 1937 we were not prepared for what followed them.

Like an army, a plague of worms crept across the dry prairie. They were tiny, inch long, green army worms. They invaded the garden, the yard and the fields. They crawled up the wall of the house. We didn't want them to drop on us when we passed through the door when we opened it, so we shook the door before we walked through. Balls of worms were found in water troughs and individual worms sat on vegetables while they fed on them. Lena counted twenty-two worms on a single green bean. They ate even the young green Russian thistle before it matured. Could the plagues of Egypt have been any worse?

Of that desperate time of drought, Annie says,

> We tried to make hay from the Russian thistles. The cows had terrible diarrhea, so you dared not walk too close behind the cows.

Henry is more graphic.

> The cows ate the Russian thistles because of the shortage of grass. The young thistle might even have been nourishing. However, it was not safe to be too close to the rear of the cows if they had eaten thistles. No Ex-lax or castor oil could have worked better. It was like a two inch water pistol, fully loaded. Cousin George Unger was at our place and came with me to get the cows. I was walking too close to old Bessie and she let go. I was marked from waist down, plus one boot was full of the gooey stuff. Poor George almost burst laughing.

When it became obvious that Dad would not harvest grain in 1937, he tried to salvage the tender green thistle for animal fodder for the winter. Again Henry writes,

Cutting the thistle for feed was terrible. To stack them they had to be dry to prevent spoilage. Dry thistles pack very loosely and are VERY prickly. While Dad was pitching the stuff onto the hayrack, I had to trample it down. The process was repeated when we pitched the thistles from the rack onto the stack. To prevent the prickles from dropping into our boots, Dad wrapped old jute bags, torn into strips, around my legs and over the top of my boots. I don't remember whether he also had some covering his boots while unloading. He too, had to stand on the load to get it off while I trampled the stack.

The thistle stacks Dad and Henry piled in the yard were black. The army worms had infested, and contaminated the thistles before Dad cut them. A news release reached us in which the government warned farmers about feeding the worm-infested thistles to the livestock. They were poisonous. So Dad had no fodder for the winter. How would the livestock survive the long cold season?

When all hope of harvesting a crop was gone, the Canadian government offered free railroad passage to any farmer wishing to move out of the dust bowl. Mother and Dad accepted the offer and made plans to leave.

In 1937 Dad was fifty-two and Mother was forty-nine. Six of the children were home most of the time. Our family had lived in this new country for twelve years. We owned the livestock and the farm implements. The years in Saskatchewan had been bitter and poor. We had harvested rocks, thistles, dust, grasshoppers and army worms. Dad had stooped to ask the government to feed his family. Canada had a good government but the land and the drought caused more than a financial depression. It had caused a psychological depression as well. The army worms dealt the final blow. We had to leave. We had been defeated. But in our hearts we carried hope. Farming could get only better.

PART II

MANITOBA TO BRITISH
COLUMBIA
1937-1948

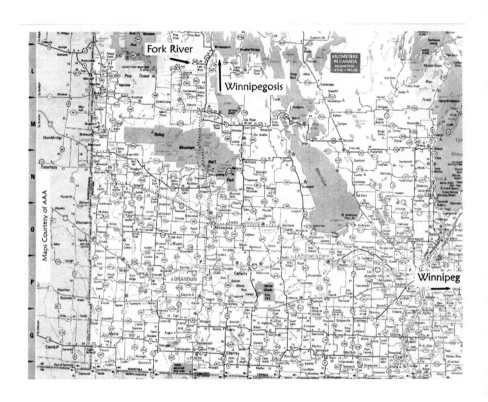

Manitoba

A New Beginning

The drought, the grasshoppers and the army worms had forced our parents into making a decision about their future. But without the Canadian government's offer to ship them out of the area, such resolve would have been in vain. Without money and without transportation they would not have been able to leave. Without knowing where they would live or what farm they would work, they decided to move to Winnipegosis, Manitoba, 360 miles northeast of Rush Lake, Sask.

Mother's second youngest sister, Margaret (Unger) Warkentin, and her husband John (Vahng) lived near Winnipegosis. Our parents never moved any place unless they had at least one sibling in that location. The drought of Saskatchewan had not extended to this pioneering area. Uncle Vahng was optimistic about farming here even though the recent immigrants were still poor.

By early September plans to move were complete. While we waited for September the eighth, our moving day, Justine and I attended the Rush Lake School for four days. In the meantime, Dad and Henry took care of the livestock, implements and our pitiful household furnishings.

Henry writes,

> We hauled our stuff to Main Centre, Saskatchewan, about fifteen to twenty miles from home, I think. We had to load it on to the Canadian National Railway because Winnipegosis was also on the Canadian National line. The cattle were driven to Main Centre and all was loaded onto one box car; all household things, machinery, four horses and, I think, six cows.

Dad and I stayed in the box car for the next three days until we got to Winnipegosis on Thursday, September 9, 1937. Since we were told that only one man could stay with the car, I had to go into hiding whenever the train stopped.

Our route took us from Main Centre to Moose Jaw, then to Saskatoon, north to Warman, then to Dauphin and to Winnipegosis.

George, twenty-two, came home with his pickup truck to take Mother and his five sisters away from the old house. The trunk-like baskets, woven by Grandpa Unger in Russia, were filled with the few clothes we had. We had a few dishes and some bedding. The top two inches of the baskets were reserved for our paper-doll houses. Our sisters carefully placed them on top to prevent crushing. I wasn't sure I wanted to play with paper dolls any more. My early childhood and childish innocence were left behind. I would be ten in November.

Annie, Lena, Justine and I climbed into the pickup bed and sat with the packed boxes and baskets. Mother and Nettie rode in the cab with George. George started the engine. We left the gray house, barn and granary behind. Two black stacks of mown thistles were left behind like two black tombstones to witness the end of farming in the dust bowl.

We drove the half mile to the Trans Canada Highway, turned right and went east to Regina, Saskatchewan's capital, about 130 miles from home. We stopped at Mother's aunt, Gretchimum, and Mother's cousin, Mary Klassen's place. George had made his home with them. Gretchimum was Grandpa Unger's half sister, Margaret (Andres) Klassen. We saw her lift her eyelids with her fingers when she wanted to see us. Her mother, our great grandmother, Maria (Neudorf) Unger Andres, had done the same, years before we were born.

Gretchimum or Mary gave us more used dolls but they did not have hair or eyes that closed. I wasn't sure I wanted to play with dolls any more either.

The next morning we were on the road again. We continued driving east and north leaving behind our beloved cousin and playmate, Mary Harms. Near the Saskatchewan/Manitoba border we came to Fort Qu'Appelle, a small town. Through the town ran a ravine that looked lush and green with trees. Never had we seen such scenic beauty in the dust bowl.

We left the scorched brown hills of Saskatchewan and admired the flat black earth of Manitoba. Clusters of trees dotted the level plains. We came to Dauphin and turned north to go the last thirty-five miles to the Warkentins' yard. Dad and Henry, with the box car full of our possessions, had arrived earlier the same day.

Uncle Vahng greeted us and invited us to come into the living room to meet Aunt Margaret. She lay in bed. Our family surrounded her bed. Accidentally I jarred the bed. She winced with pain. I felt a sense of grief around the bed. She had been in bed for the past year, since giving birth to twin girls. Agnes died but Lorena lived.

Aunt Margaret's body became infected after delivery. That infection spread throughout her body. Uncle Vahng took care of her, slipping his hands under her body to turn and reposition her. He said it felt as though there were liquid between her skin and her muscles. Sulfa and penicillin had not yet been invented.

Lorena had lived with the Peters, a church family, for the first year of her life. The day we arrived at Warkentins she was at home. Eighteen year old Elsie was the cook and housekeeper for her father, two brothers and three sisters. The family had decided that Lorena should live with her biological family after her first year. To make the transition easier for the baby, eleven year old Annie Peters came with Lorena to the Warkentins. Henry took note of this cute little girl with blond braids.

For obvious reasons our family could not stay at the Warkentins, so Uncle Vahng made arrangements with Annie Peters' parents. When the Peters had moved away from their log and mud homestead the buildings were vacant. We could occupy the house and barns without payment.

Before we left the Warkentins' house, our parents had made several major decisions about our family's life.

1. Nettie, aged twenty, would stay at the Warkentins to help Elsie. Lena writes of the arrangement, "The government had a program whereby the farmer was paid half of her salary and Nettie was awarded the other half of the payment."

2. Our livestock would eat Warkentin's hay. I think this had something to do with Nettie's work. Dad cut some hay on a meadow between the Peters' place and the Warkentins. The hay was probably of a poor quality to begin with but to mow hay in swamp fields in September guaranteed an even poorer quality of hay.

3. Lena would drop out of school because no high school was located within walking distance of the Peters' place. Winnipegosis was six miles away and Fork River was further. In this cold and snowy place there were no school buses. Our parents had no money to pay for a correspondence course. Henry, Justine and I would go to the Nordheim school, 3½ miles from the Peters' place, instead of going to Bicton Heath, 2½ miles from our new home. We would learn to read and write German at Nordheim. But at what price!

4. We would drive a horse and buggy or sleigh across unmarked fields to shelter our horse in Warkentin's barn. The school had no barn. We would walk the last mile.

5. One-year old Lorena Warkentin would live with us the first winter because Mother wanted to take care of her. This was natural since we were relatives.

Uncle Vahng recommended Nordheim School because the teacher was a German Mennonite from Russia like we were. His strength lay in the half hour of German he taught after school. This meant we could not leave school until 4:30 P.M. After that we walked to the Warkentins where Henry hitched the horse back to the sleigh. We rode home the rest of the way.

During the time we had spent with Annie Peters at the Warkentins, we children learned from her that she enjoyed going to Bicton Heath where Mr. Turner taught. We wanted to go to Bicton Heath, but our parents wouldn't listen.

The Peters' house surprised us. First, it had a built-in-brick oven that heated the whole house and at the same time Mother could bake bread in another compartment of the stove. The fuel compartment closed with a metal door. It warmed us when we stood in front of the stove. The brick was homemade. For the first time we had adequate fuel since Manitoba grew trees. Poplars were abundant. We were done with using manure chips to cook and heat the house. Warkentins allowed Dad to cut wood in their "bush" (woods in USA). The animals were less fortunate. Their barns were freezing cold.

Secondly, the house had no floors except the earth. This is the house that our daughter Pat saw in May of 1995 when Henry took us there and she stepped through the wooden floor. The house had been moved to another location and someone had put in a wooden floor.

The consequences of those early decisions unfolded the first year.

1. Nettie would never live at home again. John Redekop was a regular visitor at the Warkentin home while she worked there. Less than a year later they married.

2. Our animals almost starved on the poor quality of hay. Peggy, our horse, was ill with sleeping sickness and almost died. She was never the same after recovery.

3. Lena, age, fifteen, spent her days at home rather than in school. She became part of the youth and young adult group prematurely. She married at nineteen.

4. Henry, Justine and I went to a school we loathed. It destroyed Henry's and my love of learning. We attended only three days a week because the horses were too weak to take us every day. Justine was in second grade and too small to walk 3½ miles in Manitoba's

weather. Henry dropped out of school before he finished seventh grade.

5.   We had a baby in our home.

Annie was at home like she might have been if we had stayed in Saskatchewan. George's life remained unchanged. He had left home long ago. He lived in Regina with relatives.

Nordheim

"Nordheim"—the German word for "northern home" suggests a place that is friendly, comfortable and safe in Manitoba's cold north land. The Nordheim School stood alone in a grove of poplars far from town. The one room school house had no basement and no second level. Two out-houses stood in the yard. There was no barn for horses. The school did not look like the Rush Lake School in any way. It had a wooden frame and only one classroom.

Nordheim had been built just east of the gravel highway that connected Winnipegosis to the north and Fork River to the south. The railroad took the same route. Mossy River flowed to the east of the school to empty into the big Winnipegosis Lake.

In 1937 every child in attendance at this school was either born in Russia or was born in Canada to Russian born parents who had arrived in Canada after World War I. Henry was born in Russia. The Ukrainian speaking children in school attended either the Russian Orthodox Church or the Roman Catholic Church if they attended at all. The German speaking children were Mennonites with names like Dyck, Martens, Buller and Wiebe. We had left the world of Smiths, Hammetts, Georges and Belters in Rush Lake. Worst of all, we had left the Harms. In Rush Lake we had never thought of ourselves as ethnic, or different from the other children who may have had English speaking parents. We were simply Canadians. At Nordheim we stepped back from the broader Canadian culture. The melting pot had not yet done its work at Nordheim. Here they were either German or Ukrainian. I felt we three did not fit at all. We certainly could not identify with this teacher, Mr. Dyck.

People at Winnipegosis had an accent. Their vocabularies were limited. They used German and English in the same sentence. Grammar was sometimes incorrect. There were no eighth graders. And Henry was the only seventh grader. Why? The desks at Nordheim were double desks instead of single like we were used to. And the top of the desk had no hinges for us to open the desk. The front of the desk was open instead, and we had to bend over to look into the desk. Furthermore, things could easily fall out. Fortunately, my cousin Lena Warkentin was my desk mate. She was ten.

Mr. Dyck told Lena to draw a pig. She hesitated. I sensed that she did not know how to draw a pig. I didn't know how to either. If she tried, would it be acceptable to this hard-to-please teacher? If it weren't, what would happen? I knew how to draw a rabbit. Miss Erskine had taught us to draw a circle for his head and an oblong for his body. All we needed was a round tail and two ears. But Mr. Dyck stood over her waiting and I dared not help her out. The tension grew and stifled any creative thought she might have come up with by herself. Defeated, Lena said, "I can't." "You can't!" Mr. Dyck shouted angrily. I do not recall the outcome. But Lena told me she thought that she and I were some of Mr. Dyck's favorite pupils. We were? I had not noticed.

Another day Lena's stomach growled. We looked at each other and smiled. "To the front of the class!" Mr. Dyck commanded. We had seen others sent to the front of the class before. I knew we would have to turn around to face the class at the end of the period to tell our peers why we were being punished. I tried to think of what I could say. Surely he couldn't punish us for smiling. So just before recess he asked us to face the class and tell them. I stood nearest his desk so he called on me first. I said, "I don't know." "You don't know!" he bellowed. He asked Lena and she said, "We laughed." That was the answer he wanted to hear. He asked me again and I echoed her words. I knew we had not laughed but it was the only way we would be free to play outside and to get out of the classroom and away from him.

We were afraid of Mr. Dyck. He was an Old Country teacher with an accent. He used Old Country discipline. We learned to know what that was. In his school we did not know at first what behavior was acceptable. There was insecurity in not knowing. We were not naughty children. The classroom climate felt cold and somber.

Mr. Dyck boasted that when he was a child in school he had been able to draw a straight line with a free hand without a ruler. His teacher had suspected him of using a ruler. Now Mr. Dyck was as unbending as a ruler.

It did not take us many days to learn that the slang we used freely in Rush Lake was considered wicked in Nordheim. Our classmates informed us quickly that the golly, gosh, gee and darn would not be tolerated. It was better for them to correct us than that the teacher hear us.

Lena Warkentin did not play with dolls any more. And although she was only ten, she had a lively interest in boys. We became good friends when we shared that interest.

One fall or winter evening Mother read aloud a letter Aunt Justine had sent from Rush Lake. She reported, "Mary says that when she looks at Justine's and Tina's empty seats she feels like crying." Mother glanced at me, knowing what I was feeling. I was on the verge of crying.

I had a hard time learning anything in a tense atmosphere. I cared nothing about grades. Just to survive every day was enough. We dreaded every school day. At home I begged to stay home.

We were often late for school and didn't care. Before we were allowed to sit down we had to wait at the door at the back of the room until Mr. Dyck asked us why we were late. We used excuses like, "The clock was slow." or "We woke up late." The reasons we gave may have been true but we certainly never hurried to school. A valid reason would have included "The horse is too weak to make it trot." I told myself I liked to stand at the door because the wood heater was nearby.

From Henry: *Tina, Justine and I went to Nordheim School that first winter. We drove to the Warkentins, left our horse in their barn and then walked the last mile. We went to Nordheim and not to Bicton Heath, which was closer, because Nordheim had a German teacher, and we were to learn all the German we could.*

Mr. Dyck, the teacher, and I didn't get along very well. I was the only student in grade seven which was terrible for me and an extra grade for the teacher. Because of the skinny horses, distance and bad road, we went to school only Monday, Wednesday and Friday. That was exactly three days too many as far as I was concerned.

There was one bright spot in the first few weeks of going to Nordheim. There was a girl only one and a half years younger than myself staying with the Warkentins, and for me it was love at first sight. She says I pulled her hair which was a no-no, so the feeling was not mutual. However, I prevailed and she has been my wife for 39 years. (Written in 1985)

At home I continued to complain about Mr. Dyck. I told Mother all the terrible happenings at school. At Rush Lake she never heard us complain. I argued, "I can read and write, add and subtract. What more do I need?" I wanted to be a fourth-grade drop out. Mother never wavered. We had to go to school.

One day I heard Henry complaining to Mother. I was surprised. He was usually very quiet about his misery at school. I heard Mother respond, "Henry, don't you too, complain. It is hard enough already with Tina complaining." I was surprised again. I did not know I had any impact on her at all. But I was not surprised that we had to keep going to school.

I stood in front of the metal door of the built-in brick oven at home. I was wearing a plaid blue skirt made over from something Tante Tin Unger had given us. I stood too close to the hot door and burned elongated holes in the loosely hanging folds in the back of the skirt. I could not tell anyone. Mother would scold if she knew I had been careless. I was careful never to stand in front of anyone. There was no room for error when we were so poor and could not replace what had been ruined, so I wore the holey skirt to school. One day we practiced singing while standing in rows at the front of the classroom. Because I was so short, many children stood behind me. Then I heard them laugh. I felt humiliated.

When I awoke one morning my skirt was patched. I was overjoyed but could not thank anyone because I did not want to be reminded of my carelessness. No one said a word about the skirt. Maybe Mother was sensitive to my need this time. I wore the patched skirt proudly.

I also remember once standing on the little porch at the entrance to the school. I noted that the children were talking about their favorite foods instead of playing on the teeter totter. I realized how much I missed Rush Lake. At this school, Mr. Dyck called Justine "Justina." I could not tolerate his trying to change my sister's name. I was fully aware that there was a young woman named Justina in church. I knew he was transferring her name to my little sister. So I mustered all the courage I had and walked up to him and said, "My sister's name is Justine and not Justina." I was so afraid of him that my voice quivered and my eyes teared. I could hardly get the words out of my mouth. But Mr. Dyck remembered to call her Justine after that.

During class one day I saw Justine raising her arm and pointing her forefinger to the ceiling. At Rush Lake two fingers meant "May I sharpen my pencil?" And one finger meant, "May I go to the toilet?" I suspected the rules in this school were not the same, but I had no way of telling Justine who was not sitting close to me. Miss Erskine would simply nod her approval. Mr. Dyck saw her arm but paid no attention to the single finger. But aloud he said, "What do you want?" She verbalized her need to use the toilet. How embarrassing.

Justine and I wore long johns under our home knit woolen stockings, thanks to the relief check. Mother skimped on yarn by not making them long enough to stay in place above the knees with a circular elastic garter. In addition, the underwear tended to sag like they were coming down. Again and again I pulled them up only to let them slide down again. Mr. Dyck noticed this action and embarrassed me when he imitated me and said, "How would it look if I kept pulling up my stockings like that?" The man was totally insensitive. I had not noticed that the other girls did not pull up their stockings like I did. They had no sagging long underwear to keep them warm because their parents had not applied for relief.

I remember a classmate, Jacob Martens, who had no shoes. He wore low slung rubbers that were meant to fit over shoes to keep mud and water out. They were not lined with fleece like our overshoes were. The rubbers were several sizes too big for him so he used rubber jar rings to keep them on his feet. Fortunately the Martens lived near the school and he was not exposed to the cold for very long en route to the school.

On one occasion Mr. Dyck used a dry willow branch to hit a child's bare hand. This seemed cruel. A four inch piece snapped off the far end on impact and landed on the nose of another child. This caused some of the children to laugh. I was appalled.

Henry adds his memories. *Rush Lake School had no boundaries. In spring if there was water in the low areas, we boys emptied our lunch pails (five pound Roger's Golden Syrup pails) at noon, and then used the pails to carry water to drown gophers in their holes. We could go as far as we wanted, provided we were within the school bell's hearing.*

Nordheim was different. They had a barb wire fence on all four sides. There were strict orders to stay within those fences. However, God had created a little creek just outside the school yard. It was dry most of the year, but in spring the winter snows melted and ran into the creek. Also after a heavy rain the water flowed in the creek.

It was spring time in 1938. The creek was running. We could hear the running stream. The boys said there were fish, live fish, in the creek. They came upstream every spring to spawn. I had never seen a live fish before.

One lunch hour when Mr. Dyck was in his home at Penners having his noon meal, some of us boys went fishing—through the barb wire fence and into the creek. Someone had brought thin flexible wire that made good snares. These were fastened to long poles, and then by sliding the snare over the fish and giving a sudden jerk, we had our fish. What fun! Plus, it was food for supper. But it wasn't to be. Mr. Dyck came and took our fish for his own supper. We were severely lectured and went home empty handed.

Every day Mr. Dyck appointed one child to take responsibility for the behavior of all the pupils during lunch hour while he left the school to eat lunch at his boarding place. My turn came. I wanted everyone to behave so well that I would not have anything to report to this man when he came back. All the children ate their lunches in the classroom. The boys sat in a row next to the wall. When they finished eating they all jumped up at the same time and stampeded out to play. Was that behavior acceptable to Mr. Dyck, or not? I thought the boys were okay but would he think so? If I did not report this to him and he heard about it from someone else, would I be in trouble? I decided to be safe and to tell him. He took no action and I was relieved. But I felt like a fool to even question the boys' behavior.

Mr. Dyck was not only our teacher; he came to church and to our house. Uncle Vahng had told us from the outset about the shortage of girls in this Mennonite community. Young men were plentiful. Although Mr. Dyck was older than my sisters, they belonged to the same social crowd.

The Manitoba winter produced a lot of snow. In fact, after one storm the snow drifts reached the low eaves of one of the barns. We took the sled up to the peak of the roof and slid to the frozen ground below in one swoop. When the wind blew while it snowed, the drifts grew high in some areas while others were swept clean of snow.

Lake Winnipegosis froze over with a heavy layer of ice. Local Icelandic people fished through holes in the ice. Fish was relatively inexpensive but the heads were waste. Dad got them free or for half a cent per pound. He brought them home for Mother to cook on the kitchen stove. The stench was terrible. The heads became food for the chickens. We wondered if the eggs would taste like fish if the hens had been laying eggs. They couldn't lay eggs until the weather turned warm in spring and they could graze outside. In the meantime Mother said, "The chickens are carrying death piggyback."

About the spring of 1938 Henry writes,

> *With my hating school, maybe more so than the teacher, and with so much work to be done at home, I was able to quit school at Easter, age 13½, not completing grade seven. It was compulsory to go until age fourteen. I think Mr. Dyck approved of my quitting school and all was fine.*

That left Justine and me to finish the school year. I do not remember how we got to school after Henry was no longer available to take care of a horse at Warkentin's place. I assume we walked the 3½ miles when the weather was warmer. Before the school year was over on June 30, our family moved to the new log and mud house the family built on the quarter section of land Dad bought.

One of the last memories of Nordheim happened in early June. Justine and I now walked from Nordheim to our new farm a little more than three miles southwest of the school. We left school at 4:30 P.M. and walked past Martens' place. On the western horizon we saw a threatening black cloud gathering and mounting in the sky. We knew a rainstorm could reach us before we were home.

We heard the sound of running feet behind us. Katie Martens had caught up with us to tell us to turn around to wait out the storm at their place. Her mother had sent her to tell us. But we knew Justina Goossen was to get married in church within a day or two and we did not want to miss that wedding while we waited for the storm to pass. It would be our first wedding to attend at Winnipegosis. So we said 'no' to Katie. She turned around and went home to safety without us.

In a few minutes the dark sky flashed with lightning. The sound of thunder rolled across the sky again and again. The rain pelted against our late spring dresses until we were wet. We kept walking. We reached the two mile distance corner away from school. We still had one and a quarter miles to go. We turned left at the corner of section 25 and saw Jackie Hayward's farm ahead. We decided to ask the bachelor for shelter. We had never met Jackie but we knew of him. He lived only a mile from our place and we would not miss the wedding. Timidly we knocked on his door. We were surprised to see an old woman sitting by the wood heater, but we felt safe. She was Jackie's former sweetheart's mother. We joined her at the heater and stood there until the storm passed. Then we walked home.

We were able to attend the wedding. Now there was less than a month left in the school year at Nordheim.

Nordheim School in 1969

A post script to Nordheim:

In 1995 I wrote to my siblings to ask about rumors of Mr. Dyck going to a concentration camp. Annie writes that she had heard the following:

> *He was sent to a concentration camp in Ontario after he was married and had a couple of children. His teacher's certificate was taken away because of his Nazism. When he came home from the concentration camp they had more children, seven in all. Some live here in Vancouver but they won't give him their address because they want nothing to do with him. He was separated from his wife and they lived off welfare. He is 84. His wife passed away and he is living common-law.*

Annie didn't think Mr. Dyck ever got married again.

Annie also recalled that one time "One of his pupils was late for school and that he hadn't let the boy come in, and he froze his feet a little."

OASIS

On September 12, 1937, we saw the log and mud Mennonite church building for the first time. It was a country church. Just like the Peters' homestead, the logs were plastered with mud/clay. Dad stopped at the church door to let Mother and the family step down from the democrat, for that is what a two seated buggy was called. Dad went a little further to leave the horses at the barn. Two outhouses stood on the yard.

Mothers and fathers greeted each other in Low German when they met at the simple entrance of the church. Children and adults chattered in either Low German or English. After a full week's isolation on the farms, everyone was glad to see each other.

Women and girls removed their wraps in the combination cloakroom and nursery before entering the worship area. To use the words "sanctuary" or "auditorium" would be an overstatement. They seated themselves on the left side of the center aisle, women in the back rows, and girls in the front. Men sat on the right side of the aisle, but the young men seated themselves behind the girls. They shared a Sunday School class. The young children sat in the first rows on the right, while adolescents walked up a couple of steps to sit on the platform, facing the congregation. As you can imagine, behavior problems were nonexistent.

We younger children had never been part of a church before. We saw so many people who were all immigrants from Russia, just like us. Most of the families had children our ages. Many of the parents were the same age as our parents. A few elderly Grandmas and Grandpas lived with their middle-aged children and grandchildren. Did this congregation of poor people compare with the village church our parents had known in Russia?

Our parents recognized the three Buhler brothers and their spouses. They had all come from Grigorjewka. We children knew the Warkentins and Annie Peters.

The plastered walls inside the church were whitewashed. A metal barrel converted into a heater in the center aisle waited to be fired when the weather turned cold.

The Sunday School hour started with songs from the Evangeliumsbuch (Gospel Song Book). The congregation sang in four part harmony accompanied by the piano—if there was someone who played. The church had a young pianist who played sometimes. Above the joyful songs of this congregation we heard Mr. Ben Buhler's voice. He always sang louder than anyone else. He yelled at his horses louder than anyone else too. We would become his closest neighbors within a year.

After the songs, prayer and introductory remarks, the five Sunday School teachers took their places in front of their classes. Petite Mary Peters taught the youngest children, including Justine and me. Henry's adolescent class was taught by Uncle Vahng. Gertrude Bergen sometimes taught the women. The men's and the young people's classes had male teachers. All classes were taught in German. Young couples with children often spoke High German to their children so they would understand High German when they came to church. Learning a scripture verse at home in preparation for Sunday was a new experience for us.

We remained in our seats for the worship service. Mr. Cornelius Janzen and Abram Bergen had been elected as ministers of the congregation before our arrival in Winnipegosis. They were not chosen by lot. Both men were fathers of young children, and both were farmers. Neither received remuneration for their weekly services. The two men took turns preaching the short introductory sermon. The alternate speaker delivered the main, longer sermon. Neither man had much formal education, but Mr. Janzen studied well for he always delivered a thought-through sermon, well suited to his audience. When Aunt Margaret was well and came to church again, she remarked about his frequent preaching about the love of God. I had not noticed. Mr. Bergen's sermons were often mere stories about "the Old Homeland."

During the worship service we sang songs out of the "Gesangbuch mit Noten." (Hymnal with notes.) I did not like this song book because so many of the chorals and hymns had slow and labored tunes. There were exceptions such as "Now Thank We All Our God" and "The Lord is King." They had upbeat tunes and I understood what the words meant.

This was a grateful congregation. They had not forgotten their deliverance from their Russian hardships, nor had they forgotten their family members still living there. This group of about forty families had all emigrated from Russia from 1923 to 1930. Mr. Dyck may have been the only person in the congregation to have finished high school. Survival had been their priority.

The church was isolated from other Mennonite congregations by miles and modes of transportation. The nearest Mennonite church was at McCreary, ninety miles south. A few people had cars but the majority used horses. Southern Manitoba had large Mennonite groups who had arrived in Canada in both the late nineteenth century and in the 1920's. In southern Manitoba were seventeen different kinds of Mennonites. There were General Conference like us, Mennonite Brethren like our K. Friesen cousins, Kleinegemeinde like Aunt Tina Koop, Bergthaler, Old Colony, and more. The latter were the most conservative in dress and in cultural adaptation.

Our church was located approximately ten miles southwest of Winnipegosis on the corner of a farmer's grain field, and across the road from the Bicton Heath School. Fork River was about seven miles southeast of the church. However, the church was not centrally located in the Mennonite community. If lines were drawn between the two towns and the church to make a triangle, the triangle would have encompassed most of the Mennonite farms, but some were located outside of that triangle. Those living farthest away on South Bay did not attend church regularly. Later, when more people had cars, distance was not a problem. And still later, after we left the area, a new church was built in Winnipegosis. The old church was razed.

As in Russia, young people prepared for baptism every winter and spring. The process included learning the answers to questions in the catechism and listening to the minister preach on the catechism's teachings based on Scripture. Many had experienced the new birth long before they were baptized. We had no tent revival meetings. Rather, the local ministers presented the gospel without flamboyance. Visiting ministers came occasionally for a series of meetings and preached repentance and forgiveness. They also preached about Christian growth and depth. When I was a teenager many of us accepted Christ when our friends told us about their own new birth. We were baptized by the "Aeltester" who came from southern Manitoba to baptize and to serve communion. Our own ministers did not serve in these capacities. The Aeltester was often the leader of a group of churches rather than the pastor of just one church.

Prior to baptism each candidate met with the ministers and the Aeltester. They wanted to hear our personal testimonies. If the candidate had not experienced the new birth, there was opportunity to do so now. Every young woman wore a black dress for this occasion, emphasizing the seriousness of this solemn commitment. Baptism was done by pouring water on the kneeling youth's bowed head. Communion followed.

We had evening meetings only rarely. Sometimes a missionary or a minister from another area presented a report about their work or they provided spiritual growth meetings. The Christmas Eve program and the New Year's Eve service were annual events.

On the first Sunday of every month we stayed after church to eat a packed lunch and to participate in a "Jugendverein." The word literally means "Youth organization" or "Youth Union." We used the word in a broader sense and included everyone in church. An adult program committee assigned poems and songs to individuals. Our family was not known for its singing ability so we mastered the art of reciting poems by memory. A poem that Annie memorized and recited was "The Master Comes." The woman in the poem is aware of the rumor of Jesus' imminent arrival in their town. She cooks and cleans until all is ready for this special guest. Three different times during her preparation she is interrupted by needy people—a child, a man, and a woman. She is too busy to help them while she prepares for the honored guest. At last she is ready but no one comes. She had not recognized Him in the faces of the needy people who had come for help.

Other special calendar events were Epiphany on the 6th of January, Good Friday, Easter Sunday and Monday, Ascension Day, Pentecost—forty days after Easter, Thanksgiving Day the second Monday of October, and two to three days of Christmas. The third Christmas Day was not held in church. It was a day to visit and to eat Christmas goodies.

National holidays overlapped with some of the church holidays, such as Christmas, Boxing Day, New Year's Eve, Good Friday, Easter Sunday and Monday. We celebrated a holiday in May, which later became the Queen's birthday celebration. We also had Dominion Day on July 1, Labor Day, and Armistice Day on November 11. At school we observed this day with a minute of silence, standing beside our desk with our heads bowed to remember peace.

Children's day was neither a church nor national holiday, but the church provided a time for children to present the adults with a program outdoors close to the Mossy River. It was a day of fellowship and fun. In late spring or early summer, we packed lunches and set out to worship together outdoors in a grove of trees near Nordheim School. The children recited and sang. But the best part of the day was eating homemade ice cream. The adults served the ice cream in bowls. We went for refills of this smooth, cold and rich creamy delicacy until we were satisfied. Nowhere has ice cream tasted so good again. All of our families had bountiful fresh cream from our cows.

The poplars shaded us on this warm sunny day by the river. The church, the people of God, provided an oasis in the sea of life. It was a spiritual center, the social center and the hub of our lives. Our parents had not forgotten the church, their oasis, during the many lean and dry years in Saskatchewan. They had prepared us to recognize the oasis when we came to it. We drank deeply from its free-flowing waters.

PICKLES, PRIPS AND PIETY

WOULD YOU LIKE a bedtime snack? Yes? How about a dill pickle? Cucumbers must have been abundant in 1937. Someone gave Mother cucumbers. Gratefully she packed them in crocks and poured brine over them. We were thankful for any food that first winter in Manitoba. No doubt the cucumbers came from someone in the church family.

One Sunday afternoon we visited the Peters' home. Annie and Erna became our friends as soon as we moved to Manitoba. When Faspa was served at about 4:00 I was directed to sit on the bench behind the table. That should have been simple enough but Justine and I had a problem. Our buttocks were covered with either big pimples or small boils. To prevent the pain I sat on a mere edge of the bench. Sitting squarely on the buttocks in an unmolded seat was too painful.

The Peters served Prips instead of weak coffee like we had at home. Prips is brewed from roasted and ground wheat. It may have looked like coffee but it did not taste like coffee. It was hard to drink my cupful. When at last we were excused, I left the table and walked past John Peters, who gave me a playful swat on my seat with a pair of gloves he held in his hands. "Ouch!" I wanted to scream but I couldn't tell anyone about my sores. Mr. Dyck would not have been forgiven so easily if he had swatted me. John later became my brother-in-law.

In 1937 we had no understanding of a balanced diet. And if we had known, our diet would not have improved because we had few choices. We had no fresh fruit or vegetables. We did not know our lean diet could cause vulnerability to infection.

One winter Sunday afternoon I wanted desperately to go to Hieberts to play with Violet and Victor. They attended the Fork River town school and reminded me of the kind of children we had known at Rush Lake. I begged Mother and Dad. They resisted, then wavered, and gave in. They too, enjoyed Dad's cousin, John Hiebert, and his wife. Two horses were hitched to the sleigh and we set out to go the two or three miles to the Hiebert farm. En route we had to cross the gravel highway. The friction of the metal runners against the gravel was too much for the horses. One of them fell down. All my sympathy went out to the poor, weak horses. It was my fault for begging our parents to go to Hieberts. But when playing with the twins, I forgot the burden of guilt.

Mennonites without telephones could not invite each other to visit as they might have wished. Sometimes would-be-guests invited themselves to someone's home for Sunday dinner. The host family was honored by having guests. When possible, housewives prepared food on Saturday in anticipation of company. Sometimes guests came for dinner and stayed for Faspa, depending on the proximity of the guest and host homes. After Faspa everyone had to go home to feed the livestock and milk the cows. Faspa was a light meal of coffee and rolls or bread. When we became more prosperous the meal became more interesting. But I recall having brown lard on the bread.

The youth in the congregation, including my sisters, often met in homes on Sunday evenings. Some played circle and partner games like our parents had played in Russia. Often the young people sang folk songs to accompany the games. These games were also played in the evenings after weddings.

A conservative element in the church considered these games sinful and therefore did not play. Fortunately, our parents recognized the need for young people to get together to socialize so they could learn to know one another before they started to see one person exclusively. Many chose their life's partner out of this group.

In our community no one divorced.

Smoking in Russia had been an acceptable practice. At the Nordheim church at least two of the young men smoked. Older men like Dad and Mr. Peters smoked but the majority did not. Even before society became aware of the health hazards, smoking was unacceptable to the most pious

Mennonites in the area. It was not called a sin but was frowned upon as sin.

Other unacceptable practices included movies, dancing, make-up, and wearing earrings. Necklaces and rings were acceptable but most people had few such luxuries. We abstained from all of these without feeling deprived. These things were prohibited not only by piety but by the lack of money.

Our family accepted all that was offered us—pickles, prips and piety.

CHRISTMAS EVE

EARLY ON SATURDAY morning the children of the church community came to church from all directions. With each of the four pre-Christmas Saturdays the anticipation mounted.

Two teachers also came these four Saturdays. Mary Peters and Uncle Vahng (and later Pete Peters) were the Sunday School teachers and the program was their responsibility. In preparation for the program, Pete Peters taught us Christmas carols. Finally Christmas Eve arrived. It was the highlight of all celebrations in the church. We knew nothing about Advent, but we knew about preparing for the Christmas program.

Every child of school age had a part to practice. At home we memorized poems and dialogue parts. At church every child recited, acted or sang. We rehearsed the entire program both morning and afternoon. At home the mothers of preschoolers taught their children a few rhyming lines about the birth of Christ since they were too young to come to all day practices. But they would play a part on Christmas Eve.

When at last Christmas Eve arrived, the church families milked the cows and fed their stock early. We ate supper and were off to the church with our sleighs. Even the members from the farthest distances made their appearance on this holy night.

Adults and youth seated themselves on the church benches eager to hear their children perform. Children sat in the front benches facing the platform. Eyes glowed with anticipation. They were not necessarily thinking of gifts this night. They were excited about the parts they would play in the program. Every child was a star. Then the program began.

The joyous news of Christ's birth rang out in children's voices over and over in one poem after another, and in every song and play. A spirit of joy pervaded the atmosphere. This joy sprang, not from the material things to be received or the commercials to which we had no access, but from the news that God came to earth in human form. We never tired of hearing the message. Joy sprang from the deepest inner self like an artesian well that could not be stopped. Once a year the birth of Christ touched the hearts of all people, including the poor.

Above the congregation, the Aladdin lamps hung from nails in the ceiling, beaming their white lights in celebration. A Christmas tree of sorts was decorated with wax candles in little metal holders. Men stood by with candle snuffers on long sticks to put out a candle when it burned too low. This was the only Christmas tree that most of us would see this season. If we had obtained a tree from the wild, we would have had no balls or tinsel with which to decorate it.

After all the children had recited, sung and dialogued, the program chairman asked for volunteer items. Now the tiny preschoolers left their mothers to walk onto the platform to recite their lines. Often we were unable to understand their words but they felt they had been part of the big party.

Two things remained to be done. First those who had been part of a name exchange, gave and received gifts. This occurred after I was part of the youth group. Finally, the goodies were distributed to all the children.

Under a cold clear sky we prodded the horses to take us home in the sleigh. Tomorrow we would gather at church for another celebration of Christ's birth. This time the ministers spoke. We enjoyed the children's voices more. This first Christmas at Winnipegosis, our family was not isolated. We felt we had come home. Until now we children had been unaware of what we had been deprived of for so many years.

The first Christmas morning at Winnipegosis, Justine and I awoke to find a china tea set at our places at the table. The tea set was shown in the Eaton's catalogue. Its price was 98¢. Before Christmas Dad had borrowed the only dollar Justine and I shared. We understood the situation and were very happy with our gift.

The First Year

Dad bought a 160 acre farm of "crown land" from the government for $800. A Ukrainian was renting the land but no one had built on it. Some of the land lay in pasture, some was cultivated and the remainder waited to be broken. A peat moss layer several inches thick covered the pasture and the unbroken land. The animals grazed the pasture. They did not miss the Russian thistles of last year. Their famine was over. Brush on the unbroken land waited to be "scrubbed." This was a term used that meant clearing the land of brush so it could be plowed.

This farm had no well.

The land was located three miles south of Peters' homestead and four and a half miles north of Fork River. It was over three miles southwest of the Nordheim School and two and a half miles southeast of the Bicton Heath School. Winnipegosis, next to the big lake, was now nine miles away. Our nearest neighbors were Ben Buhlers, a quarter mile northwest of us, and across the road.

To buy this farm Dad borrowed money from his sister, Tina, and her husband, Abram Koop, who lived in southern Manitoba. Dad was in debt again but I do not know by how much.

As Henry stated earlier, he dropped out of seventh grade after Easter to help Dad. One of the first priorities was to build a house. The barn, chicken house and granary could wait to be built until after we lived on the property. As soon as the soil was dry enough after the spring thaw the land needed to be worked. Henry reports,

Dad and I got the logs from north of the Nordheim School. We cut the trees down with an axe, loaded about 5-10 on a wagon, and

horses pulled them home. I remember getting stuck and having to unload.

Before putting the logs in place, Dad and Henry dug a shallow cellar, no more than four or five feet deep. They feared ground water if they dug deeper. There was no cement wall or floor in the cellar. It was just a hole in the ground. Neither would the house have a concrete foundation. Henry says flat stones were used. A large stone was placed at each corner and smaller ones between corners. The house would be rectangular, with three bedrooms upstairs and one bedroom, a living room and a kitchen downstairs. Our parents would finally have a bedroom to themselves. And so would Justine and I.

The logs Dad and Henry laid down formed the ends and sides of the house. At the corners they were anchored in place with nails. Logs also formed the walls inside the house. Dad bought no lumber to build the house. Instead he bought an old building in Winnipegosis for $40 and took it apart. The floor of our new house came from the boards of the old building. The ceiling boards also served as the upstairs floor. We could see through the cracks to the ground floor if we put our faces close to the floor boards. The roof rafters were pitched and covered with more boards and tar paper.

The upstairs rooms were built under the eaves with enough room to stand upright. Henry had a room of his own. Annie and Lena shared a room. In the middle, and in between the rooms, was a walk-in closet without a window. The pantry was built directly under the stairway just as it had been in Rush Lake. There would be no bathroom, kitchen cabinets, running water, pump or electricity.

After Dad and Henry put up the log walls they brought clay, or loam, out of the local ditches to the house. Henry says it was hard to find clay without stones in it. Stones could cut the hands that used the clay to plaster the walls. Lena says,

Apparently in most places the soil had enough loam so we could use
it with a lot of horse manure and straw mixed into it. We usually

mixed it in a tub, but I remember once we did an awful lot on
the ground. I sat on a horse without a saddle and went round and
round through the horse manure, clay or loam mixture. I had a
sore bottom for days.

After the mixture was worked up, Annie and Lena scooped it into
buckets and carried it to the wall that needed plastering. The buckets
full of clay were heavy and the plaster was less than gentle to their hands.
Again, Lena says,

Usually three layers were required depending, on how uneven
the logs were; but usually three layers were enough, two of straw,
manure and clay, and then a layer of clay and sand to make it
smooth.

Constructing the outside of the house, the inside, and the walls
separating the rooms of the house kept them very busy. Then at the end
of the day they fetched the cows and milked them. Lena was sixteen and
Annie eighteen.

Lena remembers,

In 1938 when Nettie was at Warkentin's, Annie and I plastered
all the log buildings. Then one day Nettie said to me that Uncle
Vahng's mother, who lived with them, didn't like Nettie but she
liked me so I should go to the Warkentins. So I went and it was
haying time. I helped Warkentins all week—terribly hard work.
When the haying was done, I went home to plaster and Nettie
went back to Warkentins. No plastering was done at home the
week I was gone. I didn't get a penny for it but I didn't expect any,
so I wasn't disappointed. We all knew Nettie did not like to work
outside.

During this time of plastering the house, Justine and I were attending
Nordheim School. Everyday when we came home, we saw progress. When

the first layer of mud was dry, Annie and Lena applied another. After all the walls were smooth and dry, Mother poured cold water on powdered lime in a bucket. The lime boiled and gurgled while she stirred it until it was as smooth as paint. The inside walls were then whitewashed with the lime mixture.

Our log house with unpainted siding in 1947

Justine and I finished going to Nordheim at the end of June. We passed our grades. Of the 200 days required in a school year, we attended 125. We had survived.

Dad and Henry built the barn, chicken house and granary in much the same manner as they built the house. The barn did not have a pitched roof. It was flat. The roof consisted of logs whose ends rested on opposite walls of the barn. They covered them with straw and a layer of sod. It was not a very good roof, for it continued raining in the barn long after the rain outside had stopped. The barn was also very cold in winter.

Dad intended to live in our house the first winter without shingles on the roof. He thought the tar paper over the boards would keep the moisture out. No one expected the upstairs to be warm. Then it rained. Water came through the roof and ran through the cracks of the upstairs floor until it dripped on our parents' bed. They discovered they were assured of a dry bed only if their bed was placed directly under Annie and Lena's bed upstairs. Somehow the roof got shingled before winter set in, although I don't know where the money came from.

During the building process we found wild strawberries in the pasture. They were smaller than Oregon's blackberries, but they were full of flavor and very juicy. We enjoyed them so much that we thought we could sell them and make some money. To fill a quart jar with small mushy strawberries took a long time. Dr. and Mrs. Mead in Winnipegosis were the lucky couple we chose as our customers. I carried the berries confidently to their door and knocked. Mrs. Mead took one look and said, "No, thank you!" I was as crushed as the berries.

In 1938 Dad seeded the cultivated acres with hope. Mother planted her garden. Rain came when it was needed. Both fields and garden prospered under Manitoba's long sunlit summer skies. Our world was green.

Dad and the older siblings scrubbed the brush and stones from land that had been plowed for the first time, as they were able. Henry says it was done by five or ten acres a year. Dad hired Ike Peters, who with a tractor broke the ground. The cost per acre was $4. When we bought the John Deere tractor later, we broke some of the meadow ourselves.

Mosquitoes thrived in the wet peat moss. We called it swamp. The evening air buzzed with gray mosquitoes as they swarmed around us. We could not sit outside to enjoy the warm summer evenings. Although everybody sought shelter in their homes, no one escaped the sting of the mosquitoes. That first summer every bite seemed to fester before it scabbed over. No doubt we scratched them when they itched, which left us with scars. Nutrition was still inadequate for prompt healing. A scratch on my knee while climbing the rough framework of the barn resulted in a scar I can still find today.

Animals were not immune to the mosquitoes either. The little pests were at their worst in the evenings. To provide relief for the animals, we built "smudges." A smudge is a fire in a pot or on the ground built for the purpose of producing as much smoke as possible without flames burning up the fuel. When the cows saw the smoke rising from the smudge, they came running to the smoke for relief. Mosquitoes do not like smoke.

During the summer the cows spent their days grazing on government land whose southwest corner was annexed to the northeast corner of our quarter section of land. Before milking time in the evening, one of us called the dog, whom we called "Pup," to go after the cows. It was a pleasant chore unless mosquitoes swarmed in a gray cloud around our heads. They were worst just before a rain. They liked the government swamp even better than our drier farm land. The peat moss there was thicker than it was on our farm and much wetter. After a good rain, the swamp was so drenched that the cows sank almost to their knees with every step they took in the quagmire. Because we children were lighter, we did not sink very deep.

We found a few wild and crumbly raspberries growing in the swamp, but they were dry and worthless. Along the Mossy River, several miles away, grew chokecherries. Although they have a powerful puckering quality and are not good to eat raw, they made a delicious syrup into which we dipped our bread. Justine makes excellent jelly from these even today. Saskatoons also grew in the area and made good jam. They look like small blueberries. Poplars, birch, spruce and willows also grew in Manitoba.

On July 31, 1938, Nettie and John were married on the ground level floor of the barn loft, built on the bank of the Mossy River, on Seifert's farm, south of Winnipegosis. The Redekops, John's parents, and John farmed the land. The simple wedding was partly funded by the Redekops because our parents had nothing. Justine and John's niece, Tina Epp, were their flower girls. There were no other attendants. The girls wore white with yellow polka dotted dresses, with bows tied at their backs. I was sorry to be too big to be a flower girl but was glad to have a dress just like theirs. Nettie sewed the dresses. I do not know who paid for them.

In the afternoon of July 31, a hailstorm swept through the Redekop farm and flattened the entire crop. They had planned to begin harvesting the following day. The hail was a terrible blow. Most of a farmer's annual income should have come from that crop. Nettie and John began their married life living with John's parents.

We rode home in our buggy that evening wondering what awaited us. Our parents' crop stood as proud and tall as it had that morning, since our farm was not in the path of the hail storm. Dad was able to harvest his first crop on this productive farm. Although he had no well yet, 1938 promised a more prosperous future. Both man and beast had survived the first year in Manitoba, though the animals just barely.

In September Justine and I walked the two and a half miles to Bicton Heath School. We too, looked forward to a happier future, leaving Nordheim School behind.

BICTON HEATH

FIFTY-SIX CHILDREN GATHERED in the one room schoolhouse in September, 1938. Twenty-eight year old Mr. Turner stood before the class. His mustached face smiled. He was not a threat like Mr. Dyck had been. His presence was warm and comfortable. But he may not have been comfortable with the 56 pairs of eyes fixed on him. We did not doubt his ability to teach such a large group of children spread over eight grades. We never thought about the preparation time required each day for so many subjects.

The physical building differed very little from the Nordheim school building. The wood stove heater was in the middle of the room. The bucket of drinking water with a dipper sat on the rear counter. The wash basin rested on the same kind of counter we had at Nordheim. In the opposite corner, in the back, was the library.

Bicton Heath School in 1969

We looked for friends from church. Annie Peters, whom we met at Warkentins was there, as well as her sister Erna. These became our best friends. Our Buhler neighbors and the two other Buhler families' children attended here. They seemed happy and we felt at home.

The children we did not know had names like Lena Drewniak (pronounced Dravnak) and the two Rostatski families. There were two classmates who were fourteen and still in grade three, Chubka and Kornik. A small minority had more common names like Anderson and Little. The student body consisted primarily of Ukrainian and German Mennonite children with parents from Russia. Swedes and English also were represented. It was not overwhelmingly different from Nordheim but the sense of oppression was gone. One boy's name was Million, so we enjoyed saying there were one Million and fifty-five students in our school.

Justine was now in third grade and I was in fifth. There were about six children in grade five. The lower grades were much larger than the upper grades. School attendance was compulsory until age 14 or after the completion of eighth grade. Very few children finished eighth grade. The Rostatski children were notorious for staying in the lower grades all of their years in school. They dropped out finally when they were fourteen. They did not seem to be retarded, so I do not know what their problem was.

As I had done at Nordheim, I shared a desk with a classmate. This time it was with Lena Drewniak. She had failed a grade earlier so she and her brother Dave were both in fifth grade. At Nordheim I had had little fun. But at Bicton Heath I knew I would enjoy myself. It was fun like Rush Lake had been. At recess we swung, teeter-tottered, skipped, played hop scotch, tag and dodge ball. Later Kate Laibel and I played soccer with the boys.

But the interest I had had in learning at Rush Lake was sapped out of my young life at Nordheim. Although I liked Mr. Turner very much, he was unable to spend much time on any subject or with any one class. He assigned work for the upper grades while he taught the lower grades the fundamentals in reading and arithmetic. But I put little effort into my work. The big, flat, gray geography book about Europe seemed boring. Each chapter closed with study questions to which we were to find answers in the dull book. How could I answer the question about "what an advantage" a sea coastal country had if I did not know what "advantage" meant? I asked for little help. When I finished an assignment I closed the book and with it, my mind. The questions about natural resources meant nothing more than the necessity to memorize the list of products that a country produced. Then Mr. Turner shared a bit of wisdom—"Think of the location of the country. What advantage did coastal countries have over land-locked countries? Think of fishing and shipping, for instance." That made sense, but I needed more help in knowing how to study. It was not forthcoming and I didn't care.

History with its explorers was just as boring as geography. Why should I care about these men who died long ago? Cartier, Champlain, and Columbus. Upper Canada and Lower Canada. What did that mean? No one explained. Columbus, at least had a jingle about 1492 and "sailing the ocean blue." I liked the rhyme. But I thought he stepped on Canadian soil instead of on southern shores so far from Canada. And what use was there in memorizing the date of the Magna Charta—and what was it anyway?

Mr. Turner taught us some interesting songs. Of course we sang "God Save The King" and "Oh Canada," but he taught us more:

The Maple Leaf, our emblem dear
"Wolfe the dauntless hero came and planted firm
Brittania's flag on Canada's fair domain.
Here may it wave, our boast, our pride,
And join in love together
The thistle, shamrock, rose entwine
The maple leaf forever."

I had no idea that the thistle, shamrock and rose symbolized Scotland, Ireland and England. Did Mr. Turner not tell us or did I not listen?

He taught us "Clementine" who "drove her ducklings to the water just at nine." We liked singing "Oh Susanna," not knowing where Alabama was located. With equal enthusiasm we sang the "Beer Barrel Polka." This music had rhythm. During World War II he taught us:

"Rule Brittania! Brittania rules the waves.
Britons never will be slaves."

Mr. Turner had nothing but his voice to teach us music, and my music grades were deplorable.

Just before Christmas, Easter and final exams, I crammed. Sometimes Lena Buhler, our neighbor and my classmate, and I met in the poplar grove across the road from our house to study for exams. My grades in geography, history and music remained low but after spelling, writing, literature, art and arithmetic marks were totaled and then divided by the number of subjects I took, I ranked first in class. No one in my grade rated high marks. There was no competition in my class until only three of us were left in seventh grade, Lena, Dave and I. Dave was good in some of the subjects in which I was poor. My rank was lower than his until we had a spelling test. Then I rated high and he low, so I beat him again.

I enjoyed reading and had good grades. Repeatedly I checked out books from our small library. I knew "Elsie Dinsmore's" family well. I felt highly affirmed when checking out a book at Mr. Turner's desk he remarked that children who took books home from the library were good readers. I knew I was one of them. We heard praise so rarely that one sentence lasted a lifetime.

In Bicton Heath I learned grammar. I enjoyed analyzing sentences, finding verbs, nouns, pronouns, adjectives, prepositions, objects and subjects. It was a whole new world of fun with words.

Spelling bees, often done late on Friday afternoons, were like dessert after a meal. I was usually one of the last to remain standing. I loved words, especially English words.

Geography matches were also fun. We were given the name of a geographic place. If the first player chose a name that ended with "e" as in "Rome," the next name had to start with "E," as in England. The next player would then select a place starting with "D." The names went on and on. Eventually we all knew the same names of places, but never learned to find them on a map. Nor did we learn the significance of these names.

Memorization was, in itself, a subject. Usually I found memorization easy, but I wasn't motivated to memorize so I didn't. At exam time Mr. Turner scheduled a memorization test on the same day as a spelling test. I found myself in a dilemma. I decided to play sick to avoid the memorization test. Mother was easy to fool because I was always pale. I was pale on the day I stayed home. What I did not know was that Mr. Turner guessed my reason for staying home. When I came to school the following day, he made me write the memorization test but did not give me an opportunity to write the spelling test. It was the only time I ever played sick.

Shakespeare's "Taming of the Shrew" was introduced to us in the seventh grade. The part that grabbed my interest was the "taming" of Kate, the shrew. How crude to name her "the shrew!" How appalling, I thought, that she became so tame she conceded to her new husband that it was dark in the middle of a sunny day. Kate had been tamed out of personhood, undisciplined though she had been.

During this time Justine was doing very well at school. She had competition in her class and was motivated. Her report cards reflected her accomplishments.

Every spring Mr. Turner inspired us to observe the return of birds from the south. After roll call each morning, he asked for a report on any new birds we had seen. We welcomed robins, blackbirds, swallows, orioles, meadowlarks, killdeer, the ducks, the Canadian geese, crows, and more. We knew barn sparrows, that nested in the straw under the eaves of the barn all winter. Although we heard the whippoorwills, they were rarely seen. Erna Peters had the keenest observation skills when it came to identifying birds.

A School Enterprise

As THE GOPHERS came out of their holes in spring, Mr. Turner announced a new government program that excited us. He challenged us to take crows' eggs from their nests to reduce the crow population. For every egg we took from the nest the government would give us a penny. We must prick both ends of the egg with a needle and blow out the contents before we came to school with our proof of success. For every gopher tail we brought we would be given a nickel. This was a great opportunity to make money! For months the Buhler children and we were very busy climbing trees and drowning gophers.

The Buhlers lived a quarter of a mile closer to the school than we did. Every day Justine and I stopped at their house on the way to school. Cutting across farmers' fields on our way to school was probably a half mile shorter than if we had walked around the fields on the road. We crawled either under, over or between the barb wire fences surrounding those fields. We caught the backs of our coats on the barbs, and I couldn't understand why Mother scolded us for that. The coat was still as warm as before. And what's a tiny tear?

On our way home, the Buhlers and we looked up every tree to find crows' nests. One of us was always eager to climb the tree and to rob the nest. We took every egg home. Sometimes the eggs contained premature crows. Then we made a bigger hole at one end.

In the process of looking for the crows' nests, we found many nests of birds which were not a threat to farmers' crops. We climbed trees to see the eggs and then without touching any of the other eggs in the nest, we took one to add to our growing collection. The oriole's nest hanging from a branch, rather than sitting on the branch was the most intriguing.

I liked their speckled blue eggs the best. Killdeer lay their eggs in nests on the ground, and those eggs were much larger. We enjoyed watching the killdeer trying to lure us away from the nest by pretending to have a broken wing, making killdeer conversation the whole time. Yellow-breasted meadowlarks sang their melodious tunes from fence posts. We watched the Canadian geese fly by in V formation, honking from the air. Gopher tails accumulated less rapidly than the crow's eggs. Every gopher grows only one tail while a crow lays many eggs. And gophers did not lie still waiting for us to pick them up like eggs.

On our way home our Roger's Golden Syrup lunch pails were empty. We used them to dip water from the many ponds and puddles left by the melting snow. Next we found a stick. It took two people to drown a gopher. One poured water down the hole and the other stood by with a stick. Sometimes it took several trips to the pond before the gopher hole flooded, forcing the gopher to evacuate. Once it was flooded the gopher's chances of survival were nil. He poked out his head in search of dry ground. The stick landed on his head and he was ours.

Cutting the tail off was not fun. Who had a knife? And once the knife had cut off a gopher tail, could the knife be used for anything else? After collecting dozens of eggs and cutting off dozens of gopher tails, Mr. Turner announced to us that the government was not paying. What a disappointment! He told us we had done all the farmers a big favor by reducing the populations of predators. Only Mr. Turner could have dealt that blow without losing credibility. For us, this particular school enterprise had been a total loss.

In early spring the ponds that provided water for drowning gophers were often frozen in the morning when we were on our way to school. We slid across them with our boots. Sometimes the ice was thick enough to carry our weight but was not hard enough to keep it from yielding with our weight. It had an elastic quality. What fun it was to walk on ice that dipped in the middle but did not break. Once we stepped off the ice, the resilient ice rose to its original level surface.

Another springtime delight was the yellow lady slippers growing wild in the bushes. One day I determined to thrill my sisters with as many lady slippers as I could find. I picked until I had a big arm full. When my sisters saw the sheer quantity, they complained about not having anywhere to put so many. I could not understand how one could have too much of a good thing.

Mr. Turner left Bicton Heath School early in the war. He joined the military to help win the war and survived.

A post script to Bicton Heath:

In 1991 Justine and I drove to the place where Bicton Heath had once stood. We parked our car on the shoulder of the road, walked through the ditch and read the sign:

"This is the site of the Bicton Heath School"

Green grain, stretching tall, covered the ground where we had swung, skipped and played soccer. No single piece of lumber remained of the school house or the teachers' residence. In 1995 we discovered that it still stands but it has been moved to another location, north and west of the school. It was converted into a house.

We looked across the road to see the site of the Nordheim Church. It too, had returned to a field of grain. But the church is not extinct. Their newer building in Winnipegosis houses the people of God in that community.

Justine and I stopped in Winnipegosis in 1991 to inquire about Mr. Turner. While doing so, Mr. Turner walked into the service station. Although we were pleased to find him, he did not remember us. He was eighty. He acknowledged that he had been overwhelmed with the sheer number of children in one classroom whom he was expected to teach. Mr. Turner died in 1995.

A Manitoba Blizzard

The sharp whistling wind awoke Justine and me as it shrieked with vengeance around the corner of our crude shack. We snuggled deeper under our wool filled comforter when we recognized another howling blizzard. We would not walk to school today.

One hundred and seventy miles north of the North Dakota/Manitoba border the landscape was white with driven snow. We could not see the fertile farmland. Firmly frozen specks of snow flew horizontally from the northwest until the atmosphere looked thick and white with flying snow. Visibility was reduced to near zero. We judged visibility on whether we could see the barn a street width away. Wind velocity was not measured in the 1930s and 1940s; at least not where we lived. The temperature could easily drop to 40 below with raging winds. This was extremely dangerous weather. The cold, the wind and the visibility were hazards we respected.

No radio beamed the news to us either. We felt like we lived on the edge of the civilized world. The Canadian National Railroad Branch Line ended at Winnipegosis, about nine miles from our home.

Southeast, and only sixty miles from the North Dakota border, was Winnipeg, Manitoba's only large city. Here people lived a luxurious life unknown to our immigrant family. They had telephones, electricity, running water, cars and snow plows.

Where we lived news came mainly by word of mouth, or by the weekly Free Press the newspaper published in Winnipeg. A few families had battery operated radios. The only power we had was muscle power and the only running water we knew was running to and from the well with buckets of water. And we were more than grateful that we had a well with water. The well driller had found water—good cold water and plenty of it. During a blizzard even the running to and from the well was hazardous. It was easy to lose one's sense of direction during a blizzard. Sometimes persons wandered further away from their destination in their attempt to find it. After a blizzard we frequently heard of someone having frozen to death. It was never anyone we knew.

Watering and feeding the livestock was one of the absolute necessities during the storm. Dad and Henry, a young teenager, were the unfortunates whose job it was to find the barn and to lure the animals away from the warmth of the barn to get a drink of water at the well. Feeding the chickens and pigs in the barns was an easy task compared to taking the horses and cows from the safety of the barnyard. The well with the watering trough was outside of the barnyard on the north side of our large, now dormant, vegetable garden. Part of the trek to the well was within two parallel barb wire fences, but the areas between the barn and the fences, and between the fences and the well, were open spaces where the livestock could get lost. As long as the men could see the barn they were safe.

With the barn doors open and the animals released from their stalls, Dad and Henry tried to herd the animals to the outdoors. The cows walked through the barn doors but as soon as they felt the stinging wind in their faces, they tried to reenter the barn. But the men persisted. They yelled and directed while the dog yelped and nipped at the cows' heels until they were steered northward into the fenced-in corridor. They bucked the biting northwest wind, while being prodded from behind. Eventually, they found the familiar watering trough in an unfamiliar environment. Dad and Henry pumped only enough water in the trough for one watering episode, because to leave water in the trough today would mean ice in the trough tomorrow. The cows drank sparingly and hurriedly and then quickly turned around to go back to the shelter of the barn. The ordeal was over until tomorrow. The men shut the door and secured the animals in their stalls.

Mother and daughters were relieved of anxiety once the men reached the house safely.

Dad slipped the rubber overshoes from his knee-high felt boots. Then he took a kitchen chair to the cheap tin wood heater in the living room, and propped up his feet on a stool within inches of the heater. He sat until he recovered from the freezing cold. Henry did not complain of the cold.

Mother and Dad remembered aloud the better days in Russia before World War I and the Revolution. The climate in the Ukraine had been mild. "But," they quickly added, "the Canadian government is so good." To fill the time during the storms, we played table games, read and wrestled until Dad exclaimed with exasperation, "Be quiet! I get so tired of that eternal giggling!" For a few minutes we might be quiet.

Outside nothing changed. We went to bed with the same piercing sound of wind we had awakened to in the morning. The next morning we heard the same howl, and again the third day. Only briefly did Mr. Wind ease off to take another giant cold breath so he had renewed power to exhale with even greater intensity.

Every day the feeding, watering and milking routine was repeated. And again the wood heater was fed. We always had wood to burn in Manitoba. We had enough wood in the lean-to to last for several more days. We restocked the wood supply in the lean-to from a long wood pile buried under a deep snow drift.

Justine, after a Manitoba blizzard

A surprising knock on the door on the third day was as welcome as March sunshine in Oregon. Ben Buhler, our neighbor, a noted story teller of tales both true and untrue, was greeted with warmth. To see and to hear him relieved us of the monotony of the last three cooped up days. Mr. Buhler was seeking relief from his own brood. He walked a quarter of a mile to see us. It was an honor for us to be the chosen hosts. We also knew he had no other close neighbors. He had risked his life to come see us.

Mr. Buhler was younger than Dad and more robust. Because he also came from Grigorjewka in the Ukraine, he was practically family. He told Dad that to sit at the heater to warm his feet was not the way to increase his cold tolerance. He ought to work to get warm. But he did not tell him how to do that today, in this small house full of children. Nothing of consequence was spoken that day, and after sharing everything that he knew might entertain us, he left to go back to his own house full of children.

The fourth day we awoke to absolute silence and bright sunshine. It was cold, but today we would walk to school. A half inch of ice coated the window panes at home. We entertained ourselves by pressing warm thumbs against the sheet of ice. Gradually the ice thawed to create a small peephole from which to see the wonders of the blizzard's aftermath. Snowdrifts as high as men decorated our yard. Every shrub, building, implement and fence had played a part in the snowy formations. Areas free of obstruction were swept bare in places, showing frozen soil. The fine hard snow made firm hard snowdrifts which could easily hold our weights.

What fun to venture outside and go to school. A whole new white world waited to be explored on our two plus miles across country to the school. We did it in the excellent company of Mr. Buhler's children. Long underwear, woolen stockings, overshoes, woolen coats and helmets; we were ready to meet the cold. Carrying Roger's Golden Syrup pails that held our lunches we were ready to climb every snowdrift between home and school.

All of our teacher's fifty-six pupils had survived the three day blizzard.

FORK RIVER

THE LITTLE TOWN of Fork River is a mere dot on the Manitoba map. In the spring of 1938 Fork River became our address. We would live only a half mile from the gravel highway running between Fork River and Winnipegosis. Then an additional four miles on this road would take us into the small town.

Onion-shaped domes graced the Russian Orthodox Church on the northern outskirts of town. A small white Anglican church stood on the corner of the highway that angled its way through town. Instead of five tall elevators reaching into the sky like Rush Lake had, Fork River had only two. But late in summer and early fall these elevators in Fork River became busy as one wagon load after another unloaded their precious cargo of harvested grain. Wheat, barley and oats thrived on Manitoba's rich soil.

Three General Stores stood at discreet distances from each other. Ogrizlo and Stashko, both Ukrainians, operated two of the stores. The Red and White store went out of business while we lived there. The Canadian National Railroad station beside the track could not be ignored. It would become part of our future. The post office was managed by Mr. and Mrs. King. Some of our church children attended the Fork River School.

Our family would use all of these facilities except for the school. At Rush Lake the school had been an integral part of our lives. The school drew us to town almost daily, but this was not so at Fork River. Now the church was the social hub of our lives. It was about two and a half miles further from town than our house was. Dad had learned some Russian in the Ukraine and with the little English he learned in Canada, he became the family's main commuter to town. He picked up the mail at the Post Office wicket, including The Free Press which arrived in the mail. He also bought the few staples that we needed from the general stores. There were no super markets and there was no fresh produce except oranges and apples. The businessmen spoke Ukrainian and a little English. They understood each other.

Ukrainian farms in the area were interspersed with Mennonite farms. The men did business together in town and the children went to school together, but the two peoples who lived side by side did not socialize together. When Mary Rempel, on the fringes of the Mennonite church, married a Natrasny boy, she created a scandal in the Mennonite community. We did not hear about the reaction of the Ukrainians. Ukrainians would have been no more comfortable in our church than we would have been in theirs. Our parents had taught us to say "Ya niz nayi Peruski." (I don't understand Russian.) When an elderly Russian woman in town spoke to me, I used the sentence. She seemed to understand what I said but she spouted forth a deluge of words I could not understand.

Early on in our lives at Fork River, Mr. Hunt discovered that Annie and Lena were willing to stook (set up shocks) for him. He was a local well-to-do farmer. He lived between us and Fork River. Lena says,

We were promised 20¢ an acre. The grain was so heavy and we looked forward to stooking a field of oats which was lighter. Then Hunt said he'd pay only 15¢ an acre for that field. I still feel bad for not standing up for ourselves and telling him he promised to pay 20¢ and 20¢ it should be. If we worked from early until late we'd make $1 a day each. And then we'd be so hot and dirty and we had no bath tub—not much water—just a basin full for a sponge bath.

Summer days in Manitoba were long. Gardens, fertilized with manure, produced potatoes, tomatoes, carrots, beets, lettuce, radishes, onions, cabbage, kohlrabi, and beans. Peas were new to our family. The first time my sisters cooked them they cut up the pods like green beans. We did not like the papery lining. We discovered that shelled peas were good.

Frost often struck gardens and grain before we finished harvesting. September frosts were common. One exceptionally early frost came on August 23. To prevent tomatoes from freezing we covered the plants with blankets at night. Green tomatoes made good Chow Chow. We also picked green tomatoes, before frost could ruin them, and let them ripen on the floor upstairs. One autumn when we had picked green tomatoes which lay ripening, our neighbor asked if we would have extra tomatoes. Why had she not taken care of her own tomatoes like we had? Mother told her we would not.

We were uncomfortable hosting non-Mennonites because we were ethnic and they would not be familiar with our foods. We also felt uncertain about our customs and our humble origins. What was Canadian etiquette? Would they like our food and would they like to eat from our motley assortment of dishes? We attended summer Bible school and wanted to invite the two women teachers for dinner. Mother consented. She cooked only ethnic food. We invited them and they came. They and we survived. We did not know it then but the meal they ate (which was probably chicken) may have been something they wrote home about.

My brother, George, married Edith Wolfe in June, 1939. Edith had been born and raised in Regina. Her parents were Baptists from Austria. Edith spoke some German but her dialect was different from ours. Mother had difficulty accepting her daughter-in-law because she was not German Mennonite. Being a city girl versus a farm girl was also a problem to our parents. Edith spoke German to them but had difficulty accepting our very humble home and the farm. The animals were entirely too close to our lives. After having been instructed about the difference between a cow and a bull, she looked out the window, saw a bull and said, "That's a bull cow!"

When she came to visit I was intrigued with everything she had. She brought more than one pair of dressy high heeled shoes. Why did she need more than one pair? A different color for every color of dress? She also used Kleenex instead of handkerchiefs. She must have seen that I was intrigued with the soft tissues. She gave Justine and me each a Kleenex of our own. I folded it and kept it safely in my Bible.

After Annie and Lena were married and away from home, I wanted to make something Canadian for Edith to eat when she and George came home. We had lots of rhubarb. I baked a rhubarb pie. When I served it for dessert, George tasted it first and puckered his face. I had forgotten to put in sugar. I offered him some sugar to put between the crusts. Edith did not want a piece but she laughed heartily, saying, "George finally got something that was sour enough for him." It was probably the first pie I ever made.

Edith did not have an education but she had made her living cleaning private homes in the city. She had access to used clothes that her employers no longer wanted. She bundled these up in boxes and sent them to us. How delighted we were when we opened these boxes. Some dresses could be worn unaltered, but Mother altered others to fit whoever needed a dress. On our family photo taken when I was fourteen years old, Annie is wearing one of those dresses and I am wearing an altered one. Mine was a pretty blue.

Being immigrants, and poor, shaped us. What someone else did not want was still good enough for us. We also learned to get along with people by trying to do what pleased them, and not ourselves. The German proverb, "The smartest one gives in," or "Don't make waves," translated to: Let Mr. Hunt cheat you. Work hard. The principle of hard work being honorable was lived out every day. So no one in the family was either dirty or lazy. Annie, Lena and Henry, upon whom the burden of building the farm fell, worked incredibly hard in Manitoba.

One autumn when frost had come to stay, our parents butchered pigs. Two pigs were meant to last a whole year. Then we ate chickens. But on this autumn day when it appeared that our family had a surplus of pork to eat, a government car drove into our yard. Ham, liverwurst, sausage, cracklings, lard, head cheese and spare ribs were in the process of being made. Mother and Dad suspected that the government officials would think we could now discontinue receiving relief checks. Our parents wanted to be able to feed their family. They and the officials decided to end the meager checks. We were on our own. What sense of pride Dad must have felt. At last he could do what he had always wanted to do; take care of his family. Still we had only bare essentials. Dad was never able to repay the government for the aid we had received but his children paid taxes a lifetime.

The government officials stayed for the noon meal of roasted chicken and bubbat. Bubbat is a baking powder batter stuffing with dried fruit in it. We usually ate it with roasted chicken. They saw the dried raisins and prunes in it and assumed it was cake for dessert. We did not correct their thinking. But we ate our bubbat with the chicken and they saved theirs for dessert. It was not a sweet batter.

Life was changing for us. We had harvested a crop and a garden. We were finished with government support.

FIRE AND ICE

EMMA JANZEN, WHO was part of the church community, was home alone with her three preschoolers. In her husband's absence, she left the children in their frame house while she went to water the cows at the well. It was winter time. While she was watering the cows, the house caught fire. Before Emma could help her children out, she saw the house engulfed in flames. Two girls died in the fire, and the boy, ten months old, died later in the hospital. In lieu of a funeral home, Mrs. Penner, also church family, took care of the dead in her house. Because the dead were children, I wanted to go along with our parents to see their lifeless little bodies. The sight of the charred and pointed little fingers haunted me for weeks to come.

Another premature death was that of fifteen year old Annie Buller who died of leukemia.

I remember that Ben Buhler, our neighbor, built coffins. The lower part of the coffin was constructed of three boards. One formed the bottom, and the other two were attached at the sides at an obtuse angle. The lid was constructed in the same way but inverted. Looking at the covered coffin from its end, it looked like a hexagon. He painted it black. The women placed some bedding in the coffin on which the corpse was laid. We had never heard of funeral homes.

When death occurred in winter, the men from church worked hard to pick through many feet of frozen ground necessary to dig the graves. There were no backhoes. Mrs. Goertzen died at Christmas time when it was extremely cold. I remember how cold my feet were that day in 1947, when we all stood around the grave in December. The Mennonite cemetery was located about one mile west of the Nordheim School.

The Mossy River froze over thick and solid in winter. Horses and sleighs could cross the river safely. Dad and Henry went to the river to cut ice for our ice cellar. The cellar was no more than four or five feet deep. A roof and gables covered it. Henry says,

> *Ice was usually taken when it was about eighteen inches thick, cut in blocks of about two feet square. We cut them up with an ice saw and chisel. Then we pulled them out of the water and onto the sleigh with ice tongs. Ice here in the winter on the lake or river gets to three to four feet thick.*

They brought the ice home and stacked it compactly in the ice cellar. They covered it with a layer of straw for insulation. We did not use the ice house until the landscape thawed. The unheated summer kitchen add-on was our ice house in winter. After the spring thaw we stored our milk and cream on the ice. The ice lasted until about July or August. When the ice was gone the well became our cooler. We hung buckets of cream or milk in the cold well.

The Winnipegosis creamery's truck came twice a week to collect cream from local farmers during the peak season. Passable road conditions may have determined their hauling season. Manitoba mud is extremely tenacious. We usually shipped a five gallon can two times a week. When the truck did not run, we shipped cream via the Canadian National Railway after taking it to Fork River in a sleigh or buggy.

The men were not yet finished building on our farm. The pigs needed their own barn and the implements should be sheltered from the elements. This time Dad and Henry built with slabs instead of logs and clay. Slabs were the first pieces of lumber cut from the tree. One surface was flat from the cut of the saw but the other was contoured like the outside of the tree. Henry says,

> *The slabs were free at the mill about twenty-five to thirty miles north of Winnipegosis. The first time I recall going was with a group. All from our church, about twenty teams. It took a whole*

day across the lake to get there. We stayed in the shacks that the sawmill workers stayed in at night. That night a storm came up, dumping fresh snow on the trail. With a fairly strong wind still blowing in the morning, there was a debate—to stay another day—venture onto the lake, the same as we came, or take the land road via Red Deer Point back home. The land road was farther but safer. I think we divided in about half. One-half took the land and the other half the lake. I was one of the ones on the lake and we got home okay.

Early at Fork River Dad still hauled water either from Hunt's farm a half mile away, or from Ben Buhler, a quarter mile away. Although the distance to the wells in Manitoba was much shorter than they had been in Saskatchewan, he still had to use buckets and barrels and it was just as cold in winter. Rain and snow provided some of the water for household uses but Dad supplemented with well water. And the livestock all used well water.

Mr. Frank Peters came to "witch" our farm for water. He scoured the area with a switch of willow. He felt the pull of the switch downward and said Dad would find water between the road and the yard. He told Dad that if Dad could not find water there he would personally carry water to us with a tablespoon. Dad dug as far as he could with muscle and a spade. He found no water at the level at which he could dig manually.

Mr. Martens, a local farmer, and father of Katie and Jacob at Nordheim School, became our well driller. Rather than drilling where Mr. Peters thought we would find water, he drilled on the north side of the garden. Day after day he drilled. Although he lived only three miles away, he stayed overnight at our place. One day he walked into the house and in a defeated voice said, "I have sad news . . ." and we all feared the worst; he would stop drilling because it was futile. Instead, he said, "I have to leave you now. I have drilled into water." Can you imagine what that did to Dad who had hauled water for years and years?

The well was deep and cold. Dad enjoyed sending any one of his children to the well to get him some fresh water. We returned carrying a pail in each hand. He relished dipping into the bucket with a dipper and drinking directly from the dipper. He had never heard of germs. I can still hear the pleasure in his voice in the big "Ahh!" that followed a big drink. It was the best tasting water this earth gives forth. Dad never hauled water again. I cannot recall in what year the well was drilled but he had waited until he could afford to pay for a driller.

Henry remembers also that,

> *We had some cream spill in the well. We had white water several days and less cream to ship. It took several days for the water to get back to normal. Cream was a valuable source of income until we harvested new grain each year. We also sold a pig occasionally.*

Hope sprang anew. Life was getting better.

ADENA

HEAVY RUNNING FOOTSTEPS on the frozen ground awakened us during the night of February 21, 1940. Then we heard voices downstairs. Out of breath, John Redekop had awakened Dad to tell him Nettie's life was in danger in this time of childbirth.

Nettie and John had built a little shack on the southwest corner of our quarter section a quarter mile south of our house. They lived there only a short time. Earlier during the night John had come to fetch Mother to attend the birth with Mrs. Penner. Mrs. Penner not only prepared the dead for burial, she also delivered babies. John had fetched her from three and a half miles away. She lived by the Nordheim School. She had delivered many babies safely but now she asked for the doctor. She was afraid Nettie might not survive. Nettie was unconscious and convulsed in her bed. Mrs. Penner wanted Dr. Mead in Winnipegosis, nine miles away, to be summoned. We had no car.

At home Dad awakened fifteen year old Henry who slept in his room upstairs, and urged him to ride his bicycle to notify Dr. Mead of the need for his medical services. Alone, and about daybreak, Henry rode the nine miles and awakened the only physician within a thirty mile radius. Dr. Mead could not take Henry and his bicycle home in his car. But the doctor was on his way. In the meantime Dad had asked his brother-in-law, Abram Koop, to go after Henry with a sleigh and horses. Dad's sister, Tina, and he had moved from southern Manitoba to be our neighbors a half mile south of us.

At home Dad told us solemnly, "Pray for Nettie." We knew the situation was serious. At age twelve I knew nothing about pregnancy and childbirth.

Dr. Mead, by whatever method, saved Nettie's life. My guess is that he used an injection of morphine. He took her through the crisis of Toxemia of Pregnancy. She had had no prenatal care. She had some symptoms but no one recognized them. The doctor told John, Mother and Mrs. Penner that Nettie's life had hung by a mere thread.

Nettie had given birth to Adena, her firstborn, and our parents' first grandchild. She was our first niece and we adored her. After this brush with death, most babies in the Mennonite community were delivered in the Winnipegosis hospital.

Nettie complained of a loss of memory from which she never recovered fully. This was not evident to me. When Nettie was the mother of two or three preschool children, she asked me if I felt sorry for her children. She remembered I had told her I would feel sorry for her children when I was eight or nine. "No," I told her. She was a loving mother.

AUNT TINA KOOP

This Aunt Tina was Dad's sister and our neighbor. We knew her well. Tina, a derivative of Katherina, was a popular name. I would do errands for her sometimes on my bicycle.

I learned to ride a man's bicycle when I was thirteen and small for my age. It was the bike that my brother George had sent from Regina. I could not reach the ground with my feet; so when Uncle Kornelius and Aunt Mary Friesen with their children, Annie and Katie, visited us from southern Manitoba, I recruited cousin Annie's help. She displayed endless patience while she helped me mount and dismount the high bike.

Aunt Mary presented me with a dilemma in the gift she brought me. She knew I was the same age as her daughter Annie, but she did not know whether at thirteen I would be a child or an adolescent. She brought a red rubber ball for Justine to play with. She showed me another red ball and a pair of cotton lisle stockings, a forerunner to the nylon hose we wear now. I would have enjoyed either. It would have been my first pair of grown up stockings but the child within won and I chose the ball.

The bicycle became our second mode of transportation. We used it to follow the path through the pasture that took us to the cows grazing on government land northeast of our farm. We used it to go to town to get the mail or to get a limited amount of groceries. We learned to balance almost everything short of a hundred pound sack of sugar or flour on the bar.

On our way to town we stopped at Aunt Tina Koop's house to ask if she needed anything from town. We hoped she needed only the mail or a small object. I had not expected her to ask me to bring her a gallon of vinegar in a glass bottle on that bar. We had no basket on the bicycle. We were indebted to her and her husband for loaning us money to buy the farm, and we did not say "No" to her. And I was her namesake. I bought the gallon of vinegar and balanced it precariously on the bar for the whole four miles of gravel and a quarter of a mile on a dirt road. I delivered it intact to her door.

In addition to the money we owed her, and the name I bore, she had provided our family with two of the four pictures Justine and I have of our early childhood. We had no camera. She and her new husband had visited us in Rush Lake in about 1931 while they were on their honeymoon. They had married late in life. They had appeared to be fairly well to do. He had a car and she wore stylish clothes, which she probably bought in Winnipeg. She had worked as a maid in the big city before she married this man when she was about forty or forty-one. He had been a bachelor whose family had come to Canada in the latter part of the nineteenth century. Neither had married before.

When I was old enough to be helpful in the kitchen, I helped Aunt Tina cook for the threshing crew. I enjoyed helping her. She may have paid me a little although I think I would remember if she had. She gave me an occasional glass dish which I saved. One dish, a round serving bowl, I treasured until it finally broke after about 45 years.

Years after Dad borrowed the money from Koops to buy the farm, I was one of the happy children helping Dad in the pigpen load the pigs for shipment, when Dad announced that with the proceeds from the sale of these pigs he would finally finish paying the debt he owed the Koops. The farm was finally ours.

Aunt Tina promised to pay for the cost of my wedding gown if I married anyone other than ES (fictional initials). He was still a teenager and I was only thirteen or fourteen. He was Henry's best friend and came to our place frequently. Many years later when I planned to get married, I wrote to her to remind her of her promise. She said the price of wedding gowns was too high now, so she contributed $10 towards a $40 gown I sewed myself. I was not surprised. I had just finished two years of voluntary service and could have used the money. But I remembered she was not known for her generosity.

THE WAR

In THE AUTUMN of 1939 we heard the drone of an airplane above the Bicton Heath School. We never saw airplanes on the ground or in the air. Now Canada was at war in Europe. Mr. Turner called our attention to the airplane and invited us to leave the classroom to watch the plane from the school yard. He told us we could expect to hear more planes because the Canadian Air Force base in Dauphin would be practicing their skills in our clear blue skies. Dauphin was thirty-two miles south of our school. Seeing the airplane and hearing him tell us of its mission satisfied us and we went back to class.

Mr. Turner was married and had two young daughters. He and his family lived in the teachers' residence on the school yard. In addition to teaching fifty-six children, he was the janitor. He fueled the wood stove and provided drinking water for us. He was responsible for the water in the wash basin too. Two outhouses on the yard needed little upkeep.

One day we saw diapers drying on the line next to his house. The older children guessed that Mrs. Turner was about to have a baby. Soon Mr. Turner was the father of a son.

Two years after hearing that first airplane, Mr. Turner became part of the Canadian Air Force. Bicton Heath had no teacher in September because the men were at war. The board was unable to find a teacher. No doubt our lonely country school with such a large enrollment was not attractive to many teachers. Justine and I stayed home in the fall of 1941.

Lena married John Peters at our church on October 5, 1941, at age 19. They lived in a small house next to the Mossy River near the Nordheim School.

Annie married Pete Peters at church on November 16, 1941, at age 22. Pete had built a small house near his parents' place about two and a half to three miles north of the church and school, and five miles from our place.

John and Pete were brothers and had been coming to see my sisters regularly every Sunday evening for several years. I was 14 by the time Annie married and would have been in grade eight if we had had a teacher.

In February the school opened. A new teacher occupied Mr. Turner's chair. Would I be able to go to school and help at home too? There was no more mud plastering to do but there were chores to do. In spring we would put in a large garden and in summer and fall we would harvest the garden and the grain. We cut and stacked hay in June or July. Without much consideration my schooling was finished. I had completed grade seven and few students in the area went to school longer than that. Justine went back to school for her sixth grade, and when she was fourteen she finished eighth grade.

In the summer of 1941, Ralph Anderson used his father's horses to take Kate Laibel, Allan Hrushowy and me to see a movie in the Winnipegosis theater. I am still surprised that our parents let me go with these twelve and thirteen year olds who were not from our church.

Justine remembers that she and I took the bicycle and rode the nine miles to Winnipegosis to see "The Bluebird of Happiness," starring Shirley Temple. I did not understand acting and I thought Shirley was acting out her own life story. Justine sat on the bar of the bike for those nine miles both to and from the movie.

Ralph Anderson had been my childhood sweetheart for most of the three years that I attended Bicton Heath, although he was probably not aware of that until he was eleven or twelve. Annie Peters was my best friend. Justine became Ralph's and my note carrier for a short time after I dropped out of school but what do thirteen and fourteen year olds write about? Interest could not be maintained.

Although my zest for life had been rekindled at Bicton Heath, my love of learning was confined to English and Arithmetic. The enthusiasm I had had at Rush Lake was gone. I did not know that it would be rekindled later.

The call to war extended to the men in our isolated and small world. Several men received their "call" to military service. The church took a nonresistant stand and believed it was wrong for Christians to go to war. John Andres and Abe Dyck were drafted. Both considered themselves conscientious objectors, but they did not know how to follow the necessary procedures to obtain that status officially. They were both jailed for not reporting to service. They were released shortly when their status was cleared. Abe's brother, Jake, served in the Medical Corp. Henry Andres served in the army and married outside the church. Men who were on the fringes of the church like Dave Andres and John and George Hiebert accepted the call to military service. Dave was killed in England during the war.

Brother Henry was called to get his medical exam. He did that but claimed nonresistant status. He never heard further, perhaps because he was an only son on the farm, or perhaps the doctor found something, or maybe it was because it was near the end of the war. Or did the draft board honor his nonresistant status?

Brother George, twenty-four, and married since 1939, volunteered to serve in the navy. He was strikingly handsome in his military uniform. He never left Canadian soil but he was sent to Vancouver Island to serve.

The prices of farm products rose sharply during the war. Dad sold hogs and grain at better prices than he had prior to the war. Gasoline was rationed. Farmers could buy purple gasoline to fuel their tractors, but they could be in big trouble if they were found having some of it in their autos. For a short time before Henry married we had a 1935 Chevrolet. Sugar was also rationed. We were provided a rationing card which we presented when we bought sugar. It controlled the amount of sugar we could buy. Just when Mother was learning to can fruit and jam, sugar became scarce. Jam without enough sugar fermented.

During the war we planted sugar beets. Our parents had experienced a sugar shortage in Russia during and after World War I, and there they had learned to make sugar-beet syrup. We grew sugar beets, dug them out in autumn and scrubbed them clean and white. Next they were boiled in the large iron cauldron in the add-on summer kitchen until they were soft. We poured the mushy beets into porous gunny sacks and squeezed the sack under a plank. One end of the plank was anchored under the outside wall of the house while the other end was forced down over the sack of beets which was positioned in the middle. An apple cider press would have been a perfect implement if we had had access to one. The beet juice was collected below the sack and then boiled down in the cauldron until it was slightly thickened. It looked like molasses but was of a thinner consistency. It did not taste like sugar because it had its own flavor just as molasses does. Women learned to make a tolerable cake with it. We also poured some into our plates and dipped our bread into it in lieu of jam. We tired of the cake and we never missed the syrup when sugar was more available.

Also during war time, men came to our farm to collect scrap metal for the war effort. We found little but they took what we had. We had not arrived at the place in our lives where we discarded anything that might be functional to someone. Others came to sell war bonds.

The war seemed to go on forever. When I spent time at Nettie and John's place, John listened to the news every noon hour on their radio. I hated to hear the news because war produced tragedy after tragedy. I tired of hearing Winston Churchill speak. And how could England, the United States and France cooperate with Russia when our parents knew who Stalin was? I remember well coming to Aunt Tina Koop's house, when she promptly announced the death of President Roosevelt. How would the war ever end without him?

Dad's cousin, John Hiebert, also listened to the radio and was pro-Hitler. Dad was easily influenced by him. But I doubt that he was persuaded. Dad hung a map of Europe on his bedroom wall and watched the map as the war redefined it. He talked about end times and the antichrist. The biblical number 666 became an issue. Did the number refer to Mussolini? To Hitler? No one had any answers.

When the Mennonite Central Committee encouraged farmers to can meat, our church community slaughtered beef to feed the hungry in Europe. We were urged to send relief packages to private families. We had little to send.

At last, in 1945 the war was over.

Gerhard and Anna (Unger) Klassen Family. Back Row: Pete Peters, John
Redekop, Henry Klassen, George Klassen, John Peters. Middle Row: Annie
(Klassen) Peters, Nettie (Klassen) Redekop with Johnny, Mother Anna (Unger)
Klassen holding Adena Redekop, Dad Gerhard Klassen, Edith (Wolfe) Klassen,
Lena (Klassen) Peters. Sitting on floor: Justine and Tina Klassen.
1942.

From the Sweat of the Brow

THE GRAIN ON the quarter section of land directly north of our new farm grew tall, thick and green. The long straw supporting the heads of grain were unable to stand upright when the breezes played in the field. They bent, twisted and fell in a tangled mess. The grain was almost ripe enough to cut and bind. Had it stood upright the Warkentins would have waited until it was golden yellow. But to avoid further falling and tangling, they decided to cut it while it still had a greenish tint. Cousins Lena and Pete Warkentin sat on the tractor and binder and started to cut the field's outer perimeter. The binder dropped one sheaf after another.

Warkentins had either bought or rented this land from our neighbor, Jackie Hayward. They could work more land now that they had a tractor. We had no tractor, so we had to cut our grain with horses and a binder. Dad made a deal with the Warkentins. They would cut our grain and we would stook (shock) the fields on their new land.

Mother and I became the field hands to do the work. Our goal was to pick up each sheaf and stand it up with other sheaves to make a stook. It had to dry before it could be threshed. To do this we grabbed two sheaves by the twine that bound them at mid section and set them up facing each other in an "A" shape. The heads of grain would be near each other at the top while the straws extended away from each other on the ground. Next, we wanted to add about five or six more sheaves to make a full stook. All sheaves slanted toward each other at the top to protect as many ears of grain from the rain as possible.

On this green and tangled field we had to modify the procedure. We found that when we picked up a sheaf, it was still attached to the one lying on the ground. The straws were firmly entwined with each other. To separate one sheaf from the other, we stepped on the one on the ground and pulled up the first sheaf with both hands until the connecting straws tore lose. This was extremely hard work for Mother and me, both about five feet two. The weight of the greenish sheaves was also a challenge. We were creating order out of chaos. This was in about 1942 or 1943. We didn't buy our tractor until either 1943 or 1944. Mother would have been fifty-five or fifty-six, and I would have been either fourteen or fifteen.

Another force of nature was also at play. Mosquitoes liked the heavy, green, moist growth. They bred in the wet soil and green growth. They swarmed around our heads. Every time we bent down to pick up a sheaf, the mosquitoes met our faces. They liked Mother better than me so they attacked her with a vengeance. Her face was stung over and over. Raised, red and itchy welts plagued her long after she was bitten. She battled the mosquitoes and tangled sheaves until she despaired. Our invincible mother finally gave up. She said, "The mosquitoes are too terrible. Let's go home." It is the only time I know she yielded to a difficulty. Of course, we returned to the field the next day with renewed determination.

I remember once being angry at Dad when he sent me to harrow the summer fallow on a Saturday afternoon. I had thought I was finished doing dirty work for the day and had cleaned up for Sunday. The cows, of course, could alter the color of my face with one switch of their dirty tails, but that was to be expected. I had washed my hair and had put it into pin curls to control the frizz. This meant nothing to Dad. I went out and harrowed with the tractor and got dusty again.

Winters at home were profoundly boring. As young teenagers we learned to knit, crochet, tat and embroider. Annie Peters taught me how to crochet at school. My sister Annie taught me to tat. Mother taught me the basic knit and purl stitches. Our sisters also embroidered. I had learned to embroider when I was six. When there was something to read I preferred that. Justine read voraciously, but reading material was scarce. There was no library nearby. Our utilitarian Mother thought that time spent doing the various hand crafts was more valuable than reading stories.

Morning and evening we did chores. It meant milking, feeding chickens and pigs, separating cream from milk, and bringing in wood.

Sometimes we dug the wood out of snowdrifts. The men cleaned the barns, fed the animals and watered them at the well. They also cut logs in the bush (woods in the US) and brought them back for fuel.

The men did most of the spring field work without the help of the women. But in June and July the women helped with the cutting, raking and stacking of hay. August and September was cutting and stooking time. By the time Justine finished school we had a tractor. She and Dad cut the grain and Henry and I did most of the stooking. Justine and Dad helped us when they could.

Henry knew the field work much better than I did. He says,

> *Our fields were worked with horses until we bought our first John Deere Model H tractor in about 1943 or 1944. Dad bought the John Deere tractor from his brother, Cornelius Friesen, who still lived in southern Manitoba. He shipped it to us by train. Our first car was a 1935 Chevrolet bought at about the same time.*
>
> *I worked for the Kruegers for two weeks, mostly 'sitting on the disk,' I was told. It turned out to be mostly walking behind the harrows from 8:00 A.M. to 6:00 P.M. with a half hour lunch. Since they also milked twenty cows, the other man had to milk while I cared for his six-horse team, plus my four. That meant getting up at 5:00 A.M., feeding ten horses, cleaning out the barn, combing the ten horses as well as putting on the ten harnesses.*
>
> *Then breakfast, a day's walking on loose ground, and after 6:00 P.M. taking off ten harnesses, feeding the horses a couple of times, with bedtime about 10:00 P.M. The wages were $1 a day.*
>
> *I sent $12 to George in Regina and he bought me a used bike,* Henry recalls. Lena adds, *George added some to Henry's $12. Later George sent a couple of dollars and told us to send them back—so Edith would know that Henry paid for the whole cost of the bike. We concluded that Edith must have given George a rough time for adding money to buy the bike.*

Quoting Henry again,

I also started pitching sheaves at age fourteen or fifteen, had Dad's team and was required to work like the other men. Pay was better, $2.25 per twelve hour day. This, of course, went to pay the threshing on Dad's farm.

Henry took a hayrack to the grain fields and pitched the sheaves from the stooks on the field onto the hayrack which, when empty, was not high. But before the hayrack was full he was pitching them high over his head to the top of the load. He then rode the hayrack to the stationary threshing machine on another part of the field. Then he unloaded the whole load by pitching each sheaf into the threshing machine. This was a real man's job. We never owned a threshing machine so Dad hired the machine and the crew. If Henry had not pitched with the crew, Dad would have had to pay cash for the services. In those days, Dad was always strapped for cash.

When I was about sixteen, Henry Goertzen asked me to stook forty acres of heavy grain on a field near our place. I said I would and thought Justine would be home to help me. But she was working for Annie in the house that fall so I stooked by myself. I was paid 25¢ per acre. The price was up since our sisters had stooked for Mr. Hunt. A fringe benefit was the sight of Henry Goertzen's younger brother from time to time.

At home we all stooked without pay,

Years after Henry first fell in love with Annie Peters when he was twelve, she returned his affection. Now it was he who visited at the Peters every Sunday evening. She lived five miles north and west of our place.

I recall one evening vividly. It was exceptionally cold, but Henry wanted to see Annie anyway. Since Nettie and John lived only two or three miles north of the Peters, I wanted to go with him up to the Peters. I would walk the last two to three miles.

We rode in a sleigh and covered ourselves with blankets. But we got cold anyway. Henry realized it was too cold for me to walk so he graciously took me about a mile, or perhaps two, beyond the Peters' place. Then he unloaded me and he turned around to see Annie.

My feet were cold before I left the sleigh. I wore shoes and overshoes and all the necessities to survive in this cold climate. But I had underestimated the cold. The ground was frozen solid and the snow on the road was packed hard.

I walked on that frigid road while my feet got colder. Gradually I could not feel my feet and lower legs at all. They felt heavy and it felt like a thump when my feet hit the snow with every step I took. My upper legs felt like they were lifting and dropping blocks of ice on the hard road. The sound confirmed what I feared. I believed my lower limbs were frozen. I also knew I would freeze to death if I did not push forward.

At last I reached Nettie and John's front door. They were surprised I had come since we had no phones to communicate. At least, I was safe. I told Nettie and John about my feet. They removed my foot wear while I whimpered. John went outside to get a basin of snow. Together they knelt in front of me and rubbed my feet with the snow until sensation returned to my feet.

This incident was something I did not want to talk about because I knew it was foolish to venture out when the thermometer told me it was too cold.

For the short time we owned a car, Henry was its sole driver with one exception. I took Mother and Dad to visit on a Sunday afternoon. I think it might have been to Jake Buhlers. We could not drive the three miles straight north because the road was undeveloped. We took the long way around on dirt roads. While we were there it rained, turning the road into mud. I drove in the deep ruts left by others. I drove slowly and the car stalled again and again. Dad or I got out to crank the car to start it. He was so short of breath that he could not do it much easier than I could. Of course, I had no license to drive but I was unlikely to be stopped by anything but mud. We came home safely after a harrowing ride.

Every time Henry drove the car with Mother in it, she said, "Henry, you're going too fast." He adapted by starting out a little too fast so that he could slow down to a comfortable speed to please her.

Henry had urged Dad to buy the car when Henry became the church janitor. He says,

*Besides helping at home from 1938 to 1946, I also looked after the
church for a few years. In winter it meant getting up at 5:00 A.M.,
walking to church, getting the fire going and heating the church
until 10:00 A.M. when Sunday school started. In summer there
was just sweeping and dusting.*

*We also did some custom stooking for Mr. Hunt. That was a
family affair where Annie, Lena, Dad and I worked for 20¢ an
acre. I also hauled grain for Mr. Hunt one fall.*

When Justine and I earned money for stooking at Koops, we ordered
wrist watches from the Eaton's catalogue. Henry told us we didn't need
them. I understood that he meant they were frivolous and therefore wrong.
I am sure he does not hold that view today. But it did reflect the attitude
about anything that was fun or nonessential during those times. Now he
boasts about paying only $5 or $6 for his current watch. Justine's watch
was $11.19 and mine was $12.69 from the catalogue. We were 14 and 16.
It was our first extravagance, and we refused to feel guilty.

We washed away the sweat of our brows after each week's work, but
we could not wipe away the indelible marks left by poverty and austerity.

One autumn we were unable to gather the potatoes from the big garden
before it rained and became cold. They had been dug up but they lay in
cold mud. If we waited for the weather to dry and warm, the potatoes
were in danger of freezing. That was unthinkable. So Mother and I braved
the cold but were absolutely miserable when our hands became so cold
from the near-freezing mud and the wet potatoes. But we had potatoes to
last us until the next summer.

Quoting Henry again,

*I started farming in 1945 by renting 63 acres from Mr. Laibel
and working with Dad's machinery. In 1946 I rented Pete Peters'
and F. Peters' places, also bought the quarter section we were on the
winter before.*

*We (Henry and Annie) were married October 20, 1946,
on a Sunday afternoon. We did it without engagement rings or*

wedding rings—couldn't afford such things. Also without any excess frills such as bridesmaids and best men. All we needed was the preacher and the witnesses in those days, Henry recalls. I will add that they did not need a marriage license either. Their intentions to marry, called 'the banns,' were read in the church two consecutive Sundays prior to the wedding.

We had a ceremony and a meal in the afternoon, Henry continues, *and a program in the evening. After the evening program we hitched up our horses and went to our one-room house on the farm five miles north of the church. We still live on that farm but built a new house in 1967.* (They moved from the farm into the town of Winnipegosis in October, 1994.)

Needless to say, there were no honeymoons at that time.

Leaving the Farm

Only Justine and I were left to help Dad on the farm after Henry married in 1946. Nettie and John had three children, Adena, Johnny and Linda. Pete and Annie had Leona and Vernon. Lena and John had Luella and Alvin; then Vera was born in November of 1946. George and Edith had only Joan; Carol came along later.

Justine memorized the required 300 Bible verses in preparation for the Gimli camp sponsored by the Canadian Sunday School Mission. She had been able to go in 1946. But in 1947, just before she was scheduled to take the two-hundred mile trip, we had heavy rains. Our flat fields flooded locally and the water washed out small bridges that would have been passable in dry weather. It appeared that she could not get to Gimli camp. What a blow it was after memorizing the verses and anticipating the long deserved trip!

Justine remembers it differently. "They didn't have money to let me go to camp on the bus," she said. I know our parents worried that the young crops would drown. They expected a crop failure. The crop situation would also determine whether Justine could attend Bible School in Altona in the winter. Two disappointments were hard to take. Justine says, "I don't remember ever dreaming of going to Bible School."

At this time George wrote from Cranbrook, B.C., to say he needed help in his Sunrise Bakery. Justine jumped at the chance to go work for him. She was only seventeen.

In a matter of a few weeks, perhaps days, the landscape dried and the small bridges were repaired. The mud was gone and the crops survived. Justine could have gone to Bible School if she had stayed home. This was the summer of 1947, less than a year after Henry married.

Now Justine's sudden absence made the house seem very empty. I missed her. We shared so much life together. I didn't even like to choose a dress to buy without her input. Being home alone with Mother and Dad was no fun. Dad was getting forgetful.

That same summer Dad and I harvested alone. I sat on the tractor and Dad operated the binder. After cutting a field of grain we tackled the hard part, stooking. I was stronger at nineteen than I had been when Mother and I stooked together with the mosquitoes. But Dad was failing. He became very tired with his shortness of breath. Frequently he sat down on a sheaf to rest and catch his breath. When he rested, he smoked. Farming was becoming too difficult for him.

Since coming to Manitoba in 1937, Uncle Vahng had had a stroke and never fully regained his mental faculties. In 1938 Aunt Margaret had gone to a Winkler hospital and had come back free of infection. But she had to use either a wheelchair or crutches to get around.

On the farm we had made progress in spite of not having any modern conveniences like electricity, plumbing or telephone. We owned a battery operated radio, thanks to Henry's urging. We had a good well. We needed no financial assistance. The animals were well fed and healthy. We harvested a good garden every summer. We no longer succumbed to boils on our buns. We owed Koops nothing. We owned a tractor. We became acquainted with marriage, birth and death. Mother and Dad had numerous grandchildren. We had come a long way in these less than ten years in Manitoba.

Progress—our new barn

Justine on tractor, Dad on binder, 1945

However, before the next harvest Dad would sell the farm to his son-in-law, John Redekop, instead of to Henry, as I would have expected. Ours was better land than Henry's and he had done so much to help Dad make it on the farm. But John Redekop had been unable to purchase his late brother-in-law's farm as he hoped. He was disappointed to say the least. Now our parents were helping him out.

In 2006 John's daughter, Linda, my niece, wrote in a letter that she found this record:

> *Grandma and Grandpa Klassen bought Crown land at Fork River (160 acres) in 1938 for $800. When they moved to BC in 1948, Mom and Dad bought it for $8000 (borrowed money from Goossens). Then they in turn sold it in 1973 to move to Morden,* she adds, *for something like $20,000 for the farm.*

On March 27, 1948, our farm auction took place in our yard. Farmers from all around, both Mennonites and Ukrainians, came to buy farm implements, livestock and household goods. It hurt to see our spirited mare, Jeanie, and her colt, sold to strangers. But we preferred to see each of our animals go to strangers rather than to Mr. Buhler, our neighbor. He not only yelled the loudest at his animals, he was abusive to them. I could not bear the thought of him buying even one of our livestock. I don't think he did. Our farming days were over.

The selling price of our farm was $8,000. The auction proceeds were additional income. Dad did not give any money back to the government because they needed to build a house elsewhere, and he was not yet old enough to get Canada's Old Age Pension. Dad was almost sixty-three, and Mother was almost sixty.

Dad, Mother and I took the train from Fork River and set out on our way to British Columbia to make a new home. Nettie, Annie, Lena and Henry with their families remained in Manitoba. George and Edith lived in Cranbrook, B.C. Justine lived and worked for them. We would visit Cranbrook on our way to the coast.

The nuclear family was dispersed. It was the end of an era.

PART III

BRITISH COLUMBIA TO JORDAN
1948-1959

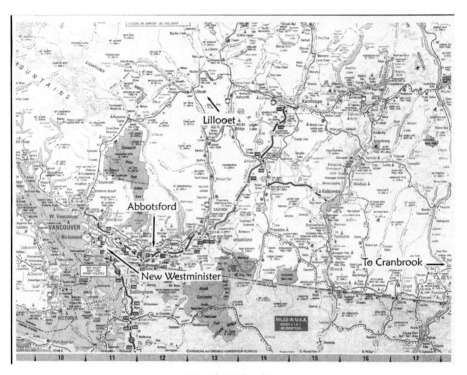

British Columbia

British Columbia

THE TRAIN ROLLED across the prairie provinces early in the spring of 1948. Mother, Dad and I traveled lightly. In western Alberta the foothills rose high above the rolling plains. Close to the railroad, the historic Frank Slide still covered the former town beneath a mountain of rocks and mud. The Rocky Mountains impressed us with their grandeur. Justine had sent us pictures of her trip to Cranbrook less than a year earlier. Now we witnessed the majesty of their snowy crowns and rugged heights ourselves.

In Cranbrook, near the Alberta/British Columbia border, George met us at the railway station. At his home, Edith was taking care of newborn Carol, born on March 28, 1948. Pretty little Joan resembled her father. She inherited his curly dark hair.

George took us to his Sunrise Bake shop on the main street of Cranbrook. The attractive baked goods displayed in the windows suggested a successful business. Every morning he rose early to heat the ovens and to start the yeast mixtures. Later his employees joined him. It was here where Justine spent her days at work.

Justine also lived with George and Edith. On Sunday evening she introduced me to her friends after church at a restaurant. I heard about "sundaes" for the first time. Roy Speirs was one of her many friends and made himself memorable by the jokes he shared with us. Justine's life in Cranbrook was very different from the isolated life she had known in Manitoba. She married Roy two years later and they moved to Regina, Saskatchewan.

Before we left Cranbrook, Edith gave me a used coat that fit me. I had been wearing a dyed-blue coat which, after I let down the hem, showed a lighter blue hemline than the rest of the coat. I was embarrassed by the coat but that was all I had.

A few days later Mother, Dad and I arrived in Chilliwack, B.C. At home we had left a few melting snow drifts but here the grass was green and the dandelions were brilliantly yellow.

Mother's sister Justine Harms and her husband Peter, with their youngest children, had moved here from Saskatchewan before we did. Cousin Mary and I could not bridge the gap between the close childhood friends we had been, and the young adults we had become. We were strangers to each other, but her sweet nature still shone through. She had integrated with Canadian culture, while I remained an immigrant child. Her mother's only criticism of me was that I was too "fromm" (pious).

Uncle Cornelius Friesen and Aunt Mary, with their children, had moved from southern Manitoba to Yarrow, a primarily Mennonite Brethren village between Chilliwack and Abbotsford. They had found a small house in Yarrow for us to rent. We now had electricity and running water.

I remember my brief stay in Yarrow for a play I went to at the Mennonite Brethren High School with my cousins. My problem was: "Is it right to spend money on entertainment?" I had 50¢ for admission but I had almost nothing else. This activity was not absolutely essential. I did not know how to say "No" to my cousins. They seemed not to have any qualms about going so I went with them. I cannot remember the play.

Almost immediately upon arrival in Yarrow, I wanted to go to Vancouver to earn money. All I knew was housework and I planned to do that until the strawberries were ripe in June. I knew I wanted to go to high school before I knew the proximity of a school to our new home.

About three years earlier I was teaching summer Bible School with twenty year old Mary Dyck, who lived in southern Manitoba. She had finished high school and was on her way to being of service to humanity. While she and I discussed her achievement and my limited schooling, I stated with resignation that it was too late for me to go back to school and finish high school. "No it isn't," she announced firmly. She planted a seed of hope in my mind. At age 17, that was a new and cheerful thought. I hung on to it.

Uncle Cornelius tried to persuade me to relax for a few weeks prior to strawberry picking. But I learned about the tram that ran from Yarrow to Vancouver and I was on it. From my Friesen cousins I had learned where the Mennonite Brethren Girls' Home was in Vancouver. That was my destination.

Both the Mennonite Brethren and General Conference Mennonite churches provided Girls' Homes in the city. This was a haven to come to on days off, or to live in until newcomers were established in the city.

A Mrs. Laidlaw hired me through a telephone conversation with the housemother in the Girls' Home. She lived on 41st Avenue in the Kerrisdale district. Later I would learn that the Kerrisdale district was one of the areas in Vancouver where the wealthy lived. I had to learn to use the city buses. Fare was 10¢ and if I wanted to transfer to another bus to reach my destination, I had to ask for a transfer slip upon payment of the fare. I did not know the streets of Vancouver and I felt very far from home.

The Laidlaws had two elementary, or perhaps middle school, children. The children laughed at me when I wouldn't drink root beer because I had never heard of it. I did not know whether it contained alcohol or not. I ate in the kitchen while I waited on the family eating in the dining room. I became acquainted with the tiny dinner bell they used to summon me. Mrs. Laidlaw was a fine mistress. She shared the household responsibilities with me and taught me what I did not know. I had a room of my own and spent the evenings there unless I went to the Christian and Missionary Alliance church. I also went to the Mennonite Brethern Girl's Home on Thursday afternoon or on Sunday after church. It was there I met the fiancée of my former boyfriend with a diamond ring on her finger. Ouch! We had broken up only four months before.

The Laidlaws gave a party for their friends while I was with them. She asked if I were willing to wear a maid's uniform. I met their guests at the door in a dark-green-with-white-trim uniform. I assume that my uniformed presence gave them added status with their friends.

After I had worked for the Laidlaws for about five weeks, the strawberries were almost ripe in the Fraser Valley so I left my job as a maid and went to Abbotsford. Mother and Dad had bought a two-acre plot on Townline Road South, between Wiebe's store on Peardonville Road and the West Abbotsford church. To live within walking distance of these two places was vitally important because we had no car. Now Mother, Dad and I found a strawberry picking job with Uncle Peter Unger, who lived on Peardonville Road, about a half mile from our new place. He and Tante Tin had moved from Saskatchewan to British Columbia since we had seen them some years before.

Our berry picking day started about eight A.M. and we picked until about five P.M. Uncle Peter was his own row boss. Tante Tin, Otto and his wife, Lena Unger, Mary and Elsie Froese, and our family were the picking crew. Berries were big and ripe. We were allowed to eat all we wanted! The season was dry and warm. We were instructed to pick rotten berries and to put them in the center of the plant to avoid contamination of healthy berries. We were also instructed to pick clean so there were no overripe berries the next time we picked the field. It was the most orderly and pleasant field I have ever picked in. At the end of each day we walked home with sore backs and knees, ready to fall into bed as soon as supper dishes were washed. By then, home was a barn built for chickens but which had never been occupied by chickens.

Uncle Peter paid the going price per pound of berries, which I think was 3½¢ a pound. After the berries had peaked he increased the pay gradually until he paid us 5¢ a pound at the end of the season. He did not want to waste good berries, and he wanted us to earn a reasonable wage. The most I picked in a day was 200 pounds.

Raspberry season followed the strawberry season as surely as August follows July. Mother, Dad and I returned to Yarrow to pick raspberries. And when the latter season was complete we took a transportation truck in yet another direction to pick hops.

In the meantime, we attended the West Abbotsford General Conference Mennonite church. In the hop fields I wondered where the West Abbotsford young people were. We discovered that the church frowned on picking hops because the hops went primarily to make beer, rather than yeast as we had hoped. I did not pick hops the next year. And Mother who became allergic to hops, also could not pick. Dad, however, continue picking hops.

By the end of the summer picking season I had earned more money than I had earned in my first twenty years. I had earned well over $100. I knew I wanted to spend it at the M.E.I. (Mennonite Educational Institute.) It was located near the Trans Canada highway on Clearbrook Road, one and a half miles from home. Mary Froese, whom I had met in the berry field, would attend the same school but she would be in grade thirteen, the equivalent to the first year of university. Her family had come from Saskatchewan and she had attended high school. I would start in grade nine if I was lucky enough to be able to skip grade eight.

The Mennonite
Educational Institute

WALKING ONE AND a half miles to the high school in British Columbia
was no problem. But how do I adjust to becoming a student when I am
twenty years old and have finished only grade seven? What if I went to
register and they refused to take me? What if I could not skip eighth
grade? And what if the person registering students refused my application
in the presence of others, thus embarrassing me? I wanted so badly to start
in ninth grade.

To avoid being embarrassed in public, I decided to settle the question
before registration. I inquired about the residence of the principal, Mr.
Isaac Dyck. He lived in the country several miles from our place. One
evening I rode Henry's bike to see him, unannounced. We had no phone.
Mr. Dyck was hoeing his garden when I arrived. I told him I was twenty
and had finished seventh grade. Could I go to school and start with ninth
grade? "Sure," was his answer. He seemed friendly and nonthreatening. I
was thrilled, of course, with his easy acceptance of my situation. Now when
I registered I could say, "Mr. Dyck has already approved my acceptance in
ninth grade." Registration was no longer a thing to fear.

The year's fee, I think, was $105. I had enough to pay for the fee and
to buy books. I made myself several white cotton blouses. I would live at
home.

When school started, I found myself in a classroom full of fourteen
year olds. The boys at this age begged for spare periods in which they
could play outside. I had come to learn everything I could in as short a
time as possible, while these boys wanted to throw away this wonderful

opportunity. My goal was to get an education so I would be in a position to help the needy people in this world.

One day when I was exceptionally disgusted with the boys' request to play, I came home discouraged. Uncle Peter Unger was visiting. He talked me into staying in school.

Fortunately a few of the girls in ninth grade were mature for their ages, and they chose me as their friend. Three of the teachers were not much older than I was.

That same fall Pete and Annie with Leona and two year old Vernon wanted to spend the winter in B.C. They liked escaping Manitoba's cold winter. Rain was not as cold as snow. Pete became the carpenter who built a small house for us. The house had two bedrooms, a living room and a kitchen. And we had electricity and cold, running well-water in the kitchen. However, we had no bathroom, refrigerator or phone. I would leave home before our parents had a phone and a refrigerator. A new bedroom was added eventually and one of the old ones was remodeled into a bathroom.

In contrast to my lack of interest in learning at Bicton Heath, now I took every subject very seriously. The work was not difficult. I especially enjoyed English and Algebra. My goal was to skip tenth grade, and I knew I had to have good grades to accomplish this. With hard work, I was able to complete ninth grade with good grades and with assurance that I could take grade eleven in the fall.

It was at this time that our family experienced a tragedy when Uncle Peter Unger was killed in a traffic accident just days before Christmas, 1948. He was sixty-two years old.

During the next summer I picked my parents' strawberries with pay. They needed me and I needed the money for tuition. Again I picked raspberries in Yarrow, but my parents did not. Instead of picking hops, I went back to Vancouver to clean houses. This time I lived at the General Conference Girls' Home. Each day some of us left the Home to clean one house. This was called "day work." We each had our own list of houses to clean and we worked eight hours a day. We returned to the same houses on the same day of the week every week. Five houses a week was a full schedule.

The wage was 65¢ an hour. That totaled $5.20 a day plus 20¢ for bus fare. We traveled to any location in the big city, including North Vancouver and the distant University area. Some addresses were hard to find, so we studied the city map before we set out to find a new home. We had no personal maps to take with us.

At the end of the day we returned to the Home to share the day's experiences around the supper table. The recent immigrants who did not speak English well had their own kind of stories to tell. They had arrived after World War II and still had many adjustments to make.

One woman reported how irate she had been with her mistress for leaving her a note telling her to eat no eggs. Lunch was provided at the place of work, so why shouldn't she eat eggs for lunch! The note said, "No eggs today." Later in the day she confronted her mistress about the impolite note left for her. She laughed when she told us the mistress meant, "The egg peddler is coming today. We don't need any today."

It was at one of these "day work" homes where I tasted celery for the first time. And avocado too.

In September, I found myself in grade eleven with students who were sixteen while I was twenty-one. Now there was just a five year difference between their age and mine. The situation was better. These eleventh graders were no longer children. I began to enjoy high school. However, by skipping grade ten I had missed theorems and history. The teacher, Mr. Bill Wiebe, reviewed geometry's theorems for an entire month. We wrote the test and I passed with a respectable grade. But I have always missed the history I should have learned in grade ten.

Our final exams in June would not be composed by our teachers. The Department of Education of B.C. prepared the questions in the exam covering the whole year's curriculum. All of B.C.'s students taking the University Entrance exams wrote precisely the same exams. I had to know theorems. I passed all the exams in fine shape.

The high school had been built only a few years prior to my coming to B.C. The Fraser Valley attracted many Mennonites, both Mennonite Brethren and General Conference. At that time, the majority of both students and teachers were Mennonite Brethren. I was one of the many General Conference Mennonite students from the West Abbotsford church.

The West Abbotsford church was a large one. Reverend Henry Epp was the lead minister. At least three other ministers preached from the same pulpit. Rev. Epp's sermons were usually about the new birth. This church was alive and evangelistic. The church had no organized youth group except the choir. With many gifted young people from three or four prominent families, such as the Epps and the two Wiebe families, the rest of us seemed superfluous. The only way to join the "in group" was to become part of the choir whether or not we could sing. I did get to know Sara Teichroew and Helen Anne Krause, who became two of my best friends both at church and school.

During the summers we were all occupied picking the berry crops. But we had time in August, too, in which we could earn additional money for school. A group, including Sara and me, went to Lillooett, B.C., to work in a cannery when the tomatoes were ripe. Lillooett is located along the Fraser River, a day's drive north of Abbotsford. The rugged gorge carved into the Rocky Mountains made spectacular scenery. We were given barracks in which to sleep. During the day we stood on our feet while a conveyer belt brought one basin full of blanched tomatoes after another. We peeled them as rapidly as possible and received a hole in our punch card for every basin full we peeled.

The peeled tomatoes were then sent on their way along the conveyor belt. The peelings went on a different belt, to a different destination. They were used to make catsup. To one peeler's surprise, she found a scalded snake in her basin. In a state of repulsion, she rejected it and erroneously sent the basin full on its way to make catsup. I have never eaten "Aylmer's" brand catsup after that.

Living in the cannery barracks, our food was served to us in a mess hall. In the evenings, I read "Gone With the Wind."

At the end of August, we returned home in time for school. I had only grade twelve to finish. No aptitude tests were available and we had no counselors. No typing was offered. What could I study? I had to learn to do something.

What was available for young women besides teaching and nursing if they could not type? Sara and Helen Anne were going to go to Nursing School at the Royal Columbian Hospital in New Westminster, thirty-five miles from home. Because I liked to be with people, I chose to apply to the same hospital, where we would live in dormitories. I reasoned that teachers were on their own, while at the hospital I would live with student nurses. I knew absolutely nothing about nursing. Nor about university.

Because the Mennonite Educational Institute offered grade thirteen (the equivalent to the first year of university), the school did not let us graduate from grade twelve. Like Sara and Helen Anne, I left without the benefit of graduation ceremonies.

We needed some money to enter the nursing school but not very much. I picked crops as usual. This time a group of us went to Kamloops in the interior of B.C. to work in a tomato cannery. After waiting several days in Kamloops, tomatoes were still not ripe. We had no time to waste. So Sara and I left and went back to Vancouver to do housework.

This time we both lived-in with the families for whom we worked. My monthly wage was $75 at Dr. Irwin and Una Horsley's home. Una was pregnant with her third child. They were strong Seventh Day Adventists who tried to convert all three adult women in the household. There was Dr. Horsley's aunt, who was a practicing Episcopalian; Mrs. Horsley's sister who was a medical student and an atheist; and me, a Mennonite. I lived and worked for them from September until Christmas and then stayed home to sew the uniforms that the hospital required of student nurses.

BECOMING A NURSE

THIRTY APPREHENSIVE YOUNG women presented themselves at the Royal Columbian Hospital in New Westminster, on January 21, 1952. We came from New Westminster, Abbotsford, Chilliwack, and as far inland as Fernie, B.C. Petite Satoye Nishiguchi stood dwarfed beside five-foot-ten Doreen Krego. Doris Madison did not look old enough to be a high school graduate, while Beth McLellan lied to qualify for the school's age limit of thirty-five or under. Beth stood apart, aloof. Sara Teichroew, Helen Anne Krause and I took comfort in knowing we had at least two friends from home.

The Royal Columbian Hospital, with its vine covered brick walls, held 400 patient beds. The general hospital housed numerous Medical and Surgical wards, Maternity, Pediatric and Communicable Disease wards, Laboratory, and a Central Supply room. The whole fifth floor was occupied by operating rooms and related work rooms. The post Anesthesia Recovery Room was housed here. Obstetrics occupied the fourth floor—labor rooms, delivery rooms, a nursery for newborns, and a large ward for postpartum patients. In the 1950s new mothers came to maternity and enjoyed a seven day holiday. The large basement held the kitchen that served patients, staff and students in the adjacent dining room.

The four student dormitories were built on the hospital grounds. Tall smoke stacks towered high above the hospital laundry roof. The newest students, the Class of 1955, were eager to explore the large hospital complex. But first we were introduced to the dormitory that would be our home for the first months. We were all assigned individual rooms, conducive to study. Sara's and my rooms were next to each other on the lower floor on the north end of the building. A housemother occupied the office.

When all thirty of us gathered for the first time in the classroom, as instructed, we brought our loose fitting blue basic uniform dresses that we had sewn at home. We also brought the wrap-around white cotton aprons we had sewn from sheeting by-the-yard. The three inch waistbands held the gathers together and buttoned in the back. One glance at the ill-fitting aprons convinced us easily that they were as different from each other as the thirty seamstresses who had sewn them. With the help of our teachers the aprons were shortened or lengthened to make the lengths look uniform. Loose waistbands were taken in to fit snugly. The hospital provided us with stiffly starched white collars and cuffs to adorn the simple blue tops that showed above the aprons. After several launderings the aprons would come back as stiff as the collars and cuffs.

We would have to earn our right to wear the coveted nurses' caps and stiff white bibs. Our registration fee was approximately $150. This covered the cost of collars, cuffs, caps and bibs. It also covered the cost of our nursing textbooks. We had bought the fabric to make aprons and blue dresses. We also bought black shoes and stockings which completed our uniform. Our list of required items included three nylon slips without lace and a hot water bottle. After paying the entry fee, I had very little money left from my summer earnings.

When we settled at our desks, an instructress informed us that we were mere "probies." We were on probation for the first four months. If we remained in the program, and qualified, we would be "capped" at a formal "capping" ceremony. At that time we would also receive our bibs. She made it clear that we were dispensable. The hospital did not need us. We sat like thirty deflated balloons.

In the classroom we learned anatomy and physiology, pharmacology and microbiology, nursing arts and nursing ethics. Early in the program the nurse-instructresses were our sole teachers. Later, physicians lectured to us.

Mrs. Chase, the dummy, was introduced early in the program. She did not respond to our treatment of her body in the same way we responded to each other when we practiced on each others' bodies. We took each others' temperatures and blood pressures. We gave each other injections of salt water in our front thighs. My needle found Doreen Krego's nerve and for a short time her leg was numb. We put stomach tubes through the nose into each other. We had to know what it felt like to a patient when he would gag and retch and tears would come to his eyes.

We were taught to respect our superiors, starting with physicians (who were self-proclaimed gods), supervisors, instructresses, head nurses, and registered nurses. We were told to stand up when a physician entered a chart room when we were sitting and charting. When asked by an instructress who was the most important person in the hospital, a naive student answered, "The Doctors." I had been thinking that the patients surely were the purpose of a hospital's existence but was afraid to raise my hand lest the all-important physicians were deemed more important. To our surprise, the student's answer was wrong. We were told the patient was most important. Before we started nursing school we could have said that, but after being indoctrinated, we weren't sure if our teachers would see it that way.

The only people who were not our superiors were the nurse aides, orderlies and cleaning personnel. We never met clerical or laundry persons.

When we were given an introductory tour of the hospital, we rode the elevators. Riding the elevator was a novelty for some students. They squealed with delight when they felt the upward-going thrill in their stomachs. A physician entered the elevator and said he knew we were probies by the noise we made. How insulting. The thrill of riding an elevator wore off quickly when faced with the life and death issues of nursing.

At first all our time was spent in the classroom. After we had learned the basics of bed baths and temperature taking we were allowed to go to the wards to provide morning care for the patients. We pulled the screen around the patient bed to provide privacy. We took the basin from the bedside stand to the faucet and got warm water. First we washed the patient's face and then dried it. Next the neck and dried it; then we washed one arm and underarm, and dried it. Then the other arm, the chest, the abdomen, the thighs, the legs and the feet, and finally we asked him to roll over. If he was unable, we rolled him over on his side and washed his back. We rubbed his back with cocoa butter. Then we put the washcloth in his right hand and instructed him to "finish his bath." Occasionally the patient did not know there was still a part of him we had not touched.

My first assignment was on the surgical ward for men where four men shared the same room. Krego was assigned to take care of two and I took care of the other two. One of mine smoked a pipe. After I had bathed him, I got him up in a chair in the middle of the ward. I gave him his pipe and lit the tobacco for him. Then he needed his ashtray, but it was across the room. Krego's patient was not using his ashtray so she handed me his. It had not been cleaned. Just then an instructress entered the room and saw the dirty ashtray. In one big swoop she grabbed the dirty ashtray and my arm at the same time and dragged me to the utility room. She put a rag and a box of cleanser in my hands while she scolded me for the dirty ashtray. I was furious. I was twenty-four and very responsible, but she gave me no chance to say a word. Any incorrect action could result in the end of a beginning career. Upon completion of my term on Men's Surgical, she wrote on my report, "Takes criticism well."

Instructresses did not understand that some of us came with higher standards than they had themselves, so everything we did was questioned. They left nothing to the benefit of doubt.

HB had been a nurses' aide prior to becoming a student nurse. She had learned some shortcuts. I saw her bathing a patient whose wet arms were both exposed and extended upwards to HB. Both arms and her entire chest were wet and exposed at the same time. "How could she get by with it?" I thought. We had been instructed to respect the privacy of the patient by covering the naked part we were washing with a towel. Then we washed under the towel. HB did not, in fact, get by with it. She never graduated. Another student, SH, while a probie, tried to take a temperature and failed to notice the patient was dead. She did not graduate either.

The capping ceremony was postponed until five months had passed. I understood that we had been too slow a class to deserve being capped at four months. I do not recall being told specifically wherein we had lacked. But at last the capping date was set and twenty-two of us were capped while we knelt before the Director of Nursing, Miss Graham. Eight students had dropped out or had been dismissed. On the big day, we recited the Florence Nightingale Pledge:

I solemnly pledge myself before God and in the presence of this assembly,
To pass my life in purity and to practice my profession faithfully.
I will abstain from whatever is deleterious and mischievous, and will not knowingly administer any harmful drug.
I will do all in my power to elevate the standard of my profession, and will hold in confidence all matters committed to my keeping and all family affairs coming to my knowledge in the practice of my profession.
With loyalty will I endeavor to aid the physician in his work, and devote myself to the welfare of those committed to my care.

We concluded by singing a song together. Our class chose "Take my Life and Let It Be Consecrated, Lord, to Thee." Until that year each class had been asked to sing a song of its choosing. After we sang our song, it became the annual capping song. I felt proud because I had chosen the song.

Gradually we spent less time in the classroom and more time with patients. We gave medications, injections and learned to process physicians' orders. We were still giving "mustard plasters" on patient chests. Antibiotics now saved lives that ten years before might have ended with a bout of pneumonia.

We spent "blocks" of time working in the hospital with no time in the classroom. Sometimes we were in charge of a thirty bed ward on the evening or night shift. A night supervisor came regularly to see that we were in control of any situation that might arise. Sometimes we had blocks of time in the classroom only. Sometimes we had classes every second day and had to leave the ward to go to class. When we worked the night shift, it was difficult to get up in the middle of our "night" to go to class.

We worked in every department of the hospital, including "scrubbing" in surgery. We saw babies born and adults die. I saw a seventeen year old who lost his arm in a traffic accident. In emergency I saw the "dead on arrival." We stayed at the Vancouver General Hospital to take our Tuberculosis training. And for eight weeks, we took the bus daily to Essondale, the psychiatric hospital. Before today's drugs for the psychiatric needs of patients, there were few medications to treat the mentally ill. Electric shock treatment was still used and so was insulin shock.

One psychiatric patient expressed herself well in her constant recitation of the horrendous burdens she bore—the weight of the railroad tracks and the weight of the mountains. Another sang, year in and year out, "When the Red, Red Robin Comes Bob, Bob, Bobbin' Along." Sometimes we laughed when we didn't want to cry.

On our days off we liked to go home or to the beach. Because the small monthly allowance did not get us far, we hitchhiked in pairs, never alone. In our first year after our capping ceremony we were given eight dollars a month. The second year we were given ten and finally twelve in our third year. It was spending money for bus tickets home and for incidentals like tooth paste. Regular commuters on the Trans Canada Highway were accustomed to seeing young women from the four hospitals in Vancouver and New Westminster hitchhiking home, or back, from the Fraser Valley. We always got a ride. Only once were we a bit frightened when the men in the car were drinking beer and teased us about being in danger.

The sun drenched beaches at Ocean Park and White Rock drew us to the warm water on hot summer days. Alternately the water cooled us and the sun baked us on the sand. We went back to work with burning red or brown skin. To plead ill after a trip to the beach was not an acceptable excuse to take off sick. I never tried it. Sunburned, yes. But sick time, no.

Of the original thirty, eighteen students survived the rigorous studies, work and discipline. Four more had left after capping.

On January 21, 1955, exactly three years after our arrival, Sara and I, roommates for two and a half years, moved out of the McAllister dormitory to live in an upstairs apartment of a private home near the tracks and the Fraser River. We paid $45 per month rent and each had our own bedroom. We earned approximately $215 per month. We worked various shifts and did not want to disturb each other. We were within easy walking distance of the hospital. We looked forward to graduation exercises, which would be held after our final exams in April.

As a new nurse, one night I experienced an exceptionally tense eight-hour shift. A man of forty-three had been admitted to the ward with a bleeding stomach ulcer. All night long a doctor and we nurses worked with him to stop the excessive bleeding. We dripped blood into him hour after hour, hoping it would clot and seal the ulcer. The doctor tried to put a coagulant into his stomach. He expelled all the blood we poured into him. When I left at 7:30 A.M I felt grateful he was still alive. He told me he had had an ulcer a long time ago and was asked to abstain from liquor. Now he had drunk one beer.

Walking home after that night's duty, the morning sun glowed as I walked toward it. I felt rewarded for our efforts, knowing we had done the very best that we could do for this man. His life hung in the balances of life and death. I prayed the day shift could accomplish more. I told God the man was too young to die. I remembered the poem that had become meaningful to both Sara and me:

The Exhortation of the Dawn

Look to this day, for it is life, the very light of life.
In its brief course lie all the verities of your existence-
The bliss of growth, the splendor of beauty, the glory of action.
Yesterday was but a dream.
Tomorrow is a vision.
But today, well lived, makes every yesterday a dream of happiness
And every tomorrow a vision of success.
Look well therefore to this day.
This is the exhortation of the dawn. (by Kalidasa.)

When I returned to work the next time, I learned that the patient died after receiving over thirty pints of blood. Although he was older than I, I knew he had been taken out of this life in his prime and I grieved his loss.

The Class of 1955 A wrote the State Board Exams after we completed our three years of work. (Class of 1955 B would write their State Boards in summer). For two days we pored over fine print, choosing and marking the right answers to the many questions. Between subjects we were able to eat a late lunch. Then we returned to the classroom for more grueling hours of exams. My eyes strained and my abdomen cramped. The exams were stiff. It was the same exam that our American sisters in nursing were taking. The failure to pass even one exam meant failure to become a Registered Nurse. We knew we would have to wait weeks to hear about the results of the exams. We also knew that our futures depended on our success or failure in those exams.

At last we heard the rumor that the exam results for all the nursing schools in B.C. would appear in the next day's newspaper. We would not be notified individually.

I worked the night shift but would be off duty the following night. After sleeping a few hours, I took the city bus to downtown New Westminster and bought a newspaper. Columns of fine print covered the pages. I found the nurses' page. Then the K's. Yes! There it was: Klassen, and Krego, Koga and Krause. I found all of the eighteen names in my class. Pictures of us in uniform verified the reality of our success. We had all made it! That day we were registered nurses. I was jubilant. I even shared my joy with the stranger who stood beside me in the bus, even though it meant nothing to her.

My name in the paper that day meant everything to me. At first sight, it meant I had passed the big Registered Nurses' State Board exams. But it meant so much more than that. It meant an end to personal poverty. I had no money in the bank or in my pocket, but it meant that I had the means to earn a living for myself. Those prospects would raise me above the poverty level of mere subsistence; above working for minimum wages. The RN signature after my name and everything I charted gave me self esteem and assurance that I was no longer dependent on the mercy of others. I had not sought fame but value and self status in the world around me. I was no longer an immigrant child working in fields or in rich people's homes. There were choices I could make. I was now a full-fledged member of Canadian society. I would not be limited to minimum wages. I had learned a skill and was capable of serving humanity.

On the Greyhound bus back to Abbotsford, I felt exhilarated. I could barely wait to tell my mother at the end of the thirty-five mile bus trip home. She had silently cheered me on my long journey to gain an education through high school and nursing school. Dad was too incapacitated to comprehend that I had made the grade. At last I had attained my goal. I had an honorable profession.

My siblings were all married by now and had families. None of them were destitute any longer. The old gray house near Rush Lake, Saskatchewan still stood, uninhabited. I would later see the house from the road when I returned in the autumn of 1955. Its deterioration was in direct contrast to the family's growth and prosperity. From 1937, when we left this "Monument to Poverty," until my graduation in 1955, we had rarely seen the house. As my family and I gradually prospered, we were able to travel more and occasionally returned to the old home place. We were able to notice the house decay slowly over the decades. We sometimes stopped at the house and took pictures. Even the Hallmark Card company thought the old house worthy of a picture on one of its greeting cards. Some of the shingles of the roof blew away, the addition to the house collapsed and the farm buildings eventually disappeared. Bitter-sweet nostalgia struck me every time we visited, when I remembered my childhood in that house. It seemed fitting that the "monument" would disintegrate and disappear after our poverty was finally eliminated.

As indicated earlier, George and his wife Edith owned and operated a bakery in Cranbrook, BC. My sister, Nettie married John Redekop and farmed on our parents' former family farm in Manitoba. Annie had married Pete Peters. Lena was married to Pete's brother, John. Both couples farmed first in Manitoba and then in B.C. Both families raised raspberries and chickens near Abbotsford. Henry married Annie Peters and farmed at Winnipegosis, Manitoba, until retirement. Justine and Roy Speirs lived in Regina, Saskatchewan. They made a living owning and renting houses in Regina. Both also worked at jobs for salaries, in addition to real estate earnings. Canada had been very good to this immigrant family.

Pete and Annie with children visit. The summer kitchen still stands.

Our house in Rush Lake Saskatchewan 1929-1937
The Monument in 1977

The Monument to Poverty on its Knees. Farewell to Poverty.

Life After Graduation

After graduation in 1955, I worked at the Royal Columbian Hospital on Men's Medical Ward E until that fall. Working on a men's medical ward suited me just fine. The hospital had offered me a job in the Emergency Room or in the Communicable Disease Department, but I liked the supervisors in Men's Medical and chose to work there. While I had been in school, my friends and cousins were busy finding their life partners. Becoming a wife and mother had always been a cherished dream. But I wanted an education too. By the time I finished nurses' training, I discovered most of my peers were married and raising families. They continued doing so and I felt alone.

Before going out into the world to serve, I wanted to be grounded in my faith. I had been tested during my nursing experience and during my housekeeping in a Seventh Day Adventist home prior to that. So, when I left the Royal Columbian Hospital in 1955, I went to Winnipeg to attend Canadian Mennonite Bible College. It consisted of one large private home renovated to accommodate classrooms. The girls' dorm was a separate building, also a former private home. The city bus provided transportation to the college in the mornings and back to the dorm in the evenings. I remember that first autumn in Winnipeg and the huge trees along the college street. I still remember stepping down into those leaves—big, brown and crunchy—as they fell fast and thick. I wondered at the works of nature even in the big city.

In the dorm, we took turns cooking the evening meal for everyone. One very large table accommodated the eighteen women living in the dorm. Married students lived independently. And men lived in the college building. On the weekends and evenings the girls' dorm buzzed with activity while we were doing our laundry, cooking, and occasionally cleaning our rooms. There was always plenty of conversation. The enrollment of the college was about 100. Here I was not lonely.

Our classes were varied. We were taught Bible, of course, but studied various other subjects. We took Old Testament History, the History of Christianity, Mennonite History, Cults, Philosophy, Ethics, Apologetics, and How the Bible came into being. Here was a shocker! Human beings were writing the books of the Bible and choosing which writings qualified as Scripture and were suitable for inclusion in the final canon and which were not. My roommate, Irma Wiens, and I discussed this problematic revelation and decided to talk to the professor. He listened, but I can't remember a word he said. But I do know that I decided to trust the Holy Spirit to have guided the authors and the editors. Apologetics entered into my thinking also. What other religion or philosophy stood the test of truth better than the Christian faith?

In 1956, CMBC moved to a brand new college building located on Shaftesbury Boulevard on the outskirts of southwest Winnipeg. Now we ate our noon meals in the dining room with everyone else, and our main meal was prepared by a very capable cook. The library was huge. We had a nice chapel for our many meetings and programs. We produced dramas, which gave me a chance to act and direct a play. Music rooms sounded with piano lessons. We still took the bus to and from the women's dorm. But when a big snow storm left large snow banks, we had to trudge through them in the bitter cold. However, in contrast to my childhood deprivations, we were well protected now by overshoes on our feet, mittens and warm coats.

Our professors were all male, except our piano teacher, Esther Wiebe, wife of George Wiebe, from whom I took beginner lessons. These two were valuable members of the musical world at CMBC. History belonged to Mr. Lohrenz and Mr. Adrian. David Jansen, a much beloved Professor, was in trouble with the conference for being too modern. However, as students we were not fully aware of that. But I do remember him going to the blackboard in the beginning of a class and writing:

"I AM NOT A LIBERAL"

"I AM NOT A FUNDAMENTALIST"

"I AM A MENNONITE"

He did not say a word more to clarify what he meant. To be Liberal was always a negative, I had been taught. But how is a Fundamentalist different from a Mennonite? I had to wait many years to find some answers to that question.

While at college I sought help for the problem of eyestrain. The ophthalmologist gave me little comfort when he said I might find some relief after about age 45 when people begin holding their papers farther from their eyes to focus. Later I learned I also had astigmatism, and later yet, that I have dry eyes. Astigmatism is an irregular eyeball surface which makes it hard to focus. And dry eyes make the eyes feel constantly irritated. Consequently, I have lived with this affliction since I was twenty seven-years old.

During my second year at college I worked many weekends to pay for tuition and board and room. The St. Boniface Hospital had a place for me to work in the Post Surgery Recovery Room. The ward had only twelve beds of critically ill post-operative patients who needed more care than the general wards could provide. Today, I see it as a forerunner of critical care units. It was in this hospital I met my cousin Tina Buhler, a student nurse. I also met intern Corny Unruh, whom I met again in Jordan about a year later. The hospital offered me a job in post recovery, but I wanted to do something more useful than to stay in Winnipeg. I became part of a MCC unit during the summer of 1957. We lived in the college dorm until September, when the students came back to school. I worked in the Queen Elizabeth Hospital which, in spite of its royal name, was a nursing home. During this time I was preparing for my next MCC assignment.

For the previous ten years I had been consumed with getting an education. I also worked to pay for that education. Now I wanted to serve, and MCC offered me that first opportunity.

JORDAN

THE MENNONITE CENTRAL Committee needed a nurse in the Evangelical Hospital of Nablus, Jordan. Nablus is Shechem in the Bible and is the place where Jesus met the Samaritan woman at the well, which still exists. Samaritans still live at Nablus and worship in their temple.

The Evangelical Hospital had been staffed by two women from The Netherlands, one a physician and the other a nurse. They were leaving and MCC wanted to staff the hospital with me and Dr. Corny Unruh from Winnipeg. His wife, Katy, would be with him. As stated earlier, I had met Corny at the St. Boniface hospital in Winnipeg. The hospital needed a Matron and an instructress for student nurses. I told MCC, while still in Winnipeg, that I was not able to instruct because of my eye condition and did not have enough experience to be a matron. They wanted me to come anyway. They thought that foreign hospitals were often sub-standard and I would be fine. I was afraid, but thought with Corny and Katy being there, it could work out.

Corny and Katie came to Jordan a few weeks later than I did. I discovered that the physician the hospital had hired was an Arab man who had just returned from England after getting his Fellowship in surgery. An expert no less! And the Matron they had hired was a delightful 25 year old Arab girl who had just returned from the USA, where she had been on a Mennonite traineeship. Afifeh's strength came from having been trained in this very hospital where she knew EVERYTHING. It was a small hospital, in contrast to the big city hospital where I had trained. She was an expert in all departments. I never felt so useless before or after in my nursing career. Neither was I ever so lonesome in my life. Someone else was hired to teach, and the Matron herself became the scrub nurse. I was able to manage the ward. After seven months I asked for a transfer to Jerusalem.

Corny and Katy Unruh had come to Jerusalem a little earlier since he was never able to get his license to practice medicine in Jordan. He and Katy remained in Jerusalem, and we became very good friends. Corny worked in a Jerusalem hospital, but needed to ask a local physician to sign all his work. He and Katy lived in the MCC house located north of the city walls. And I came to join them after having lived in a large house in Nablus with Afifeh. Ernest and Mary Lehman were our hosts and leaders. This was "home", a center to all of the MCC workers and Pax boys working in Jordan. On weekends, MCC personnel converged from Amman, Jericho and Hebron to be "home" at every opportunity they had. This was our family. There were seventeen MCC staff and Pax fellows in the family. This number changed as members came and went.

Living in "the Holy Land" for two years had sounded very attractive. Geographical places printed on the pages of the Bible became actual soil and meant interacting with real people. The hospital where I worked, Spafford Memorial Hospital, was named after Horatio Spafford, the author of the lyrics to the hymn, "It is well with my Soul," and survivor of the Titanic shipwreck. His 80 year old daughter still had ties to the hospital while she lived in the USA, where she actively solicited money for Spafford Memorial. I met her at the hospital once while she was visiting.

The hospital was staffed by an Arab Muslim physician, who visited at least once a week. The matron, the lab technician and three nurses were Armenian women. The matron gave me a project which made my work meaningful. My job was to keep a little boy, Saleh, alive and to nurse him back to health. He was born to a family of several girls and being Arabs, the family wanted a boy. Their wish was fulfilled, but the mother appeared to be middle-aged and was ailing of a heart condition. She was unable to take care of Saleh and probably had no milk. At five months old he weighed seven pounds. He looked old and his little buttocks were flat instead of the round little buns I was used to seeing in Canada. His face, arms and legs were equally emaciated. He was unable to keep milk in his stomach and therefore would die before long if no one intervened.

Not having seen anything like this in my nursing career, I had no idea how to treat him. But the Matron did; instructions were to give him a teaspoon of weak tea frequently to establish adequate hydration. It was a simple prescription, but what about calories? His stomach couldn't handle calories. Teaspoon by teaspoon was poured into this little being, both day and night, by whoever was on staff. When he was able to keep the tea down, we experimented with giving him a teaspoon of milk at a time. Very gradually he was able to digest milk and then semi solids. When he was no longer in danger, the matron hinted freely that MCC personnel take him home and take care of him. Dr. Corny and Katy Unruh, RN, were capable and willing to nurture him until he could be released to his family. Little Saleh was very dear to me and leaving him in the hands of different caregivers was something I had not planned for. In my heart, he was my son. His mother had died and although his father wanted him, he was unable to care for him. The last I knew of Saleh was that he had come to the USA.

In another situation a baby girl had been admitted to the hospital. She too was malnourished and needed help. She was a twin to a boy. She had beautiful natural curly black hair and became somewhat of a nurse aide's sweetheart. She too thrived and eventually went home. But months later her mother returned with her. I did not recognize her. Alice, the aide, burst out with, "Miss Tina, do you know who this is?" Unkempt and starving, the child whimpered when a nurse tried to give her intravenous fluids. Her veins were small and collapsed. The mother had milk for only one twin and had let the girl deteriorate until it was too late for us to help.

All too often these little patients were admitted with a diagnosis of gastroenteritis, which meant diarrhea and vomiting, accompanied by malnutrition. Another diagnosis was parasites, which was often deliberately misdiagnosed as appendicitis and followed by surgery, because surgery was financially more beneficial to the physician. A dose of medicine would have been effective for what ailed them.

Mahdiyeh, an aide and a Muslim of 17, told me her own story. She spoke English well, although some of the aides were not as fluent. Mahdiyeh was the oldest of her family but had a younger brother and two younger sisters living at the Mennonite orphanage in Hebron. Their mother also lived in Hebron. Their father had left them to live with his second wife in another village some miles north of Amman. The second wife was pregnant and about to deliver when Mahdiyeh was 12. She became her stepmother's helper before and after her delivery. One day the stepmother gave her some money and sent her to get some groceries. But before Mahdiyeh left, she heard her father making a deal with a man in the next room of the house. Her father would permit this man, who was about her father's age, to marry his 12 year old daughter. She did not say what her father would receive in exchange. But she exclaimed, "He had only one eye and he was my father's age!" She could not allow her father to do this to her. So she took the money her stepmother had given her and went to town to take the bus to Amman, to her uncle's house and to safety.

Later, she returned to Hebron and worked at the hospital. Before I left, she gave me a lovely photo of herself and her young cousin in Amman to whom she was engaged to marry. He was a handsome young man and she was happy. Her siblings were in the orphanage for safekeeping lest they fall into the hands of her father. She was grateful that a "religion" like the Mennonites had helped her family when her own religion did not.

Jordan proved to be a difficult place to work for many of us. I think of Corny being unable to get his physician's license, Leron and Wilbur with a problematic agricultural situation, my need to leave Nablus, and Wayne having to leave Jordan. Married couples seemed to fare better. Katy could support Corny. Bob and Virginia Lapham, formerly with MCC, now served with Church World United. Virginia established a baby clinic in Hebron, weighing infants so mothers could see progress while learning how to feed their babies powdered milk.

During our two years in Jordan we visited many of the places mentioned in the Bible. We saw the Dead Sea which did not let us sink into its salty water. We discovered that Jericho is really hot in summer time because of its low altitude and Jerusalem is relatively cool because of its elevation. Some of us walked the approximately eleven miles across country from Jerusalem to Jericho. We became familiar with the hills and valleys and the rocks and dirt. We slept in sleeping bags under the clear sky of Damascus. We visited Petra in the desert and saw the hewn out rooms on the sides of the rocky gorge where there are still "high places" (altars of sacrifice). We saw Solomon's stables under the former temple; we walked through Hezekiah's tunnels into Jerusalem, which were used during the time of siege. We visited the Garden of Gethsemane, the Mount of Olives, the Place of the Skull in Jerusalem, and the hills of Bethlehem where we ate roasted lamb in a cave on Christmas Eve. We saw so much more than the tourist sees in a few days.

Tourist guides took us to the Bible places so dear to Christendom and our hearts were thrilled. However, beneath all the beauty of these famous places, the MCC workers saw something more than the "Holy Land." We met the poor who were unable to get an education and therefore could not attain a decent living. For these, the future was uncertain. The Bedouins lived in tents, sometimes far from water for cooking and sanitation. Parasites plagued the population. Sanitation for the poor was often not available. In the hospital I saw it all: dirt, poverty, lice, worms, ignorance, and lack of adequate clothing. The land did not feel holy and I wondered how it felt for God to come in person to this troubled part of the world.

We volunteer workers were able to return to North America to work and to thrive. But part of us remains in Jordan where the need is great. We served our terms, but what difference did we make to those we served? In a nutshell, I would say we learned more from our experience than they benefited by us having been there. I came home in December 1959. I had no money but my future looked bright. My thoughts were turning back to Canada, the country I loved. My passport was Canadian, as was my nurses' registration. It was Canada that provided all my memories. But it was also where my parents were refugees. We had been poor and needy, but poverty is relative. This was where I had once been the poor child with little more than a dress of seven scraps. To this day I make comforters for the needy and remember the multicolored dress on a little patient, which was made of seven different scraps of fabric.

EPILOGUE
PART I

REFLECTIONS ON MY PARENTS

DAD

WHO WAS THIS silent man under his short, heavy frame? He measured only five feet and five inches tall when I knew him, and I knew him only as an old man. How tall was he really before his back stooped? And before a roof fell on him in Russia that crippled his hip? How tall was he before World War I and the Russian Revolution? And before his defeat in his battle with Saskatchewan's dust storms and depression? Or before he was himself depressed?

Dad was forty-two when I was born. He was probably forty-four or forty-five before I recall memories of him. His big, work-worn hands and bunioned feet told me he was strong. The way he hoisted the hundred pound sack of flour or sugar from the wagon on his humped back and carried it up a full flight of stairs at Rush Lake reinforced my image of his strength. With a sigh he plunked it down on the floor of the junk room that held our few possessions. After the task was done he came downstairs to reward himself with a home-rolled cigarette.

As a little girl I watched him often while he sat at the kitchen table on a straight-backed chair and rolled these little sparks of pleasure. Taking a pinch of tobacco from a round tin can, he placed it on a very thin piece of cigarette paper and spread it along one side of the paper. He used his thumb and forefingers to roll the paper around the tobacco to shape a cigarette. Then he raised the cigarette to his lips to lick the loose side of the paper with his tongue. Now he pressed the wet edge along the full length of cigarette to seal the tobacco into a tiny roll. He rolled enough cigarettes at one sitting to last him several days. Now he was ready to smoke.

He put the end of the cigarette between his lips and with a cigarette lighter from his pocket he lit the other end. He drew and he puffed until the cigarette glowed with burning tobacco. Ah, the sweet aroma of fresh tobacco as the smoke wafted and curled over his head! A look of contentment on Dad's face translated to me a feeling of well-being in the midst of poverty. Dad held his cigarettes between his thumb and right forefinger. I had seen other smokers hold their cigarettes between the forefinger and middle finger, which looked much more sophisticated. I wished Dad had held his that way. I tried to light straws of grain in the grate of the kitchen stove but without tobacco in them the fire went out as soon as I withdrew them from the grate. Dad's cigarette would burn shorter and shorter until it almost reached his lips. He would then remove it and crush it in a saucer. But he saved the butts, Henry says. When Dad accumulated a certain amount, he took the paper off and used the stubs of tobacco to roll new smokes.

In 1994 I learned from Cousin George Unger that Mr. Harms ordered a cheap brand of tobacco especially for Dad, and kept it in the back of the store. Art Harms had shared this information with George when they were boys, snooping around.

We were unaware of the stale odor that pervaded the whole house. No doubt the many cracks in window and door frames allowed enough fresh air into the house to defuse the odor. Mother complained that we had no money but there was always money for tobacco. Dad argued that smoking was the only pleasure he had. He did not approve of smoking himself. He promised George a golden watch if he never started to smoke. What deterred George was not the empty promise of a golden watch. He tried to smoke and the smoking made him very ill.

Mother's complaint was validated one day when Dad reached into his pants pocket and pulled out three Canadian pennies. "That's all I have!" he exclaimed. Someone in the family suggested cheerfully that he could buy a three cent postage stamp to mail a letter. Dad was not comforted.

I remember how Dad's poor vision plagued him. He told us of the days he spent in the darkness of a bedroom when he was only eight years old. Dad was extremely nearsighted and his gray eyes were very sensitive to the glare of sun and snow. The dark room would have given only temporary relief. In today's world he would have glasses to fit, and sunglasses for the glare, enriching his life. As it was he had not completed grade school. He could not find lost animals. He could not see the tracks of a drill when looking in the direction of the sun. His reading was limited to the Bible and the *Rundschau* although Mother usually read from the latter. He was barely literate.

His vision and his ability to trust that poor vision were tested one dark night when he led a horse either through the pasture or on a country road. The fear on his face and the rapidity of his words, when he burst through the door that night, were unmistakable. Never had we seen him so frightened. He prefaced the telling of his visual experience by saying we must tell no one what he was about to tell us. Then he told us about unexplainable lights he had seen on the road. The lights were as tall as a man. He thought they had writing on them but when he walked towards the lights to read them he could not see well enough to be sure there was writing on them. Together he and Mother pondered aloud whether perhaps God was trying to tell them something. Long after he experienced this unusual sight an article in a Saskatchewan newspaper said many people had seen the same kind of lights at that time, and no one could explain them. Unfortunately the news item appeared fifty years too late to alleviate Dad's doubts about his sanity.

It was with awe one day that we witnessed the one occasion when Dad was playful. Only once can I recall that he played with one of his children and Justine was the lucky one. He took her hands and played Ring Around a Rosie. He played it with such gusto that when he fell down, like the song suggests, he fell on his seat and exaggerated the fall by throwing his feet into the air.

One other time he voiced pleasure with Justine when she sang "Bobby Shafto" from her perch on the wooden kitchen bench. He enjoyed music and recognized bad music. Hers was good and mine was bad. Like Mother, I could not hold a tune.

Dad survived the eight years of drought, climaxed by the green army worms that ended his farming in Saskatchewan. But he had courage to start over in Manitoba. It would give him another chance to succeed. He did succeed in raising our standard of living.

He made a great attempt to break the smoking habit. Neither the Manitoba church nor the West Abbotsford church condoned smoking. He felt the disapproval. He struggled. It was incredibly difficult for him to stop, but he succeeded at last. He never smoked again. Once he was rid of the habit, he detested it in others.

The flip side of the coin was that he gained weight. Weight had never been a problem while he smoked. He became obese. He had to work harder to walk, to carry wood to fuel the stove, and to just breathe. He had no understanding about what foods made him fat. He loved fatty meat, fat-fried potatoes, bread, pasta and cookies. He did not like vegetables. The forgetfulness we had noted in Manitoba became worse. He forgot the words he was trying to say. His lungs were not providing his brain with enough oxygen. I could not find a radial (wrist) pulse. He coughed, spit and panted.

Dad often spent his time at the kitchen table with his head bent over the Bible, trying to understand the words. And just as often he sat there tapping the table with his fingers, driving Mother crazy. When he wasn't at the table, he lay on the couch napping and moaning while he rested. He brought in firewood for as long as he possibly could, but it took all the breath he had.

For the first few years in B.C., I was the only child living with or near them. I believed they needed me nearby. But Lena and John with their first four children moved to B.C. during this time and I felt free to leave. At some point when Dad was quite senile, he said I should always stay with Mother. He would not be here very long and she needed me. I considered him incompetent at this time and I thought, "Dad, you got married and lived your life. I need to do the same."

After 1955 I never lived at home again. Actually, I left in 1952 but came home on my days off. Lena wrote to me in Winnipeg that Dad had dreamed he heard angels singing. He wanted to die. When Ray and I came home for New Year's Day in 1960, Dad did not know me. He had deteriorated. Seven months later he died. Apparently it was a stroke accompanied by pneumonia. Mother took care of him to the end. He was seventy-five.

I asked, "Who was this silent man who didn't know me, and whom I felt I hardly knew? Who was this man with whom I rarely had a conversation?" Dad had usually removed himself from our childish endeavors and entered his quiet world of smoke and thought. He had not built relationships with us. He was an Old Country father who was always preoccupied with trying to pull himself out of poverty.

But I remembered the occasional simple philosophies he verbalized. When we were children I remember him telling Mother "Let us not blame one another for a breakage. To know one has broken it is enough punishment." Or to me he said, "A girl does not need an education," when I was twenty and wanted to go to school. When I was doing housework in Vancouver to earn money to go to school, he remarked, "I don't like to see you in a position of having to clean up after rich people." About farming and business he said, "A man needs to be his own boss. In working for wages he makes money for the owner and not for himself." These were little gems uttered in an often gray world of poverty and depression.

What kind of man would Dad have been if World War I had not strode into his home and life in 1914? What if he had not been pulled up by his roots because of the Russian Revolution or had not been sandblasted by the dust storms of Saskatchewan's winds? George called Dad a "gay-blade" in Russia when he was young. He and Mother had fun quadrilling and playing *Mensch Aerger Dich Nicht* with a passion.

So how tall a man was he? He was tall enough to take responsibility, to work hard, to persevere, to have a conscience, to have faith in God and in the Bible, to believe in freedom of speech and religion, and to appreciate the good government in Canada. Underneath his silence and withdrawal, we knew he wanted what was best for us in his Old Country way. He lived long enough to see that each of his children lived with the values that he and Mother had instilled in them. Underneath his bent frame and quiet demeanor, there stood a man, straight and tall.

MOTHER

We did not have to ask who our mother was. She had given birth to us and nursed us. We knew her well. She spoke what she thought and sang what she felt. She was verbal enough, but did we understand her?

Could we put ourselves in Mother's position in Saskatchewan? She lived in an old, ugly house. In winter it was cold. She had inadequate fuel to keep herself and her family warm. In summer the dust blew into the house and left layers of grit on the window sills. When the windows were open the flies swarmed in. How did the dreariness of the unadorned house affect her? The old plaster walls were never painted in the eight years we lived there. She had no money to change anything.

Imagine trying to feed a family without meat. She was not a vegetarian, and would not have had enough vegetables if she had been. She made many meatless meals. Because of the drought, the garden had to be watered by hand from barrels. When eggs in the cellar were no longer fresh, she had to cook without eggs. How could she make noodles or roll-kuchen? When she had no fresh produce, what were her options? How did it feel when the fuel was dry cow dung which produced smoke? And even the cow chips had been picked from another farmer's pasture.

How must she have felt when her daughters had only one dress? She enjoyed sewing but how could creativity be nurtured when she had no means with which to buy fabric and thread? How did it feel to use only one or two towels for eight or nine people? How did she adjust to seeing us in less than clean clothes because we lacked clothes and water?

From visiting cousin, Nettie Peters, I learned something about dirt and clothes when she stayed with us while our parents went to Manitoba to visit. We were five and six years old. While we played outside, Nettie scooped up some dirt into her upturned skirt. When her skirt was full of dirt, she lowered the hem and let the dirt slide out. I warned, "You are soiling your skirt." She replied, "That's the idea. Then I get to wear a clean dress." This was a novel idea but it would not have been tolerated in our family.

Being cut off from family and friends in Russia was difficult. Mother was without a church. How did she keep faith when there was little to encourage faith? We know she had a song to sing for every mood. She expressed her sorrow and her thoughts in the words of the songs she had learned in church and school. She developed some philosophies that helped her cope. She adjusted, although with difficulty.

She learned something about the loss of young children when her oldest two died in Russia. Her grief had been overwhelming at the time, but after experiencing the war and revolution in Russia, and the poverty in Saskatchewan, she said she was glad they had died. They had been spared the devastating poverty. They were happy in heaven. She said, "Parents who lose their children to death, need not cry. But one has ample reason to cry for children who lose their parents." She may have thinking of her sister Margaret Paul's children who were left orphans after their parents died.

She also had an opinion about gender preferences in newborns. She had little sympathy for a Rush Lake woman who complained about giving birth to another baby of the same sex. Mother simply said, "God determines what we get. We must be grateful as long as the child is healthy."

Other philosophies were expressed in proverbs: "Der Kluegste gibt nach." (The smartest one gives in.) This translated to an attitude of "peace at all costs." Our parents had few quarrels to settle among their children. We were pacifists before we knew what the word meant. "Wer einmal luegt, den glaubt man nicht." (He who lies once will not be believed again.) "It is not a shame to be poor, but it is a shame to be lazy and dirty." Sometimes poverty led to dirty. When a cat squealed when Mother accidentally stepped on its toes, she said, "Put your shoes on." When she pulled feathers from the breast of a duck, she said, "It doesn't hurt me a bit." Yet she scoffed at the woman who said, "If it doesn't burn me, I will not blow the burn."

Mother was not overly sensitive. But she was capable of sensitivity as demonstrated on Christmas Eve when she prepared me for the next morning's gift in the form of a tin car. I remember the affection in her face and heard the tenderness in her voice when she held Justine on her knee and said, "Justine will always stay with us. She will never leave us."

When I was a preschool child, Mother wanted to take a nap. She told me to wake her up when the hand on the clock reached a certain number. I watched the clock. Five minutes until the appointed time, I went to her bedside to tell her, "You have five minutes left." Of course I woke her up. I remember this only because she saw the humor in it and reported it to someone within my hearing.

We called our parents "Ma" and "Pa." The "a" was not said as in "mat" or "pat" nor was it "Maw" and Paw". It was sounded as in "Ha, ha" or as in Vietnam. Mother was comfortable in her maternal role. Ma and Pa did not quarrel. Mother's rare gripe was about his smoking, and his worst insult was to say, "What's for dinner?" when he did not like a meal. She had to improvise as she did when she put sauerkraut into borsch because she had no cabbage left.

In Saskatchewan we saw a part of Mother that was not as noticeable in Manitoba—irritability. But she knew exactly why she had been irritable as evidenced later when responding to George's statement made in B.C., "Mother, you aren't as irritable as you used to be." Emphatically she said, "George, are you surprised? We were so desperately poor." And she was right.

She did the best she could with what she had and we understood that.

In Manitoba she had what was essential to life after the first year. Now she was not as irritable. She had been slim until now but in Manitoba she gained weight as we prospered. She was happier. She laughed until her round belly shook. The church gave her the social life she had craved. She was able to buy the fabric she needed. She enjoyed sewing, knitting and crocheting. She also liked gardening. Manitoba's long summer days and fertile soils produced excellent gardens. She no longer worried about what she had to make a meal with.

Mother was happy in B.C. My parents lived within walking distance of the store and the church. They needed little else. They had no car. The house they built cost about $1,000 for materials I think, and the labor was free, but she liked it. They received old-age pension at sixty-five. So Mother had to wait for five years before she was eligible. They had no financial worries because they were satisfied with very little.

In spite of the fact that I lived at home and was not self supporting while I went to the Mennonite Educational Institute, I felt Mother's approval about getting an education. The evening before I left for nursing school she asked me to pray with her. This was a first, and I was uncomfortable. I was used to praying in English. She prayed that I might be "bewahrt" (preserved) in a secular environment. But I think she was looking for a companion to replace Dad. He was becoming increasingly more senile and she no longer found companionship in him. Mother had become his caretaker and, although Mother was strong, being the caretaker took its toll.

In July, 1960, Dad died at home. He was seventy-five and she was seventy-two.

When we left her after the funeral she seemed like a tired old woman. She stood in the yard with a shawl over her head, a dress that was too long, her hands folded at her waist, and a sad and weary look on her face. What did she have to look forward to?

Four years later we went to her wedding. She was marrying Diedrich Braun. I had never met him. Now she wore a hat, a new dress, and a happy face.

Diedrich Braun had been widowed twice before they were married. He had come to see her earlier, seeking her hand in marriage. She said, "No." She did not want to remarry. But she felt guilty for turning him down. She believed the Lord had directed him to her. Either Pete and Annie, or Lena and John, took her for a ride past his place at Aldergrove. He had seen her ride by his place and he came to see her again. This time she consented. They did not know each other but both of them had a good reputation.

Mother sold her property on Townline Road and he sold his at Aldergrove. Together they bought a house in Clearbrook. For the first time in Canada, Mother lived in a nice house. She wanted for nothing. Mother said the marriage was better than the first. For five years they lived happily together. Mr. Braun's first wife bore him children. His second wife raised the children. Mother had no major responsibilities.

The carefree circumstances of this marriage suited both of them well. He had a car and could drive wherever they desired. He was quite deaf but she could visit well. He could hear her at least. He was proud of her and she was happy with the life he provided her.

In the summer of 1969, Mother did not feel well. In autumn the doctor found a mass in her abdomen. In surgery they found colon cancer that they did not remove. George had died of the same problem a year and a half earlier. We saw her in the hospital in September when we were in B.C. for Vernon Peters' and Arlene Vogt's wedding. She came to the wedding, but she returned to the hospital after the wedding.

When we went to say good-bye to her she sat on the edge of her bed facing the window. She did not see us arrive but I heard her moan with pain. She explained that the pain felt like labor pains without periods of relief. I asked the nurse for a pain killer and was disappointed when she gave me a codeine tablet to give to Mother. I suggested Demerol. I do not know whether it was ordered. We left her with her pain. I wanted very much to stay behind to sit with her day and night to take care of her. I wanted to relieve the pain. But our daughters were eight and six. They needed me.

She died a month later, on October 21, 1969. Diedrich Braun loved her so much, he said he would like to have her body preserved and put in a cabinet in the living room. She was buried in the cemetery beside Dad.

EPILOGUE
PART II

Ray and I and our Children

I FIRST MET Ray Kauffman, my future husband, at an MCC (Mennonite Central Committee) orientation in Akron, PA, in November 1957. He was on staff there going on two years, and was also headed overseas. I wanted to buy a new camera to take with me to Jordan. Another MCCer, Stan Yake, offered to make the purchase for me. When he brought it back to the MCC main house and we were tinkering with it after a meal, I noticed that Ray went out of his way to stay and help me learn how to use the camera. Later I discovered he was more interested in me than the camera. However after inquiring, I found out that he was an OM (Old Mennonite) and I being a GC (General Conference Mennonite) wasn't very interested in striking up a romance. My knowledge of OMs was mostly hearsay; I had had little exposure to them in Canada. I imagined him in a plain suit (conservative dress) and holding to traditions that were not a part of my faith. However, that proved not to be the case.

While I served in Jordan, Ray served in Europe for two years, during which time he came to the Middle East twice, and we corresponded. We married in Germany in November, 1959, at the conclusion of our terms. We settled in his home state of Oregon and have spent over 50 years here. Nursing part time was my occupation while Ray taught in Albany high schools. We both retired in 1990. We are both active in the Albany Mennonite Church.

Our daughters, Pat and Lynette, were born and raised in Oregon. They remained in Oregon, except for several years of college out of state, until they married. Then both moved away with their husbands, Wayne Stutzman, and Brian Plank, and live in Idaho and Pennsylvania, respectively. Our one and only grandchild is Nathan Plank.

Appendix I

NAMES

WHEN I FIRST came to the Lebanon Hospital in 1960, I worked in the obstetrics department on the night shift. Ray and I were planning to have a family and I was interested in names. What names were young parents giving their newborn babies? What would we name our own?

In the labor rooms I monitored the progress of the young women. At the right time we called the physician while two nurses wheeled the expectant mother to the delivery room and readied the room for imminent delivery. Eagerly we watched for the little jewel to make his debut into the world. Anxiously we waited for his first breath and his first cry. After that first big howl, we ourselves remembered to take our next breath. I was the nurse who wrapped the baby in a warm blanket and whisked the bundle to the nursery where I bathed, weighed and measured him. I wrapped him up again and lay him in the plastic, transparent bassinet. I wrote his surname on a card and immediately slipped it between the bassinet wall and the mattress. When the parents chose first and middle names, we recorded them in a hospital records book. On less busy nights, I read all the names of the babies born recently.

Harold Wayne Stutzman was born six weeks after I came to Lebanon. I noted the name "Harold" and wondered if the name was a fad. I did not know his mother. Twenty-one years later he married our daughter, Pat. His mother remembered me. I had given our future son-in-law his first bath. The little card with "Stutzman" on it was written in my handwriting. The name Harold was not a fad in 1960. "Wayne" may have been. That is the name he uses. His paternal grandfather was Harold Stutzman and the name had meaning to his family.

I recall the first time I witnessed the revival of the name "Tina." The only "Tinas" I knew were all either born in Russia or they were daughters of people from Russia. It was a very German ethnic name in Russia. In 1960 and 1961 it was a fad name. I was astounded that this Old Country name was so frequently attached to these helpless newborn babies in the U.S.A. "Tina Marie" was my favorite combination. My name was simply Tina. But my name had meaning. Did theirs? Was it just a cute name to the parents? These parents had no ties with Russia or with Catherine the Great. Was she the reason there were so many Tinas? I did not know the answer to that but I knew Mother and Dad each had a sister by the name Katharina. We called them both "Tante Tin." Undoubtedly they were called Tina in their earlier years. Uncle Peter's wife was named Tina and so was Uncle Jakob Unger's second wife.

In German the "h" is silent when it follows 't' and the "r" is rolled. It is pronounced Katarina. That has four syllables, and so most Katharinas became Tina as children, and Teen, Treen or Tinchi, as they grew older. Mother used all these names to address me. Afraid of having missed any nicknames, she also called me Katie or the Russian "Katya." The names were all acceptable to me but there were entirely too many Tinas in our ethnic circle. It was as common as Mary and Martha.

When Dad registered my birth he must have been weary of registering children. Did he not tell the registrant that my full name should have been Katharina? Or perhaps his inability to communicate in English was the reason I do not have a complete name. Consequently, it has always been Tina, a diminutive of Katharina. No one was given a middle name then.

At the time of my graduation from nursing school, each new graduate's name was called slowly and clearly to come to receive her diploma. How elegant to hear "Patricia Elaine Barkley." How plain it was to hear "Tina Klassen." It sounded clipped and abbreviated, as though I were not quite worthy of more syllables in my name. My Old Country ties showed up again. But I became a registered nurse in my own right, as legitimately as any of my classmates who had beautiful or even graceful names.

In my parents' culture as in most cultures, it was important to know to which family a child belonged. They had a system for identifying children, which was that children were identified by using their father's name. I, for instance, was Gerhard Klassen's Tina. In a few families where the fathers were brothers and they named a daughter after their paternal grandmother, the girls, too, were informally called in a similar manner, e.g., Mary Jake Buhler or Mary Ben Buhler. The boys used their father's first name initial for their middle name when they grew up.

My brother George's name was not the English 'George' that he became in Canada. His given name was Gerhard, after our father, Gerhard Klassen. Dad's father's name had been Gerhard. Dad went by Gerhard all his life and used G. for his middle initial to indicate who his father had been. Dad was the fifth male child to be born to his parents, yet he was named after his father.

Dad's oldest brother's name was David, because his maternal grandfather was David Loewen. Sometimes naming a child after a grandparent was more important than naming it after its parents. David's initial would have been G. for his father. Dad's next oldest brother was Abram. We did not learn to know our paternal grandparents' siblings, so we don't know where the name comes from. He, too, would use G. for his middle initial. The third and fourth sons were named Gerhard after their father, but they died four and three weeks after birth. The parents still wanted a namesake when Dad was born. He survived and bore his father's name.

The Gerhard story continues. Dad married Mother in 1911. When their first son was born, he was named Gerhard after his father, grandfather and great-grandfather. He was a year old when he died in 1915. But Mother was pregnant with their second son. When he was born in July of the same year, they named him Gerhard. The name Gerhard was used as long as they lived in Russia, but it became George as soon as they came to Canada in 1925. But when the family became naturalized citizens in 1931, Dad still registered him as Gerhard. In English he was George, in Low German he was Yiet, in High German he remained Gerhard, and occasionally he was called Yehor. I am guessing that Yehor is Russian.

Our maternal Grandmother's name was Helena. Consequently, all of her surviving children named one of their daughters Helena. The "e" in German can sound "e" as in egg or "igh" as in "night." Our parents' first daughter was called Helena, but she also died, in 1915. This time our parents shelved the name.

Their second daughter was named Aganetha, but the "e" sounds "igh", and the "h" is silent, so the name is sounded "Aganighta." In Canada she became Nettie. Mother had a sister Aganetha. We called her Tante Nighta, mother of Jake Harms and Tena Neufeld.

Then came Annie who was named after Mother, whose name was not Annie, but Anna. Mother appears to have been named after her father's sister. Our sister Annie was called Nyut, as in Newt. It comes from the Russian Anyuta. We simply dropped the first and last letters of her name. We moved from Saskatchewan to Manitoba on her eighteenth birthday and she requested her family to drop the Nyut and to please call her Annie.

Next, our parents used the name they had shelved for ten years. Lena was given the beautiful name of both her grandmothers, Helena. We called her Lighna in German, and Lena in English. Many Helenas became Helens in Canada.

Justine was named after Mother's sister, Justina (Unger) Harms who had assisted with her birth. She, in turn, had been named after her maternal Grandmother Justina (Driedger) Nikkel, who was born in 1815. The "J" in German sounds like an English "Y" so she was Yustine.

Only Henry, or Heinrich in German, was not named after anyone. Relatives expected our parents to name him Peter after his maternal grandfather, Peter Unger. Mother said she refused to do so because his name would have been Peter Klassen. There was another Peter Klassen in the village of Grigorjewka, who was retarded. She chose Heinrich and was accused of naming him after Dad's deceased half-brother, Heinrich Schroeder. He had been killed while serving with the Russian army.

Having a child named after a relative was an honor. Therefore the names were used over and over. Mother and Dad honored both of their mothers, one of their fathers, four aunts and uncles, and themselves. If they had had more children they could have honored siblings Jakob, David, Abram, Maria, Margaretha, Elizabeth, Susanna, Johann, Kornelius, Julius and Franz.

Dad's mother had given birth to sixteen children from three husbands. Mother's parents had twelve. I am sure they were glad when their biological clocks stopped at last.

Ray and I named our daughters Patricia Sue and Lynette Rene, after no one in particular. Should we have been more mindful of our families' histories?

APPENDIX II

LETTERS

LETTER TO
PETER UNGER IN GERMANY FROM HIS
PARENTS IN RUSSIA

(While Peter the younger was enroute from North America to Russia)
Grigorjewka, Charkow
May 8, 1921

Dear Children, Peter and Tina,

Hearty Greetings! We received your letters on April 28, all three at the same time. I was just on the street preparing to leave home when M, A and G (their children) called after me, raising their letters high. "From Peter and Tina!" What a joy!

Now we know you are already in Germany. People get ideas but God carries out his plans. Did you not receive our last two letters? We sent them along with a speculator. Peter, you raise the question about whether we use stamps here. Money is worth less than nothing. We are sending this letter along to Charkow with a speculator. He promised you will receive it.

According to your letter you will arrive here after the sun has climbed higher. We would be happy to see you before the harvest, in spite of the fact that we don't have much to live on. All we have is the home place, fifteen acres across the tracks and four acres with the well on it. On the other side of the village they are building the third row of dwellings; the Russians have divided up the remaining land. We have only limited horse power, as I wrote you in the last letter. Up until now we had a German servant but he wants to quit. He wants to go to Germany too. We gave him a sack of wheat as wages from May to August.

In Bessarabia they have received many letters from Germany. Peter, don't get the idea it's great over here. You probably won't be able to do any mission work over here, but then again, I don't know. They are having a tent crusade in Padonoka. What shall I write? I can't write anything good and dare not write anything bad.

Are you going to come pretty soon? When you do we'll have lots to talk about. H has been fired as Kontorist and is now living with us. N is living with her mother-in-law. They are working the land and are taxed 25%. JP would be quite well off except they have seven kids plus an extra one (their orphaned nephew, Heinrich Pauls) and they too, are taxed heavily.

Gerhard Klassen and Warkentin—(author's Dad and Uncle Vahng)—live on the other end of the village. They are very poor. Last year they did not sow much. They did not have enough feed or firewood, so we helped them out. Now we are without feed, without straw for bedding, without corn: everything.

GK is still walking on crutches. January 12 we had the biggest snow storm on record. The roof fell on top of him and he is still sick even though he has been to the doctor twice. They thought he was dead. When the village heard about it, everyone came and cleaned up his stuff. (Dad's hip was fractured and was never set correctly. Author's addition.)

Last week a lot of people went to Molotschna to buy bread. A lot of people from Ignatiew went too. There was still a lot of wheat there, but now they (Russian government?) are taking everything including ours. They are taking all kind of things along for barter. For a pound of spray (for trees—George Unger's parenthesis) they receive a sack of wheat. Gerhard brought home 26 sacks of wheat and four pounds (? probably should be the Russian 'pud' or 'pod'; one pud equals about 36 pounds) of flour. Maybe that will last him until harvest time. He has sown only four acres of which he has to give a bunch to his mother.

Recently we received a letter from Jakob (son). He is working for the government. He wants to come here too. We received a letter from (daughter) Tina in Arkadak. They are very poor. Things look pretty grim. We have very little clothing, which is expensive. For a pound of sugar we have to pay two pounds of butter. When you come, be sure to take along enough food for the trip.

From your parents, Peter Ungers

A LETTER FROM
JAKOB UNGER IN SIBERIA (UNCLE TO THE AUTHOR, TINA KAUFFMAN) TO HIS PARENTS, PETER AND HELENA UNGER, AND JACOB'S SEVEN SIBLINGS IN CANADA

The 10th of September, 1933
Will mail the letter the 18th of September.

Dearest Parents and Siblings all!

Since we, dear parents, received your letter of July 23 a few days ago, (Also received one from Peter), I visit with you today, Sunday, in spirit, with all of you so far away.

Have written to Peter. (his brother in Saskatchewan—parenthesis mine. T.K.) He enclosed a dollar, which we received. From what he writes, they haven't had a very good year. The grasshoppers take it all. It appears that in the whole world there is an "Oh!" and a "Woe!" From wherever we hear, there is much left to wish for. We have finished the threshing but the harvest did not produce as it promised, but we hope to have bread for the winter.

We have dug out the potatoes whose tops were dried out. We have about 125 Pud. About 40 more Pud are still in the ground, which are still to be dug up. We will have enough potatoes. I want to dig a hole in the shed to bury the seed potatoes. Outside we have a nice cellar built of kiln baked brick. We have to destroy it because of its frequent visitors, who want help, or better said, share or take everything. And we are of the opinion that we grew them for our own use. Several times they have dug up potatoes in the garden. I think they took about four Pud from the garden.

Well, Mama, you write about Papa going to visit with Buhlers (his youngest sister, Elisabeth). We would like to do that too but here it has gone out of style. This summer we have not . . . and the way we heard, we should have received a little girl a week ago. (??) Next Sunday we want to walk there if it remains nice. It is far but we can't think of driving.

You write about having to drive cows. We would be glad to chase cows if we had them, but unfortunately we have only one old one. She comes home alone. Every few weeks we make about a pound of butter to sell. We need the money so badly to pay and to buy, for everywhere we fall short. Butter was ten Rubel per pound but now is only eight Rubel. Eggs are eight Rubel for ten. They are expensive but whatever we buy is expensive. Tina (his second wife) said if only sunflower oil were available. There is no lard. For this fall we have only two small pigs, one about five Pud and the other about three Pud. And for the near future there is nothing. So we will again have no lard. We bought a two week old pig a month ago for 60 Rubel, and so the butter money is spent right away. Yes, we always wait for the butter money.

I have to pay the village council 50 Rubel. We have said often to each other, when we sit at our table, how we would like to sit at the table of our parents and siblings. How that would please us.

Our baby often yells out, "I want syrup bread!" Yesterday Tin made some peppernuts and he likes those very much. I have often said the boy doesn't learn to like good food. (His name was Bernie.)

The potatoes baked in water really taste good. Well, you wouldn't think so, and yet, if we were asked, like the disciples, "Have you ever done without?" we would have to say "No, Lord, never," for we always have something to eat.

We are all well, for which we cannot thank the Lord enough, and hope to have bread in winter. Yes, we have learned to do with little. And when the need is the greatest, the Lord is the nearest. We have experienced that. And so I will stop my song of complaints for it could get too long. But what the heart is full of, flows over from the mouth. (German proverb.)

If the harvest had been better we would not have been better off because according to the government, their plan is okay. We do not have to give them much, for the winter wheat did not survive well. Must close.

Thank Netha (his sister) heartily for her letter. None of the other siblings have written. I have often said, when our dear parents are no longer able to write, we will no longer get any letters.

Well, good bye! May you all live well until we see each other again, if not here, then let us strive to meet each other over there.

So hearty greetings from your loving children J and T Unger. (Jakob)

About the Author

I was born in Saskatchewan to German speaking parents of Dutch heritage who were born and raised in Ukraine. My story is about a family's journey from war-torn Russia to drought stricken Sask. and onward to Manitoba where we slowly prospered. My parents and I moved to British Columbia where they retired. My own journey led me to the Royal Columbian Hospital nursing school where I earned my R.N. diploma. Degrees were not in my vocabulary then. The R.N. signature opened doors for me to serve humanity as well as to serve God.

After a career in nursing, I am now retired, as is my husband, and we live in Albany, OR. I love to sew and read. We are both active in our church and community, taking part in volunteer, academic, religious and cultural pursuits. We have also traveled to Western Europe several times, and to Russia and Eastern Europe. TKK

CPSIA information can be obtained at www.ICGtesting.com
Printed in the USA
BVOW020341281212

309275BV00002B/166/P